O N
the market

O N

<u>the market</u>

surviving the academic
job search

edited by
Christina Boufis
and Victoria C. Olsen

Riverhead Books
New York

Riverhead Books
Published by The Berkley Publishing Group, a member of Penguin Putnam Inc.
200 Madison Avenue
New York, New York 10016

First Riverhead edition: September 1997

The Putnam Berkley World Wide Web site address is http://www.berkley.com

Library of Congress Cataloging-in-Publication Data

On the market : surviving the academic job search / edited by
    Christina Boufis and Victoria C. Olsen. — 1st ed.
        p.   cm.
    Includes bibliographical references
    ISBN 1-57322-626-2
    1. College teachers—Employment—United States.   2. College
teachers—Selection and appointment—United States.   3. Job hunting—
United States.   I. Boufis, Christina.   II. Olsen, Victoria C.
LB2331.72.05   1997
378.1'2'02373—dc21   97-8549
                                                                                           CIP

Printed in the United States of America

10   9   8   7   6   5   4   3   2   1

Acknowledgments

Every book is a collaboration, and this one perhaps more so than others. We would first like to thank the many people who were so willing to share their personal experiences of being on the market: those friends, colleagues, and strangers who candidly told their stories, who sent us essays and e-mail, who referred us to books, websites, and other resources, and who created the book with us. Our contributors are an impressive group of people and we learned as much from their examples as from their essays.

We are extremely fortunate in having a reading group that sustained us through our own job searches and that supported this project from its beginnings. Laura Mann, Lisa Nakamura, Christina Olsen, and Susie Wise gave invaluable advice, listened patiently, and cheered us on throughout. We are ourselves a microcosm of market demographics: four of the six of us have Ph.D.'s and only one of us is working full-time in academia.

We are also truly grateful to Rachel Brownstein for both the enthusiasm she has shown for this project from the start, and for putting us in touch with the right people, especially our editor, Celina Spiegel, whose faith and skill turned the project into a book.

Acknowledgments

Finally, we extend our love and thanks to Scott Peterson, Joshua Seiden, and Naomi Olsen Seiden, who have lived with this book and who realize the happy intersection of the personal and the professional.

O N
the market

Doonesbury

Doonesbury

BY GARRY TRUDEAU

Contents

Acknowledgments   v

Introduction
Christina Boufis and Victoria C. Olsen   1

1. First Words: The Application Process

Introduction   17
    Lisa Nakamura, Department of English,
    Sonoma State University

Remembering the Battlefront: Notes on the Academic Job
Search in the 1990s   22
    Joseph J. Basile

It's All Uphill from Here: Confessions of a Ph.D. Job
Searcher   32
    Barbara Bennett

Six Shards from a Search   38
    Dave Williams

Contents

Planning, Persistence, and Politics: Do's and Don'ts from
a Job Search in the Physical Sciences   51
    Kurt T. Bachmann

2. Cattle Call: The Academic Conference and Interview

Introduction   63
    Daniel Born, Department of English,
    Marietta College
Scenes from the APA, or Odysseus Looks for a Job   67
    Michael O'Donovan-Anderson
My Journey Through the Job Market in Mathematics   79
    Howard Wachtel
Feminists Face the Job Market: Q & A (Questions &
Anecdotes)   87
    Elisabeth Rose Gruner

3. The Aftermath and Beyond

Introduction   103
    Barbara Louise Ungar, Department of English,
    College of Saint Rose
Grape Expectations   108
    Joseph O. Aimone
There's No Place Like Home   111
    Martha Hollander
The Sound of the Mail Truck, or How I Learned to Stop
Worrying and Read Rejection Letters   125
    Anahid Kassabian
"Cadences of Rejection"   129
    Daniel Brownstein

Contents

4. Identities and Politics

Introduction   137
    Elizabeth Freeman, Department of English,
    Sarah Lawrence College

White Men Can't Teach: Affirmative Action and the
Academic Job Search   142
    Gene McQuillan

Where's the Closet at the Hilton? In or Out While
You're On   155
    Julie Vandivere

My Life Part-Time: Reflections on Damaged Goods   161
    Brian Caterino

Of Job Trails and Holy Grails for Feminists Out There:
A Postmodernist Cautionary Tale   174
    Sivagami Subbaraman

5. The Professional Meets the Personal

Introduction   191
    Carrie Tirado Bramen, Department of English,
    SUNY-Buffalo

Portrait of the Ph.D. as a Young Woman   196
    Ingrid Steffensen-Bruce

(Academic) Sense and Sensibilities: Confronting
Ambivalence About the 1990s Job Market   203
    Diana Dull

The Sad and Candid Story of an Immigrant Woman in
Canada and Her Unsuccessful Job Hunt   212
    Veronica Vazquez Garcia

Contents

6. Different Paths

Introduction   225
    Victoria C. Olsen

The Gypsy Scholar: Making a Living as a Full-Time
Adjunct   229
    Marilyn Bonnell

Life-Path Sexism   235
    Eleanor B. Amico

The Job Search As Career: 1983–1997   242
    Allen G. Hunt

Ordinary Women: Teaching at the County Jail   253
    Christina Boufis

7. Alternative Careers

Introduction   265
    Christina Boufis, Institute for Research on Women
    and Gender, Stanford University

If You Can't Join Them, Beat Them   269
    Eliene Augenbraun

How I Got to Collegiate   275
    Adam Bresnick

Ex-Philosopher   287
    Brian Ulicny

Expectations   295
    Victoria C. Olsen

Contents

8. Where Do We Go from Here? Critiques of the Academy

Introduction   301
> *Anne M. Menke*, Department of Modern Languages and Literatures, Swarthmore College

The Economy of Letters   304
> *Lesliee Antonette*

Hidden Injuries of the Job Market   309
> *John Dixon*

Independent of What? Rethinking Academic Marginality   319
> *Laura Stempel Mumford*

Afterwords

> *Louis Menand*, Ph.D. program in English, The Graduate Center of the City University of New York   339
> *Michael Bérubé*, Professor of English, University of Illinois, Urbana-Champaign   348

Appendix of Useful Resources for the Academic Job Search   364

About the Contributors   371

Introduction

Christina Boufis and
Victoria C. Olsen

"Let us have a conversation about a profession that eats its young."

—Cary Nelson[1]

This book was born out of an equally profound sense of both hope and despair. Perhaps it was first conceived in our reading group, which itself began as an intellectual resource for grad student friends and has evolved into an emotional support group for unemployed new Ph.D.'s and former academics. On the other hand, it may have begun in 1991, when we met at Dickens Universe, a summer camp for graduate student Victorianists, and a model for an intercampus academic community that other institutions and fields would do well to emulate. But maybe the book really began, for all of us, in the late 1980s, when widely reported demographic research on higher education led us, and hordes of other eager scholars, into graduate school expecting a hiring boom when we resurfaced in the mid-1990s.[2]

As we all know now, and none better than our contributors, that hiring boom, which was supposed to occur when a generation of tenured faculty reached retirement age, never happened. Faculty members aged predictably enough and enrollments rose substantially in the past ten years, but budget cuts and hiring freezes more than kept pace, resulting in an unusually depressed job market in almost all fields of university employment, even by historical standards. Of course we had heard certain rumblings of possible job shortages even before we completed graduate school—and it was true that the job market in academia had been steadily constricting since the 1970s—but like many others, we felt that these warnings would not apply to us. Like good students everywhere, we had internalized the rules which said that the key to landing a job was to work hard and to do well: to research and write good dissertations, publish articles, and establish good relationships with people in the field. But such rules, we soon found, were almost obsolete in the catastrophic academic job market of the 1990s. Like many new Ph.D.'s, we graduated only to find ourselves facing several difficult professional choices: endure low wages and no job security while juggling adjunct teaching jobs and jockeying for permanent positions, "wait out" the market with other paid work while trying to keep up the publications and credentials necessary to get hired "later," or leave the field one has spent five to ten years apprenticing to enter. This then has resulted in a generation of scholars in limbo, who occupy a murky and largely undocumented area known as being "on the market."

The numbers tell one side of the story: the number of full-time tenure-track positions in English and foreign languages, for example, has declined by almost 50 percent in the past seven years alone. The placement rate for new Ph.D.'s in many humanities fields, like English and history, during this same time, has hovered around 45 percent.[3] But add to this that the total number of doctorates in all fields, according to the National Research Council's 1993 Summary Report, has more than tripled since 1963, and you have a staggering number of Ph.D.'s who are either un- or underemployed.[4] That number is still growing. Even the sciences don't fare much better; according to one industry report, the " 'natural production rate' of science doctorates exceeds the demand from all sources by about 22 percent."[5] Ph.D.'s, especially in physics, were particularly hard hit by recent cuts in government spending, and those in other sciences, once secure of finding positions in industry, now find those promised jobs also disappearing.

2

And what about the human side of the job market search? For numbers, while helpful in assessing what is happening or is not happening in the job market for recent Ph.D.'s, cannot portray the personal consequences for candidates. Where were their stories? We had heard anecdotally about many academics who had spent years looking for a job, moving from one-year position to one-year position (if they were lucky) until they had spent the better part of a decade in a constant state of search and upheaval. What toll does all the years of waiting and hoping, while living indefinitely on the economic sideline, take on job seekers? What about the many recent Ph.D.'s who turn the economic and political into the personal, and make the entire experience of the job search—despite the increasingly long-shot odds—into a narrative of professional "failure"? How do they deal with this crisis?

From the beginning we conceived of this project as an emotional guidebook to the academic job search by the candidates themselves, both newly hired and still looking. By addressing such questions, it would help others navigate the rough seas of the job search process. Moreover, while there are many career planning books for academics in every field, and many departments have their own handouts and counselors to aid their alumni, what we felt was really lacking as we went through our own years of job searching were personal stories. Sure, job placement rates of new Ph.D.'s in all fields, according to the NRC's Summary Report, are at roughly 53 percent, down from 64 percent in 1973, but what kind of jobs are these 53 percent getting? How did they get them and how do they feel about them? Are those jobs worth struggling for, and if not, what other options are available? What about the large percentage of people (and that number increases every year) who never find a position in academia? Where do they end up? Within a department such an information search and the community building that goes with it are often stalled by the inevitable competition among job seekers. As John Dixon notes in his essay, the competition for scarce jobs often makes an already difficult search even more isolating, as candidates hoard tips and contacts and avoid talking about their multiple rejections.

This is not to say that academic job candidates are not willing and eager to reach out to one another. From the many queries we received, to the sustained commitments of our contributors to pull together to make it happen, this book has been an exercise in the construction of a community across disciplinary, generational, and hierarchical lines. Newly hired assistant professors attest to their efforts to make the process easier for the rest of us, and those still searching or on the sidelines have all confronted and revealed the varying anger, pain, shame, and new hope that their experiences have taught them. It isn't easy to talk about a job search that almost always—and sometimes only—includes rejections, but all of our contributors have done that.

We believe that talking about the job search may be our best solution to its hardships. This whole book is built on the assumption that telling and hearing people's stories is indeed therapeutic and empowering. Many of our actual and potential contributors wrote to express this very same thing: they told us how relieved they were to be able to write their stories (even if we didn't use them); just giving voice and shape to an experience that previously had felt so amorphous, powerful, and beyond their control, they wrote, was cathartic.

Our own stories overlap with the stories in this volume, and many others. We both came out of well-respected English programs in 1994 with Ph.D.'s and with the support of enthusiastic advisors. We both have teaching experience in our home institutions and publications. We both ended up on the market for three years, as ABDs and then as new Ph.D.'s, but despite some good interviews between us, neither of us has come close to a tenure-track job in our field. For both of us this led to depression, resentment, and then personal and professional stock taking. After all our years of hard work, we felt entitled to decent jobs—full-time, relatively secure, with varied teaching and research expectations. We were willing to relocate, though with certain conditions and not every year. Yet these expectations, we were told, were "unrealistic"—as our experience on the market seemed to prove. We ended up caught between our own sense of self-worth as to what we should and could

4

accept and the market's ruthless leveling of all egos. The only way to preserve our precarious self-esteem seemed to be to get off the train, even if that had other pitfalls.

And what else could we do? It is often difficult enough to explain to anyone outside of academe just what it is one has spent perhaps ten years preparing for. It was already clear from numerous cocktail parties and family Christmas gatherings that Ph.D.'s were not widely valued by the American general public and were already viewed as hopeless dreamers for having stayed in school so long. We felt too that it was way past time to get a job: we were in our thirties and had lived like students for long enough. But if we left academia, we feared we would only be qualified for entry-level jobs, which added extra humiliation to our situations.

We had both enjoyed our graduate work immensely, and had no regrets about the value of the education we received, but we had still thought of it as a means to an end (a job and an income). It was a shock to reconceive of our graduate work as an exercise in self-development, but that is what the market seemed to be saying to us. "It was a luxury to spend seven years in full-time intellectual pursuits," we told ourselves many times. "It is a privilege to be a Ph.D.," we repeated to each other, "and we are better human beings for it." But there were those doubts that, after all, that wasn't primarily how our graduate work was represented to us at the time. Besides, it begged the question of what to do next.

That is where our paths diverged. Victoria had a baby just as she finished her Ph.D. and decided that if she couldn't get a full-time, tenure-track job in her field she would work part-time at home until her daughter started school. This had drawbacks: it was frustrating to continue being dependent on her husband's income and it was hard to adjust to such an overwhelming shift in identity from academic/career woman to mother/part-timer. But it had its advantages too, and editing this book and transforming part of her dissertation into a biography have provided a sense of continuity as well. Christina moved cross-country, finished her dissertation, and soon found herself going through a divorce. Unwilling to pick up and move again, she began writing freelance articles and adjuncting at local community colleges. This led her to her current job, teaching women in the San Francisco county jail, which she is developing into a book.

Our contributors pose similar questions about how to construct a career and a professional sense of self in the transitional time on the market, but they sketch partial answers too. Perhaps the most common denominator among all the contributors—regardless of discipline, employment history, or personal situation—is the difficulty of creating and maintaining any sort of academic identity in the current job market, where full-time and permanent jobs are scarce. We all want to belong, especially after the often intense identification with a graduate department and after the long apprenticeship of doctoral work. A few live happily in their role of "gypsy scholar," roving from job to job. But most of us struggle to define ourselves in a profession that doesn't seem to want or need us, or doesn't want or need us as we are—as experts in Jane Austen's juvenilia or ancient Chinese music, as openly gay scholars, as younger or older men or women, as parents or caregivers, as people of color or people of a recognizable class. As many of our contributors attest, in this market any public or private identity can be a handle for rejecting an applicant, and can be cause for speculative self-doubt among candidates. The wild talk that goes on in all academic circles about the effects of "political correctness," affirmative action, and "trendy" specialties and identities is a tribute to the lack of real information about the job market and the lack of security that almost everyone feels in the academy now.

But our contributors also demonstrate quite creative and resilient ways of carving out new identities and professional selves in this uncertain time. Martha Hollander had such a strong sense of an academic identity that her years of marginal employment only strengthened her resolve to persevere until the academy acknowledged her existence. Victoria's experience has been more like Laura Stempel Mumford's and Sivagami Subbaraman's: if the academy has no place for her, she will attempt to be a functional academic without the name tag—to research and write and give talks and publish "on the margins" even if that identity is almost totally self-generated. We know others who have tried to keep as much of the academic role—of researcher or teacher—as possible without preserving the core identity at all. But as Mumford and Subbaraman relate, such a balancing act is rarely accomplished without crisis, without an interim sense of having no identity whatsoever. And the strain of constantly defining oneself in relation to the academy and its hierarchies ("What do you do?" "What is an independent scholar?" "Where do you belong?") can be exhausting.

Our intention in assembling this collection was to strike a similar balance between personal and institutional perspectives. We looked for interesting, well-written accounts but also for representative issues and experiences from many different fields; however, no anthology could hope to be fully representative of such a varied and wide-ranging profession. Nonetheless, our focus on anecdotal evidence provides the emotional driving force of the book. From the start, we were impressed by the flood of interest and emotion this topic elicited from job seekers eager to tell their stories.

We organized the essays around parts of the job search process (from applications to campus interviews) as well as around thematic issues. Such categories inevitably overlap, and the reader will find that all the essays deal with parts of the process as well as with emotional concerns. They are filled with advice, but the advice emerges from the contributors' personal experiences. We then assigned the task of introducing each section to experienced candidates and newly hired professors, who offer more generalized guidance and contextualize the material covered in that section. In general we have also tried as much as possible to let people tell their own stories in their own ways and with their own opinions, so the voices are all individual and the essays may even be contradictory. Such discrepancies only point to the fact that there is no one "right way" to navigate through the job market; it would be foolish of us to suggest otherwise.

We begin the first section, "First Words: The Application Process," with an essay by Joseph J. Basile, an archaeologist, because his essay embodies both what is best and what is worst about a career in academia. Given the current state of the job market (let alone the ten-year average time to degree), it is often difficult to explain why anyone would choose to go into this profession in the first place. But it is clear from Basile's essay that a love of teaching (with research as a strong second) underlies his decision. So despite the thousands of dollars in debt (evidence suggests that for some recent Ph.D.'s that number may be at least as high as $20,000),[6] the five hundred applications sent out in three years, and the numerous other sacrifices of time, money, and self-esteem, what keeps Basile, and so many others like him, going is the sheer love of teaching ideas and subjects that are close to one's heart. Certainly, this kind of passion cannot be calculated in dollars and cents, yet just as certainly, such commitment does get tested in the harsh economic realities of the job market.

The other essays in this section shed light on the coping strategies that job seekers construct to deal with the pressures of looking for an academic position: both how to handle the sheer weight of the paperwork involved, and, more intangibly, how to reckon with the emotional highs and lows, the doubts and disappointments that seem to plague all job seekers. In Barbara Bennett's essay, a sense of humor, as well as a one-day-at-a-time attitude, go far toward easing some of these pressures. As Dave Williams's essay demonstrates, establishing routines can indeed help one better cope with the arbitrariness and inscrutability that appear to govern the entire process. As all of these essays show, learning how to ride the emotional roller coaster that accompanies the job search requires innovative strategies.

The next section, "Cattle Call: The Academic Conference and Interview," shows that despite the initial "success" one might have in getting a conference or campus interview, most candidates are still puzzled by the "rules," a set of intangible requirements and procedures that they imagine help land candidates full-time jobs. As Michael O'Donovan-Anderson satirically illustrates, conferences can take on epic overtones to a young scholar: one's entire fate seems to hang on the almost superhuman actions of hiring committees who are far removed from the hero/job seeker. Or, as Howard Wachtel, a mathematician, recounts, figuring out how to fly to several cross-country interviews may be a fortunate dilemma but it might require a degree in airline scheduling and an unlimited expense account. Furthermore, as Elisabeth Rose Gruner shows, many unspoken assumptions concerning a candidate's marital status or sexual preference can and do (illegally) influence the final choice of a hiring committee. Kurt Bachmann reports candidly on how he learned the rules the hard way.

For many of the essayists in the next section, "The Aftermath and Beyond," means learning to deal with rejection. Coming in second in this race, while one may have indeed victoriously crossed several finish lines—completing the dissertation, getting the degree, going through the application and interview process—does not necessarily mean getting a job, as Martha Hollander's essay poignantly shows. Joseph Aimone chooses to handle the disappointment of near misses by sharing comic poems with other job seekers. But on a more serious note, the numerous rejection letters one receives may foster a kind of self-scrutiny in which one takes painful stock of oneself as both a scholar and a person. Anahid Kassabian attests to the long afterlife that rejection can have, even after one finally gets a good job. Academia in general seems to call for constant self-assessment; but job seekers can be especially vulnerable to this reflective process—particularly when there are no real guidelines or answers. It is this lack that leads Daniel Brownstein to speculate on the lives behind the signatures that pen his rejection letters: the need for analysis of some kind is clear in his essay, even if it means one must construct meaning from the weft and weave of the paper itself.

The next section in our anthology, "Identities and Politics," makes clear that despite—or perhaps because of—the fact that there are so few positions, job hiring has become a politically charged battleground in which there are no real winners. Gene McQuillan, a "white male," writes of the numerous and contradictory feelings that arise when job ads invite women and minorities in particular to apply. Should one read them with anger, dismiss them, or take them as a "warning" not to apply? What or who are hiring committees really looking for? And how is a candidate to know? These questions underlie all of the essays in this section, from Brian Caterino's indictment of hiring processes to Julie Vandivere's investigation into the ''coding'' of queer identities on the market, to Sivagami Subbaraman's confusion over the contradictory ways people label her and her work. All of these essays question the way in which labels—white male, working-class, gay, postcolonial, woman of color—may be at once too narrow or too balkanizing to adequately describe the candidates and their work. As these essays demonstrate, when questions of identity politics are factored in hiring, the search becomes that much more shrouded in mystery.

As the essays in ''The Professional Meets the Personal'' section make explicit, it is almost impossible to separate emotional from intellectual decisions in the academic job search process. For there is perhaps no other profession in which the mandate to relocate is so absolute. The difficulty of weighing this imperative against personal ties—one's partner, community, or family—is tellingly illustrated in both Ingrid Steffensen-Bruce's and Diana Dull's essays. In the case of Veronica Vazquez Garcia, the job search is inherently tied to making major geographic moves—in her case from Mexico to Canada. But as all three of these essays make apparent—and it is significant that they are all written by women—a career in academia mandates not only that one relocate, but also that major life decisions, from having a baby to buying a house, must wait, sometimes indefinitely, until one finds a job. How painful this waiting becomes is evident in all of the essays, particularly, as Diana Dull writes, when one's common ''sense'' of the job market comes into conflict with one's ''sensibilities''—those immeasurable things that a person wants out of life. In a profession that often leaves so little room for personal choice in where one may live, how long one will live in this limbo is sometimes the only real decision to be made.

While many people already established in the profession advise ''waiting out'' the market for several years (one study suggests five or more)[7] until one lands a full-time tenure-track job, the essays in the ''Different Paths'' section show that there are alternative possibilities to this main route. For Marilyn Bonnell, a one-year position becomes not only a job, but an opportunity to try on a new locale and meet new people. Her optimistic approach and willingness to uproot every year are indeed assets for living the gypsy/scholar life. But for others whose plans did not turn out as expected, and they include many in this volume, the bigger dilemma is what to do while waiting out the market. Eleanor B. Amico's essay describes one such path: her reentry into academia after first rearing children attests to how difficult it is to make the transition to a permanent job, despite many years of both work and "real-life" experience. Allen G. Hunt chose to retrain himself in a new academic specialty, and he details the difficulties of that path. Christina Boufis has found rewarding work, but wonders how relevant it will be to her long-term career goals.

What many of these essayists share, some explicitly, and some only implicitly, is that despite all the odds and risks, the desire to get a doctorate and go into academia is akin to a calling that is almost impossible to disavow. But there comes a time for many when waiting it out while adjuncting, taking one-year positions, or temping is no longer a viable option. The essays in "Alternative Careers" show what life is like outside of academia, or outside of what one thought one would do with a doctorate. Victoria Olsen confronts the consequences of her choice to step out of academia to straddle two ill-defined "careers": independent scholarship and parenthood. Eliene Augenbraun's essay reveals the exciting possibilities of turning a career in biology into one in multimedia, and how such a route both is and is not circuitous. Similarly, Brian Ulicny has made a successful switch from linguistic philosophy to computer science while remaining true to his original interests. Adam Bresnick has found that teaching at the secondary school level is, in many ways, more satisfying and rewarding than teaching at the university level. Given the increasingly difficult odds of landing a full-time job in the academy, such rethinking of the uses of one's degree may indeed become a necessity.

We hope that the essays in the "Where Do We Go from Here? Critiques of the Academy" section are not the last words on the job market discussion. Rather, as Laura Stempel Mumford, Lesliee Antonette, and John Dixon all argue, we need systemic changes in the academy. We offer some critiques here, and we hope that they are a spur to further dialogue and discussion. We can start, as Mumford points out, by recognizing all of the people who do intellectual work—whether "officially" supported by a university or not. And we can acknowledge, as Antonette's essay does, that going on the market means we are selling ourselves as commodities: to pretend otherwise is to ignore the market forces at work, much to our detriment. As Dixon points out, such selling need not make us become competitive and hostile toward one another, but rather can lead to cooperative communities that will ultimately benefit us all.

In this vein, it would behoove both those of us "in" the profession, as well as those looking to become part of it, to work together to change some of the iniquities that have now become almost part of the academic hiring process. We should resist what Michael Bérubé in an Afterword labels the "adjunctification" of the professoriate in which full-time lines are replaced by poorly paid adjuncts. This process serves no one, even though many of us depend on such subsistence positions for our livelihoods. And though market forces are largely responsible for the lack of academic positions, as Louis Menand explains in his Afterword, graduate programs can work to make their programs shorter and more humane, thereby lessening the psychic damage done to their graduates. It may be time to rethink the Ph.D., as both Bérubé and Menand point out, but it is long past time to listen to those who have battled for years in this merciless job market. We present the essays in this volume to offer solace to job seekers, to communicate honestly and personally about our expectations and our disappointments, and, more hopefully, to foster a dialogue that will continue beyond these pages.

Notes

[1.] Cary Nelson, "Lessons from the Job Wars: Late Capitalism Arrives on Campus," *Social Text* 44, Vol. 13, No. 3 (Fall/Winter 1995), p. 130.

2. See Howard R. Bowen and Jack H. Schuster, *American Professors: A National Resource Imperiled* (Oxford: Oxford University Press, 1986) and William G. Bowen and Julie Ann Sosa, *Prospects for Faculty in the Arts and Sciences: A Study of Factors Affecting Demand and Supply, 1987 to 2012* (Princeton: Princeton University Press, 1989).

3. See Bettina Huber, "Recent Trends in the Modern Language Job Market," *Profession '94* (New York: MLA, 1994), pp. 87–105; David Laurence, "From the Editor," *ADE Bulletin* 111 (Fall 1995), pp. 1–3; Louis Menand, "How to Make a Ph.D. Matter," *New York Times Magazine* (September 22, 1996), pp. 78–82.

4. *Summary Report 1993: Doctorate Recipients from United States Universities* (Washington: National Academy, 1995).

5. Jocelyn Kaiser, "Is It Time to Begin Ph.D. Population Control?," *Science's Careers '95: The Future of the Ph.D.*, Vol. 270 (October 6, 1995), pp. 123–34.

6. See Stephen Watt, "The Human Costs of Graduate Education; Or, The Need to Get Practical," *Academe*, Vol. 81, No. 6 (November-December 1995), pp. 30–35.

7. See Jack H. Schuster, "Speculating About the Labor Market for Academic Humanists: 'Once More Unto the Breach,' " *Profession '95* (New York: MLA, 1995), p. 60.

One

First Words:

The Application Process

Introduction

Lisa Nakamura
Department of English, Sonoma State University

n my conversations with other recent Ph.D. and ABD job seekers, the most common word I have heard used to describe today's academic job market is "crapshoot." The dismal state of the market has seemed to instill in many a sense of the randomness of the process. There is also an almost addictive quality to the job application process; with the odds of finding a job so very slim, there is the sense that one must roll the dice as many times as possible in order to improve them. To extend the gambling metaphor further, however, each roll of the dice costs—each application uses up time, money, and energy, scarce and precious resources indeed in the lives of scholars who are just settling down from (or are still engaged in) the Herculean tasks of writing dissertations, teaching, getting published, and finding ways to pay off loans.

The job application process in academe is an all-consuming activity and becomes a way of life. The separate parts of this process are individually arduous and collectively overwhelming: combing multiple publications and bulletin boards for openings, which involves research in the libraries, placement offices, and on the Internet; researching the institutions one might apply for; preparing, producing, and paying for the myriad (and sometimes rather eccentric) documents necessary for each application; faxing, mailing, and making phone calls to track applications. The process requires organizational skills, energy, and emotional stamina which can tax a highly trained Ph.D. to the limits of his or her ability. And then this daunting series of tasks must be shoehorned into a tight schedule of teaching, writing, and researching, and it sometimes displaces these activities. All three essayists in this section succeeded in finding jobs, and with the incredible amount of work, ingenuity, and emotional toughness they put into their searches this should not surprise anybody. Their ingenuity and persistence can teach their fellow academic job searchers a great deal.

The level of commitment each of these essayists displays puts that venerable job-hunter's guide *What Color Is Your Parachute*'s advice to readers to put "at least 30 hours a week" into the task of job hunting in a different perspective indeed. Joseph J. Basile, Barbara Bennett, and Dave Williams all dramatize the extent to which the application process becomes a more-than-full-time job. Basile even calls his job hunting a "second job" and developed an application "system" that eventually led to his present position. Bennett's "day in the life of a job searcher" describes how the application process becomes a routine, a ritual, and how the punishing effects of constantly receiving rejections while sending out applications can be mitigated by support from colleagues. Williams describes the ingenious emotional self-maintenance techniques he employed to stay sane.

Coping with multiple applications, for positions ranging from those at elite research universities to those at much humbler institutions that stress teaching, presents an enormous challenge; for each application demands that the applicant make him or herself out to be the "best" person for that job. The constant alternation between identities means that one may be describing oneself in radically different ways each time one writes a letter. Bennett writes about producing letters that make her out to be the "perfect candidate for all four jobs," and Basile stresses the importance of developing second and third specialties so that one can apply for as many jobs as possible. While necessary, tailoring each application letter to each job results in a carefully governed variety of multiple personality disorders—like a method actor, you have to imagine yourself in several different identities, sometimes ones which differ radically from the one you identify most closely with yourself. The additional difficulty is that you cannot know precisely which role to choose, because it is impossible to know exactly what employers want, sometimes because they themselves have only the vaguest idea. However, choosing a role in which you feel comfortable will result in a more coherent and convincing performance. A glance at a job ad for a specialist in children's literature at a good university not far from one's home can lead to reveries such as "Well, my dissertation is on feminist theory and doesn't address children's lit at all—but I remember liking *Harriet the Spy*. Maybe I could make the case that Harriet is a feminist, and therefore . . ." or "The job description says they want children's lit, but maybe they really want . . ." The sometimes irresistible desire to roll the dice yet one more time can lead to the slippery slope of rationalization—but while fibbing to yourself about your real qualifications is unavoidable, and to be expected, it is also to be resisted.

With those general caveats in mind, here are some specific pointers for coping with your mass mailings:

- *Prioritize*. Applicants should anticipate running out of gas at some point, and therefore it is important to do first those applications which are closest to your heart. Being exhausted makes one emotionally susceptible and psychologically tender; the sections of Williams's story entitled "Rebellion" and "Rudeness" detail with remarkable honesty the unanticipated and sometimes unwelcome emotional side-effects of the process.

- *Be familiar with the contents of your application materials, including recommendation letters*. In this market even a single negative comment in an otherwise positive letter can undermine an application. If you waive the right to see them, and you are lucky enough to have an advisor or administrator friend whose judgment you trust, ask him or her to look at your file and give you an honest assessment. Sometimes letter writers can be remarkably dense; though they may honestly think that their letter is an asset to you, it is best to get a second opinion if possible.

- *Conserve your resources.* Some schools advise their students to apply for every job they see, for the main purpose of getting practice interviewing. Try to arrange mock interviews at your home institution instead, preferably with faculty members who do not know you well; they are far less expensive learning experiences since they don't involve purchasing new suits and plane tickets, and you are more likely to get detailed and honest feedback. Many mentors, advisors, and placement officers encourage what Williams calls a "no-holds-barred-damn-I-want-a-job-apply-for-everything" attitude, but it is also important to pick one's battles carefully. And here is a very subjective piece of advice, arising from personal experience: don't go on the market with only one chapter. Derailing and disrupting your dissertation for the opportunity to compete with those who already have their degrees worsens your odds, and an unsuccessful year on the market at that stage cannot benefit your work toward the degree. The added sense of confidence, legitimacy, and accomplishment that comes from possessing the degree, having it "in hand," contributes toward the resiliency that one is absolutely guaranteed to need during the application process.

- *Keep in mind that hiring does occur during the "off" season, or at the last minute.* Though a measure of despair is unavoidable after receiving numerous rejection letters, it is wisest not to succumb to it too early in the process. The number of job seekers I know who got their jobs quite late in the year exceeds those I know who got them during the "season." This may be because increasingly tightened hiring budgets seem to get firmed up relatively late, or because positions sometimes become "unfrozen" in the spring rather than the fall. Community college jobs in particular open up all year long.

- *Most importantly, keep in touch with other job seekers.* Don't let competition divide you from those who can offer you the most support. You can always make it a condition of your interactions with colleagues that you refrain from sharing specific information about who got what interview where, etc., as a jealousy prevention measure. As the job search becomes more protracted due to market conditions, these friendships may be the primary support that keeps you forging ahead amid a flurry of rejection letters. The academic job application process can be peculiar, arcane, and more or less incomprehensible to those who aren't engaged in it. Finding fellowship with those who are also on the market can help to keep you going over the long haul.

Remembering the Battlefront: Notes on the Academic Job Search in the 1990s

Joseph J. Basile

I received my Ph.D. in classical archaeology and art history at an Ivy League university some four years ago, on what was probably the coldest, wettest Memorial Day recorded in New England. And my own heart was as dark as the sky.

Sorry to be so melodramatic, but I was genuinely depressed. I had worked hard for my degree, which, over the five-year course of my graduate career, had often seemed unattainable. So I suppose I should have been proud, and I think I was, deep down. But there were other things on my mind, and bleak reality was setting in. My dad was just recovering from surgery and was walking around in the cold spring drizzle aided by a cane. When I was a kid, my dad seemed omnipotent and immortal; now he just seemed old, and it frightened me.

The previous summer, I had excavated with the American Academy in Rome, a prestigious position. But the work had brought me little joy; it was a constant source of friction between me and my girlfriend, and it was an economic hardship not to work at a real job that paid more than airfare, room, and board over the summer. So the very night I received my degree, I had to tell the director of the excavation that I couldn't return. He told me that career-wise I was making a mistake, and I knew he was right, but try explaining to Visa and MasterCard that you can't pay them because of the demands of an academic career. When their bills come every month, they want their money, and no excuses, please.

The reality of my student loans was also setting in: over $30,000 worth, coming due in December. The payments would be something like $300 a month—where would I get that kind money? I was working, doing research, and making maybe $900 a month, and my girlfriend's job paid only a little better. After rent, food, heat, phone, electricity, etc., had made their demands on our budget, how would we pay?

What was most on my mind, however, was securing a job in academia. As a naive undergraduate, I had assumed a Ph.D. would assure me a job in research or teaching. As an only slightly less naive graduate student, I knew that few people in my field could hold down a purely research-oriented position, so I shifted my focus to teaching (which I had come to love, anyway) and assumed that my top-notch advisors and Ivy League degrees would win the day. Also, this was the eighties: scholars and pundits were making the rounds at universities all over the country, heralding a new golden age in academia, when, they predicted, factors like the growing economy, government funding (especially in the sciences connected with the defense industry), increases in the population of college-bound students, and decreases in the number of professors (due to old age and retirement) would combine to create a bull market for recent Ph.D. recipients. We all waited for the job offers to come pouring in.

Well, as we all know, none of this panned out. The economy stopped growing under the Bush administration, the Cold War ended, and the defense industry collapsed. Many of the demographic arguments concerning the college-age population were found to be flawed, and universities eliminated the positions occupied by their retiring professors, replacing them with part-timers who would work for a fraction of the cost. Recent graduates were told that there were no more tenure-track jobs out there (to hell with academic freedom—tenured professors cost universities a lot of money), that they would have to work part-time with low pay and no benefits, and when their services were no longer needed, well, bye-bye. When there were full-time slots, prospective hires were told they would have to teach four or sometimes even five courses a semester, yet continue to research and publish, with no guarantee of contract renewal. All of this since the mid-eighties, when work was supposed to be falling in our laps. The pundits seem to have thought that somehow the job market in academia was independent of the economy at large. Too bad they were so wrong. Instead of a boom time, we've arrived at a bust: colleges now borrow management models from big business in order to cut corners and save every possible penny—terms like "cost accountability," "jobs of work," and "downsizing" have crept into the vocabularies of our academic administrators. Students are "customers," their education a "product." The desire to create an elite organization with top-notch faculty and research facilities clashes with the need to streamline, cut costs, raise funds, and keep tuition competitive with peer institutions. Thus, we have arrived at a new corporate climate, where recent recipients of advanced degrees are used as a cheap part-time labor force in the same way that big business uses temporary workers to keep from paying good salaries and full benefits. The way things are, it's a miracle anybody gets a job these days.

So as the luminaries occupying the stage at my commencement ceremonies made their speeches, and slapped one another on the back, and spouted little Latin phrases, this is what I was thinking: I had been looking for work since I had begun my dissertation, a year and a half earlier, and it had become like a second job. Poring over issue after issue of the *Chronicle of Higher Education* took up half my day. Cover letters, c.v.'s, teaching statements, writing samples, letters of recommendation flowed from my home by the hundreds. My thesis advisor, who had sensed the shift in the job market, took me aside one day and advised me to cast my net wide, hope for the best, and not expect too much. Other members of the professoriate were (and still are) oblivious to the dire nature of the situation. "No interviews?" they would gasp, when inquiring as to my fortunes.

"You applied for a job *where*?!?" they would exclaim, when I would ask them to send letters of reference to Northeast State Municipal College and Vocational Technical School, Southwest Backwater Campus. Most of my peers, who had received their degrees in the few years prior to my own graduation, still didn't have permanent positions. What fate would await me? Was I much better than they were? Would I, somehow, be spared the unemployment line? My future, which had once looked so bright, began to seem pretty bleak indeed.

It's not that there were *no* jobs advertised, or that I didn't receive *any* interest in my applications. In the five months prior to commencement, I had exactly three interviews. I subsequently discovered that for one there had never really been any funding for the position, so the search was summarily terminated. For another, I never had a chance; there were inside candidates, and I didn't have the credentials for it, anyway. And for the last, well, I had to spend my own money (really, my parents' money) to fly out for the interview, and when I called a few months later to inquire as to the status of my candidacy, I discovered that my materials had been lost. Apparently, the college—a small fine arts school—was on the verge of losing its accreditation, had been censured by the AAUP for its administrative practices, and had fired a variety of deans, chairs, and professors in a housecleaning operation. In the confusion, all memory and evidence of my interview was erased. Looking back, I realize that I probably dodged a bullet by not getting that job, but it didn't seem that way at the time.

So by the end of May 1992, I had my degree, no work (except for my research post, which paid an hourly wage), little hope, and even less self-esteem. December rolled around, and my first student loan pay-stub book arrived. By scraping, saving, and asking my family for a lot of help, we managed to pay the bills, but just barely. Any unforeseen expense—repairs for the old clunker of a car I was driving, a trip to the doctor (I had no health insurance at work and couldn't afford it on my own)—could push us over the edge. Without the support of my girlfriend, my former professors, my boss at the research institute, and my family and friends, I probably would have given up. But in those depressing months, I discovered the most important trait that someone looking for work in academia can have: patience. The job search is demoralizing and dehumanizing, sure. But if you expect to work in academia, you have to stomach it. This is the current climate, the reality, and we can't change it from the outside. With the advice and help of others, but mostly by trial and error, I kind of developed a "system," which was not a smashing success, mind you, but which did eventually land me a position. Actually, two positions. First, with the help of one of my professors, I landed a spot with decent pay and benefits at a prep school—not what I had originally intended to do with my degrees, but a place to start, nonetheless (also, it turns out, one of the most satisfying teaching and personal experiences of my albeit young career). This position led to my current post, a full-time position at a fine arts college (*not* the one I mentioned above), with a reasonable teaching load, salary, and benefits. So, you're asking yourself, how'd he do it?

Well, the first step is to be aware of all of the resources at your disposal, and then to cast your net wide. Aside from the name recognition of my program, the contacts of my professors, the job placement services of the professional organizations in my field, and the career office at the university, I explored some avenues of my own. Probably the best thing I did was to read every issue of the *Chronicle of Higher Education* from cover to cover. It may sound self-explanatory, but you would be surprised how few graduate students do this. They assume, I think, that all of the good jobs that are worthy of them will appear in professional journals specific to their disciplines. But *everybody* is applying for those jobs; a glance at the *Chronicle* will reveal positions in affiliated areas, at schools with fewer resources, and at less "traditional" institutions. Maybe these kinds of jobs don't interest some; well, I admire those who shoot for the moon, but if you're holding out for that endowed chair at Harvard, maybe you're being a little unreasonable.

The job candidate can't afford to turn his or her nose up at any bona fide position, period. If you don't like where a job is, remember that it can be used as a stepping-off point to a better one next time.

There are so few positions now that you really can't pass any up, whether you think one is beneath you or not. By using the *Chronicle* in this way and broadening my horizons (that is, my definition of an acceptable position), I must have tripled or quadrupled my applications; in three years of job searching, I probably sent out five hundred application packets for colleges big and small, community colleges and prep schools, correspondence schools and "great books" programs, anthropology and art history departments, full-time and part-time positions. That's not hyperbole; it's what I think it takes to get a job these days. Had I stuck to classical archaeology programs at "known" schools, I'm sure I would still be looking. The word processor is a savior here: I had a number of cover letters, reference letters, and related materials stored on disk. I could tailor each application to specific requirements, yet mass-produce applications if need be. The only hurdle was the postage, but I saw it as an investment, so it didn't bother me too much.

Beyond this, I recognized from the start that I would have to be willing to move *anywhere* for a job. Mobility is key. The days of regional jobs are over; if you get your degree in New England, don't count on working there. For all you know, the next crop of jobs may be in the Southwest or the West. Such market forces are beyond our control; you can only react when you see shifting trends. The job candidate needs to be able to move where the work is. Put down no roots, make no commitments, until you have a position with some security. So, for instance, I applied for work in Missouri, Arizona, California, and Alaska, though I had never been west of the Mississippi. As a lifelong Northeasterner, I had trepidation, and wondered how I would get to a good research university from, say, Nome. But I got over my xenophobia, eventually, and even started looking at jobs in American schools and English-language schools opening overseas: Germany, Turkey, Bulgaria. Well, maybe Bulgaria seems extreme to some, but I was prepared to go, if only to have the experience and a full-time position on my c.v.

Writing dozens of applications to diverse schools and programs had a number of side benefits too: I honed my application writing skills to a fine edge. One thing I came to notice, for instance, was that many positions required that applicants have varied backgrounds and second or even third specialties. Colleges that are hiring know that it's a buyer's market out there, so they can demand more of their applicants. In my own field, for instance, jobs for people who can only do ancient art are few and far between. Why hire a one-trick pony, and have to hire a Medievalist, and a Renaissance specialist, and a Modernist, and a non-Western specialist as well, when you can demand (and get) someone who can teach in two or even three areas? So I brushed up on my art history, ancient history, Greek, Latin, and anthropology, and played off of the interdisciplinary nature of archaeology. In my case, I can teach in a non-Western specialty, and I was willing to do surveys of Medieval, Renaissance, Baroque, and Romantic art. I know for a fact that this played a role in my successful candidacy for the position I currently hold; graduate schools would do well to train their students in a secondary specialty.

I also began to notice that while most position announcements still stressed research (especially for positions at "known" schools), there was a growing emphasis on teaching skills. This was lucky for me, as I enjoy teaching more than research, and had spent a good chunk of my graduate career mastering these skills. After graduation, and while I was searching for work, I continued to teach—sometimes for free—in continuing education programs and secondary schools. The lesson here: teach whenever you can in graduate school; seize every opportunity. Teach at community colleges, high schools, retirement homes, whatever. Just teach. Once upon a time, research was the determining factor in securing a job; with the exception of the big research universities, those days are gone. Publishing is how you *keep* a job now; to get one, you need teaching experience. Look at what is happening in state houses all across the country: legislators, most of whom haven't seen the inside of a classroom since they were students themselves, are "reexamining" the teaching loads of professors in their state universities, looking for ways to get academics to teach more students more often. The importance of research, sabbaticals, and academic freedom as guaranteed by the tenure system is becoming less and less obvious to politicians and (in all fairness to politicians) many taxpayers, who want to see more "work" out of academics on the government payroll. And if you think private schools have been spared, think again. Try explaining to a parent spending $15,000 in tuition why it's important that Sally's professors only have a 2/3 workload. It's tough. Thus, the emphasis at most schools has shifted to teaching, and without proven experience in the classroom, you don't have a chance.

So, how did all of this pay off for me? Well, one of my professors, knowing I was casting my net wide and would take whatever (reasonable) position came along, recommended me to a colleague of hers who was developing an ancient history and culture curriculum for a new prep school opening up in Boston. Turns out this colleague was also a student of my dissertation advisor when they were both at Princeton. So I went to interview for the job, which was only part-time. I'm sure some of my friends and professors thought I was nuts: training to get a Ph.D., spending five years and thousands of dollars to teach at a glorified high school? Well, the meeting went great, the part-time job suddenly became a full-time position, and I was offered $32,000 a year with benefits. I was given carte blanche in my classroom, gained valuable experience developing a rigorous program which touched on all areas of ancient civilization, and plunged headfirst into teaching seven hours a day, five days a week, two hundred and fifty days a year. Plus, the kids were fantastic, my colleagues were top-notch, and the facilities first-rate. By the end of that year, I had more real, nitty-gritty, down and dirty teaching experience than I would have received from any four years of college instruction. I guess some might say that I just got lucky, or that I benefited from the "old boy" network; *I* think, though, that I made my own breaks by letting people know that I was willing to do whatever it took to get in front of a classroom.

Actually, I would have stayed at that job, if they had let me. Sure, it was never my intention to teach at the high-school level, but I loved it so much it was hard to leave. Leave I had to, though, because we didn't enroll enough students by the end of the year to support my position. I was angry at first, then sad, then panicked.

Then I resigned myself to going back to the job search. This time, however, there was a marked difference: now I had *real* experience, full-time for a year, and more schools looked harder at my applications. Just a couple of weeks after hearing I wouldn't be back for the 1994–95 school year, I made the short list at a fine arts college looking to expand their art history program. I interviewed and promptly got the job. So, here I am. It ain't Yale, but I kind of like it. There's no tenure track (I'm up for contract review right now, with no guarantee of renewal), the library is small, and there aren't million-dollar research grants to support my work (I got $600 to excavate last summer), but I'm happy. My students are bright, the pay and benefits are (almost) reasonable, I get to teach seminars in any area of ancient art that I choose, and I get to stay on the East Coast, near libraries, resources, and family. Who would have thought it possible? Happiness seemed remote not so long ago.

Yet despite my recent, modest success, my own advice to the new generation of graduate students is realistic, sometimes harsh. When my undergraduates approach me concerning an M.A. or Ph.D. in art history, I tell most of them to forget it. Unless they want the degree for their own edification or sense of accomplishment, or they know that the academy is the *only* place they want to be and they are willing to do and endure *anything* to get there, I send them away. This may seem mean, but it's responsible. I don't see the job situation changing much in the next five or six years, when today's first-year graduate students will likely receive their degrees. If anything, money will get tighter, and the corporate mind-set will be firmly entrenched. The mercenary class of part-timers and replacements that the system has created will continue to do most of the work for almost no reward—what financial incentive does a college have to hire someone full-time, on a tenure track, when there are dozens of good teachers and scholars who, to put food on their tables, will teach on a per-course basis for $3,000 or $4,000 a pop? I refuse to participate in the creation of the next generation of unemployed and underemployed academics.

But I still get the occasional student who is not put off by my advice, and I try to guide that student based on my own experiences, as I would anyone thinking about academia as a career. That's what moved me to write this essay, despite the highly personal nature of some of the episodes I have just shared. Beyond that, there's nothing more one can say, except to warn the job seeker to expect hard times, demoralizing moments, dehumanizing demands, fatigue, debt, and grief. After all that, if you prepare well, stick to your guns, get some practical experience, and are willing to pack up and move at a moment's notice, you just might get your first full-time job. And when you do, remember what you had to do to get there, and try to change the system from the *inside*. Be a true mentor to students exploring the idea of a career in academia (in other words, do the responsible thing and tell them the truth), and to your graduate students as they enter the job market. Defend the rights of part-time instructors, while at the same time arguing for the replacement of part-time positions with full-time ones. Join organizations like the AAUP and defend the rights of the next generation of scholars to reasonable teaching loads, good salary and benefits, sabbaticals to do research, and tenure and academic freedom, before these once basic job offerings are eroded away completely. Without the efforts of the current professoriate, the system in place now will not change, and we will condemn future graduate students to the dismal rat race that is the academic job search in the nineties.

It's All Uphill from Here: Confessions of a Ph.D. Job Searcher

Barbara Bennett

Welcome to a day in the life of a Ph.D. job searcher; it is a Wednesday, sometime in February:

7:40 A.M. I teach an English 101 class no one else wants (which I'm happy to have), even if the class *does* contain twenty-five freshmen who registered too late to get a better time slot. Needless to say, these procrastinators are all late to class on a regular basis.

9:30 A.M. I check my campus mailbox. There are two letters from schools which I wait to read until I get back to the office I share with three other people. One letter, a rejection from a community college in Texas, begins "Dear Applicant." The other is a rejection letter from a small school in Iowa, informing me that my application was one of 435. The letter, though, is written with compassion, commiserating on this difficult job market and wishing me luck. Amazingly, the letter also reminds me that this rejection in no way reflects on my "excellent qualifications." I don't care that it's a

" It's All Uphill from Here" will appear in a forthcoming issue of *Concerns,* the journal of the Women's Caucus for the Modern Languages.

32

form letter; the sincerity and sympathy elicit tears from my eyes. But then, these days, even Johnny on Bud Lite TV commercials affects me the same way.

10:00 A.M. I allow myself fifteen minutes of pure self-pity, facedown in a Norton anthology on my desk, during which I seriously consider becoming a Peace Corps volunteer.

10:30 A.M. I'm on my way to teach class #2 (which I'm glad to have) when I meet two full professors giving a campus tour to a job candidate. The first professor introduces me as *Ms.* Bennett. When Professor #2 reminds him that I'm now *Dr.* Bennett, I make a mental note to send her flowers and offer to paint her house.

Noon I check my e-mail. I decide not to answer immediately the one from my baby brother who got a master's degree in international business and was offered $52,000 for his first year's salary by a company in the south of France. I conclude that his success is probably my punishment for locking him in his closet so often when he was a child.

I also check *The Chronicle* on-line and find four possibilities for jobs. I wonder how many are "real" jobs and how many are already decided upon, the ad only a requirement to fulfill affirmative action. I spend the next two hours working on letters that make me sound as if I'm the perfect match for all four jobs. I refuse to look up the cities of the four schools on a map unless the schools show interest.

2:40 P.M. On the way to class #3 (which I'm thrilled to have), I pass three more colleagues, two of whom find somewhere else to look in an attempt to avoid my eyes. Many people have started doing this since the end of January. I think they're embarrassed to keep asking if I've heard anything. The third person is one of my office-mates, who looks me straight in the eyes and says, "Remember, Barbara, you're brilliant, beautiful, and in big demand." It's sort of a deal we have.

4:30 P.M. Home for a few hours to feed the cat and check for phone messages. There is only one—from my mother. I call her back, and she asks if I've consumed anything yet today besides coffee. I lie and say yes. She's happy.

I glance guiltily at a stack of ungraded freshman narratives about broken romances and tragic childhoods and turn on my computer instead. I waste an hour designing new layouts for my vita, attempting to make it stand up and shout. For a break, I print up a fake vita with three books listed, published by Cornell, Johns Hopkins, and LSU Presses.

6:30 P.M. I teach class #4 for today (which I'm lucky to have) at a local technical college. My students are returning adults. They come directly from work and wear suits, skirts, and blazers. I console myself with two thoughts. First, I *do* have my degree in hand, and second, in the academic world, there is the distinct possibility that I'll never have to wear heels and panty hose again in my entire life.

9:00 P.M. I stop on the way home and have food and drinks with a friend who is on the job market in biology. He has had no luck either, especially since his area of specialty is "freshwater fish"— and I thought I had it rough. We talk about everything *except* jobs. There is the familiar look in his eyes, though, of despair and helplessness, but also a stubborn unwillingness to give in to either. Finally we part, chanting clichés like "Hang in there."

11:00 P.M. Home. No messages. I grade some papers and prepare for classes tomorrow. When I fall asleep, I dream of affirmative action surveys and short lists.

This day I've described is not *one* day, but *many*. Fortunately, my individual story has a happy ending. A job in California advertised in October was filled in early February by a man from Texas, leaving his job open. In March, the job in Texas was accepted by a woman from a small liberal arts college in the upper Midwest. That school, Marian College, advertised a job opening in early April, interviewed me by phone in early May, and brought me to campus three weeks later, offering me the job the second week of June. In August, I found myself driving two thousand miles from Tempe, Arizona, to Fond du Lac, Wisconsin, proud owner of a tenure-track assistant professorship.

My individual success does not, however, lessen my concern

about the miserable job market. My friend in biology is still searching for a position, and I have numerous graduate school friends approaching with terror what they perceive as the hardest test of all: not oral or written exams, not dissertation defenses, but The Job Search.

In writing this paper, I wanted to reach two groups: first, graduate students and recent graduates who need to prepare themselves emotionally, financially, and professionally. They need to seek out support from family, friends, and fellow searchers. They need to know that feelings of rejection and self-doubt are normal, and that, as that kind letter I received said, rejection letters are not an indication of self-worth. Finally, they need to understand that the MLA conference is not the end of the market for the year; it is the beginning. Persistence into the summer months may well pay off.

The second group I wanted to address includes the university faculty members who admit graduate students to their programs, mentor them through the years, and serve on search committees. The job market has changed since many of them were hired, but the university system has not—or is not changing fast enough. There are many problems, and I'm feeling *just secure enough* in my humble new job to be honest and spell out five major problems as I see them:

1. The number of students admitted to Ph.D. programs needs to be indicative of the number of people who can be placed in jobs, rather than of long-established numbers or the number of English 101 instructors needed.
2. The market has changed. It is now the exception rather than the rule for ABD's to find jobs. What does this mean? It means that universities need to find a way to support Ph.D. job searchers who need the extra year or two, with degree in hand, to seek a position—by offering adjunct positions and instructorships on a widespread basis. It simply isn't feasible to expect graduates to leave school and go directly to a waiting job.

    Another solution, proposed by Sander Gilman in a

35

recent issue of the *MLA Newsletter* (Winter 1995), is to set up two-year "postdoctoral mentored teaching fellowships" with a matching system much like the one used to place medical residents—fellowships which would include limited benefits, replace the "masses of graduate assistants" admitted to teach courses, and "offer meaningful, serious employment" to recently graduated Ph.D.'s.

3. Mentors need to understand the intense competition for jobs and emotionally support job searchers. I can't tell you how many times I heard the comment "I just don't understand why you aren't getting offers." This *did not* make me feel better. In desperation, I once photocopied my "prize" letter from a school in Oregon, the one informing me I was one of *853* applicants. I highlighted the number *853,* and put copies in the mailboxes of everyone I could remember ever questioning my perseverance in the job market, and I never heard that phrase expressing doubt again.

4. When many of the now full professors were on the market, it was possible to get that First Job as a Ph.D. at a big research-oriented school. This is also the exception in the system now. Mentors need to prepare students to have realistic expectations. Entry-level positions at research-based universities are much less common than jobs like mine, at schools with a teaching emphasis and little or no interest in publications. Teaching loads of four and five courses a semester are the norm. Reality is a long way from what graduate students see at their large universities: full professors with reduced teaching loads and plenty of time and motivation for research.

5. Finally, search committees need to remind themselves to be human. The large number of applicants mandates the use of form letters, but those form letters *can* be sensitive to the intense stress accompanying the whole process.

The Application Process

The original title of this paper, which I eventually discarded as too pessimistic, was "Here's Your Diploma. Here's Your Prozac. Welcome to the Job Market." That title says much about the mental state so common in the job searcher. But I contend that with a little human compassion and a lot more reality, we can create fewer Prozac junkies and more success stories.

Six Shards from a Search

An academic job hunt may not be as stressful as freeway driving, being tossed into a pit of cobras, or ordinary daily life in Sri Lanka or Rwanda. Still, anyone who has ever conducted one knows that it has immense power to make life chaotic and painful. The very nature of the experience resists any attempt to shape it into a coherent narrative; thus, I have chosen to represent different aspects of my recent job search as "shards." Even so, thanks to the natural human desire for mental coherence, a narrative of sorts does eventually emerge.

Without further ado, then—

Shard the First: Routine

My field is theatre. To apply for an academic job in this discipline requires many different materials. First and most important is the curriculum vitae, or c.v. The simple question it intends to answer is "Where have you been, and what have you done?" However, there are all sorts of minutiae that must be observed in terms of form and content, and specific guidance can be found in books, or from any school's job placement office. Second in importance is the cover letter, which restates the c.v.'s information in prose, and should present the applicant's authentic voice (as much as possible without overstepping the bounds of propriety: hot pink paper is not a good idea, no matter how authentic to your personality it may be!). Next in importance are the letters of recommendation from professors, employers, or colleagues. Rather than bother my professors for a separate letter for each application, I took advantage of my university's credential service. Observing strictest confidentiality, the professors wrote only one letter, which the Career Center would then send out with every application. Academic transcripts complete the picture.

The paperwork required has a negative side, but an even more powerful positive one. Naturally, assembling all these documents takes a lot of time and a fair amount of money; this is particularly true if one is conducting a no-holds-barred-damn-I-want-a-job-apply-for-everything search, as I was. However, this work serves a very useful psychological purpose, which I came to appreciate more and more as my search went on. The hard fact of the matter is that a job applicant is almost completely helpless in getting hired. One is simply unaware of exactly what a prospective employer is looking for, and consequently has no clue as to how to present oneself most attractively. Added to this uncertainty is the sheer quantity and quality of the competition. You know that every job is going to attract over a hundred applicants or even more, all of whom have been in or directed a certain number of plays, taken a certain number of courses from more or less qualified institutions, published a certain amount, etc. By submitting an application for evaluation by established academics, one is permitting them to control one's destiny. This is not a comfortable prospect for anyone, least of all people who have shown the initiative and determination to strive for an advanced degree. The routine of collecting, processing, and submitting application materials, however, is completely under the applicant's control. Within the larger context of helplessness, such islands of autonomy are extremely important. They may provide only the illusion of control, but (as plays have shown again and again), illusions of a certain type are as necessary for survival as air.

My routine worked like this: every Wednesday, off to the public computers in the library, when the current issue of *The Chronicle of Higher Education* comes on line. No time for the articles: I cut right to the "Jobs Available" section, category Humanities, subcategory Theatre. First, I scan the ads, discarding only those that hold out no hope whatsoever ("Established department seeks chair . . . " "Musical theatre specialist wanted . . ."), and then print out the realistic possibilities. I keep an ongoing list of positions I've applied to, and the names and addresses of that day's postings join it, on a separate page. I print out two copies of this page, one for me and one for the Career Center. The names and addresses then get plugged into my form letter requests for transcripts. A quick glance at the Other Humanities category sometimes turns up an interesting possibility as well ("For the current academic year, the University of Qatar is seeking . . ."). I also print out the necessary application letters, suitably adjusted for date and type of job. Theatre positions are somewhat different from others, in that some schools are primarily looking for theatre practitioners, some primarily for academics, and some, occasionally, for a combination. I also run off a few c.v.'s whenever necessary. All this must be done on a laser printer, at 15 cents a page.

After this, it's off to the university's Career Center. I give them one copy of my printout, and $4 for each name on the list (double that amount for an overseas job). They will then send out my dossier of credentials. Yvonne, the secretary in charge of this service, is always pleasant and sympathetic, no matter how much paperwork I saddle her with. Her husband is also a desperate graduate student (in mathematics, with employment prospects about as bad as my own), so she understands my situation. Small comforts like my conversations with her help me maintain my fortitude. After talking with her, I visit my final stop, the Administration Building, to request my academic transcripts. I fill out the necessary forms, and pay my $2 for each name on that day's list.

On odd weeks, there is also a trip to the Theatre Arts Building to check out the latest issue of *Artsearch*; if suitable positions are advertised here, there then follows another session on the computer. Besides increasing my chances for employment, this little epicycle keeps my routine fresh. That ends my activities on the campus . . . but there is more to do at home. My transcript request letter with that day's possibilities goes to the university from which I received my MFA, draining another $2 per application from the family resources. The cost of each single application is not that serious, but over the weeks and months, it begins to resemble a minor hemorrhage. Still, there is no choice: you wanna play, you gotta pay.

My copy of the address list of that day's applications then goes up on a wall in our living room. Because academic hiring is seasonal, the list starts out small in September, but it eventually nearly covers the wall, with over two hundred names and addresses. As the list grows, my hopes rise; surely with so many applications out and expecting a response, there will be one university, somewhere, who will look at my soon-to-be-granted (later, in-hand) terminal degree from a pretty hotsy-totsy school with more-than-decent grades, my other degree in hands-on practical experience, my membership in Actors' Equity, my records of performance, publication, and service activities, and hire me. . . .

As the time passes, however, this does not occur, and the wall takes on a particularly foreboding character. As each rejection comes in, I cross off the name of the school. My personal record was five letters of rejection received in one day. In my mind, the list of schools applied to and rejected by eventually became known as the Wall of Shame. What can the people making hiring decisions possibly be *looking* for? Week by week, one by one, I see the ad, send the application, get the rejection, cross off the name. The seemingly invariable pattern is depressing, and yet comforting in a perverse and illogical fashion. As assurance that the universe runs along orderly, predictable lines, the blizzard of rejections from an academic job search is hard to beat. Still, the cost to one's professional and personal self-esteem is high. Anyone who doesn't feel emotionally lacerated during an unsuccessful job search is either stoic beyond belief, or already dead.

One of the reliable ways for protecting oneself during this difficult time is routine. For every rejection that comes in the mail, there is another advertisement somewhere else. At the full peak of the hiring season (usually in November/December), there are even more possibilities opening up than those that are closing down. Routine is also a useful corrective in adjusting one's expectations to reality; it may just be the case that I am not as indispensable to academe as I would like to think I am. This is painful, yes, but the way of the world is that there is no wisdom gained without pain. The possibility of pain endured without gaining wisdom is itself too painful to contemplate. Even long after my search has ended, my memory of these and similar emotional gyrations and distortions remains vivid. One cannot hope for emotional growth under such conditions: simple survival is already a success, and the routine of concentrating on the practical actions of application is a great help to this end.

Shard the Second: Rebellion

One aspect of the job search that deserves a special section of its own involves the inevitable arrival of the "affirmative action" (read: "quota") form for each position applied to. This is a thorny issue, and this essay is not the right place for an involved discussion, but a basic statement of my principles is essential for an understanding of my reaction. In brief: being a straight white man does not make me any better than anyone else, but I'll be boiled and starched if I'll let anyone tell me that it makes me worse.

My reaction to the arrival of this form had both constant and variable components. The constant reaction was to the statement on the form that the information I provided would not affect my candidacy, to which the only reasonable response is "Yeah, right." I have a friend, a full professor, who has told me that on at least one occasion, their department arbitrarily decided to hire a woman, in contravention of federal law, academic integrity, and any reasonable standard of morality. Information concerning my race, gender, and age (all completely irrelevant to my abilities as a scholar, teacher, and artist, by the way) will always be susceptible to abuse by those who are more interested in fulfilling a social agenda than in hiring the best candidate. Should I take only their assurance that they will allow a member of the allegedly oppressive race, gender, and sexual preference to compete on a level field? I think not.

My variable response involved the form as a whole. Most of the time I lacked the spunk to do anything other than sigh and acquiesce. I would check the appropriate boxes, and chuck the wretched thing in the mailbox with equal loathing for the process, the recipient, and myself.

However, on several occasions, I would assert a more playful and anarchic spirit. The oatmeal-brained bureaucrats responsible for creating and implementing this policy are completely vulnerable to, and completely deserve, some zesty ribbing à la Abbie Hoffman or Shel Silverstein. Metaphorically, the affirmative action forms are the most dismal shades of Stalinist gray; splashing some nice Day-Glo colors on them is tremendously therapeutic. The forms themselves provide an abundance of irresistible opportunities for pointed japery.

One such opening occurs when the writers leave one blank for "date of birth" and another for "age." Why not put down a date and a number that don't match? Hey, if the affirmative action officers don't realize the redundancy, let them figure things out when the answers don't match! Another similar possibility involves mismatches of name and gender. A woman named Robert? A boy named Sue? "HOW DO YOU DO!"

It was the "Race" category, however, that always presented a cornucopia of possibilities. For one, I was born in the United States; according to the valid (i.e., pre-PC) definition of the term, that makes me a native American. Well, gosh, there just happens to be a space defined by that very term, think I'll check it. Another bit of casuistry worth deploying relates to the origins of humanity. Archaeology has proven beyond any possible dispute that Homo sapiens evolved in

Africa; therefore, every single person on the planet is an African-something. I must be an African-American. The space; the check mark.

Some forms had a box marked "Other," allowing the respondent's own self-definition. Now if we're going to play the victim game, the Jews have as good a claim as any people for that special status, and better than most. An atheist by creed, I am one-quarter Jewish by descent, but for the purposes of the form, I became one hundred percent Israeli-, Jewish-, or Hebrew-American. *Mazel tov!* Another response which made a far less subtle point was to check the "Other" box and write the single word "Human" in the following blank. This was the closest I came to expressing my contempt for the form's mind-set. I wish I had had the courage to leave the entire category blank and write something like "Race is an artificial construct; what are you, a bunch of essentialists? And what could race possibly have to do with my skills, anyway?"

I make no apologies whatever for these responses to the quota forms. Again, the issue was control; I could do nothing to counter prejudice against who I was, but I could make my resentment at being thus "processed" known. It brightened many a dark day to know that I had done my small part in ventilating the smelly little orthodoxies that infest the academy of our time.

Shard the Third: Rudeness

For anyone who is not a saint, a long-term, unsuccessful job search generates considerable bitterness toward oneself and the world. This is only human nature; however, as Katharine Hepburn said in *The African Queen*, "Human nature . . . is what we are put here to rise above." I admit to being less than exemplary in this regard. Most of the time, I could bear up reasonably well under the strain, but more than once, I mistakenly believed that my own distress gave me license to behave badly to others. This is the story of my deepest plunge below the line of civility.

In addition to looking at jobs at colleges, I also conducted a job search among private schools. (Incidentally, this is a subsection of the job market not to be overlooked. Many private schools have extremely good facilities and pay quite nice salaries. These positions lack the prestige of a professorship, but all things considered, one is better off at a good private school than at a bad college.) The conditions are somewhat different from the freelance college job search. There are several agencies that represent candidates to private schools, and if one wants to be taken seriously, representation by these agencies is almost essential. The agencies are not exclusive; in fact, because each one deals with a special geographical area of the market, candidates are encouraged to sign up with as many agencies as possible. The candidate pays no fee to any agency; instead, the agency receives payment from the school if it sends a successful candidate.

One of my agencies secured me an interview with a private school on Long Island. I traveled there, had a very enjoyable experience, and, I thought, presented myself well. However, I did not get the job. One of the responsibilities of a candidate represented by multiple agencies is to keep all of them aware of the current status of the job search; so I had to tell all my agencies of this rejection. My hopes had been raised and then dashed, so I was feeling even more bitter than usual. In the middle of one call to a job counselor representing an agency other than the one that had sent me, I found myself making one of the few remarks in my life of which I am completely ashamed. She responded to my news by saying (and meaning, with genuine sympathy) ''That's too bad.'' In a completely inappropriate cutting tone, I responded with ''Well, you should be glad; one of your competitors sent me to that interview.'' My meaning was that her agency's hopes for making some money from me were of course more important than my disappointment. Looking back, I am appalled at the cynicism, misdirection, self-pity, and downright rudeness of such words, but at the time, they flowed from me with tidal force. Much to her credit, the counselor did not respond with the appropriate chastisement, but calmly said, ''I'm sorry, could we start this conversation all over?'' I immediately apologized, and later wrote her a short note apologizing again. Still, it is true that words are like arrows—once they are launched, nothing can bring them back.

The incident was ultimately for the good; it brought home to me with great force the point that my difficult situation did not entitle me to renounce my responsibility for courtesy to others. From that time on, no matter how many rejections I received or how dark my prospects seemed, I was able to discipline myself from poisoning the well of public conversation. Still, anytime I want to feel like sinking through the floor (as I have since had to do for a play I was in), that incident remains completely effective in pushing me there.

Shard the Fourth: Recharging

One of the more insidious difficulties of an academic job search is that it occupies far more time and energy than it ought. Those who have tremendous willpower, or those who are incredibly busy all their waking hours, can probably handle the aftermath of an application the right way: send it off and then forget about it. After all, once it is in the mail, there really is nothing more that can be done except wait. Any reliance on magical thinking to increase one's chances for employment is just so much mental and emotional energy wasted. However, since all of one's hopes (not to mention those of one's family as well) are riding on the outcome, forgetting an application once sent is, putting it mildly, a challenge. The situation reminds me of an old joke about a carpet with a special power. To make it fly, a person merely had to sit on it and not think of a white rhinoceros! Achieving serenity with several job applications outstanding is a similarly impossible task. In addition, each rejection received makes a positive response from each prospective employer not yet heard from even more crucial.

The nervous system is simply not built to withstand such uninterrupted and ever-increasing tension. One of the most helpful things I found to get me through this time was this: as I lay in bed at the end of every day, I would take a moment to recollect and savor the single best thing that had happened to me during that day. After all, even the flattest county in Kansas does have one highest point. No matter how depressing the day, I always did find some small moment of value, and I would take a few minutes to relive it. If I had had a pleasant run, I would recollect the feelings of my legs pounding smoothly, my heart thumping, and the air rushing in and out of my lungs; if the sunset had been spectacular, I would re-create the colors and the warm breeze; and so forth. The point was not so much the manifest content of what I found, but rather the reinforcement of my sense that even though career matters were proceeding dismally or not at all, the world still held beauty and pleasure. Although I'm no psychologist, I think that having that thought as my last conscious impression every night gave me some strength upon waking to face the next day.

I did not do this for the first few months of my search, and in some ways, they were harder to bear than the later months, even though the job search had dragged on for a longer time. I'm not sure exactly how I got the idea, or even when it became a routine. As corny as this may sound, I do know that it was the single most valuable thing I did to maintain my perspective and sanity. I found coping mechanisms that were suggested to me by anyone else to be of small or no value, and therefore this end-of-day meditation may not do much good for anyone else. I am not prescribing this for anyone, but I would urge everyone in similar difficulties to evolve your own equivalent and personal way of recharging; and the sooner the better.

Shard the Fifth: Redemption

My search does have a happy ending, but with more compli-cations than were perhaps necessary. The situation resembled the city-bus effect: you wait for a bus for an hour at the bus stop, and then a whole string of them arrive at once. Just as I was becoming resigned to another year of non-academic work, frustration, and poverty, good news came, from not one but two places at once. Quite late in the hiring year, at the end of July, I received a phone call from the chair of the English Language Department of Providence University—on Taiwan! She did not even want an interview: she offered me a job on the spot, and would be mailing me a contract immediately. I told her that I was immensely pleased, but I would of course have to discuss the matter with my wife. Certainly, a move of this magnitude was not to be undertaken lightly.

As if the prospect of moving halfway around the world weren't a sufficiently thorny question in itself, that very day, the issue became more complicated still. A letter came from the chair of a small school in North Carolina who was also interested in my application, and would I please send some photographs of sets that I'd worked on? Although not quite as straightforward as the Taiwan offer, it was clear that I had a real shot at this position as well.

It really is true that a sudden change of fortune for the better is nearly as stressful as one for the worse. In a span of three mere hours, I had gone from being the world's doormat to a more-or-less hotly desired commodity. While this all sorted itself out, I found myself being more unstable emotionally than I am comfortable with, this, of course, at the very time when I needed my logical faculties more strongly than ever, in order to do the best thing for myself and my family. A full description of all the ins and outs and backs and forths is not necessary here, but the upshot was our decision that if the North Carolina school came through with a firm offer, we would go there. Meanwhile, of course, we let the hiring process continue at Providence, and kept both places informed of each other's administrative progress or lack thereof.

The North Carolina chair, however, never brought herself to the point of making a definite offer. She soon informed me that she had chosen to bring another candidate to the campus for an interview; this, coupled with the fact that the deadline was fast approaching for a yes-or-no decision on the Taiwan job, more or less clinched matters. I profusely thanked the North Carolina chair for her interest, and called the Providence University chair to accept her offer. It was a great relief to disentangle ourselves from the final set of complications in which this job search had wrapped us, and to begin the physically hard but psychologically straightforward tasks of packing and moving. Probably my case is not typical, and most people will receive a single offer at a time. However, one must be prepared for anything; the universe seems not to let go of its playthings without a final reminder of who's really in charge.

Shard the Sixth: Reprise

I have thrown myself into my work at Providence with a will, and I have established myself as a worthy teacher, actor, director, scholar, advisor, and committee member. As a result, my job here is probably secure for as long as I would like it. I am reasonably satisfied with my work, colleagues, students, and opportunities, and I know that I am a thousand times better off than I was at this time last year. However, various aspects of the physical and social environments have led me to begin another job search. (The air is filthy, and the drivers have to be the world's rudest.) This search's emotional contours, however, are completely different from those that characterized my first one. Most important, the sense of desperation is entirely absent. I no longer feel bound to apply for *every single job* that is remotely related to my expertise; this alone is an extremely liberating development. Instead, I can afford to be selective.

As before, I now find myself regularly staring at my computer screen, checking out advertisements in *The Chronicle of Higher Education*. This is thanks to the Internet, and it would have been completely impossible only a short time ago. I am no follower of Coué, insisting that every day in every way, things are getting better and better, but it is nice that in at least one concrete way, there has been significant improvement. In the future, the Internet can only get more and more important; I've already seen a few web pages created by job seekers. One of the useful things a candidate could do to improve the chances of getting hired is to learn as much about this exciting new medium as possible, and then plunge in.

So far, I have applied for only two positions and recently received word of rejections from both. Instead of beating myself up over them as in my first search, I can now afford to say, "Eh—their loss," and mean it. I am in a win-win position. If I get hired elsewhere, great; if not, I can continue helping deserving students, and piling up teaching experience, publishing and artistic credits, and money. I will always be profoundly grateful to Providence University and to the chair; however, I don't think I want to settle in Taiwan. (This is more for the sake of my children than for my own.) Even if my job search from an established position turns out to be longer than I would like, it is already shaping up to be a far more pleasant experience than standing outside the candy store with my nose pressed to the glass.

To close the circle of this essay: despite its potential for fragmenting one's emotions, perceptions, relations, and personality, conducting a job search is like writing a linear narrative, with, we all hope, a happy ending. The painful truth, however, is that this happy ending will not come about without some cooperation from some other, somewhere, which we are almost completely powerless to bring about on our own. Given this situation, it is only natural that feelings of helplessness, inadequacy, anger, frustration, and despair crowd the emotional landscape. In particular, it is extremely painful for people whose academic excellence demonstrates superior initiative to be defined merely by so many c.v.'s, cover letters, recommendations, and transcripts (cf. *A Chorus Line*: "Who am I anyway? Am I my résumé?"). The best we can do is to write our portion of the story with as much grace, intelligence, and resiliency as we can. No question, the satisfaction from doing our best is meager in comparison to receiving a job offer from that glorious, high-prestige, high-salary, tenure-track position, but until such an offer arrives, it will have to do. The knowledge that others have been in this situation before us, or are there now, is similarly cold comfort; yet it is also not entirely to be disregarded.

Good fortune to each and every reader contemplating a job search, actively engaged in one now, or recuperating from one.

Planning, Persistence, and Politics: Do's and Don'ts from a Job Search in the Physical Sciences

Kurt T. Bachmann

In late August 1995 I began my current job as assistant professor of physics at Birmingham-Southern College in Birmingham, Alabama. I consider myself extremely fortunate to have this desirable academic position at a small, high-quality, private undergraduate college, and I am able to pursue my goals of being both a quality educator and an independent researcher. This account describes my job search during the 1994–95 academic year, including my applications to over seventy academic institutions, my education and experience, the unflattering comment on one of my reference letters, and my work toward getting a high-school teaching certificate when my prospects for a college teaching job seemed particularly bleak.

During the summer of 1994, I turned thirty-four years old. I was also beginning my second year as a "junior scientist" at a well-known national laboratory, a contract position that had the potential of being renewed after the initial two-year period, but not into anything permanent. I knew that I had little chance of a tenure-track position in solar research because my work involves analysis of data rather than instrumentation or theory, and because the resources devoted to solar research are small compared to those devoted to other fields of astrophysics. Also, a tenure-track position in this laboratory had just been filled by a young Ph.D. from Europe.

My own education and experience are reasonably prestigious and diverse. I received my B.S. with honor in physics from Caltech in 1982 and my Ph.D. in high energy particle physics from Columbia University in 1988. I discovered about halfway through my graduate years that two reasons for the large number of high energy physics graduate students were to rationalize the "educational value" of high energy physics to the federal government, and to provide cheap night watchpersons for the large detectors. Nevertheless, since there were many undergraduate teaching positions open at that time, I persevered with my final two years of analysis while teaching two courses each semester as an adjunct lecturer at two well-known universities, both in the New York City area. Since the year of my Ph.D. was 1988, this teaching experience allowed me to obtain a tenure-track position relatively easily at a mostly undergraduate university near Philadelphia that had a small engineering school.

However, the downsizing of the United States' military-industrial complex in the late 1980s hit small engineering schools hard. Our introductory physics enrollment dropped by more than half during my three-year sojourn; engineering faculty members were taking over courses traditionally taught by physics faculty members; and one physics faculty member who had been a full-time administrator decided to return to teaching. Although I enjoy teaching very much and my second-year review was quite favorable, my department head told me candidly that the tenure committee would probably be very tough on me because my position was essentially superfluous at that point. I therefore decided to take a research position in a new field more amenable to me than high energy physics.

With the help of a tenured professor I knew, I obtained a two-year post-doc in Boulder, Colorado, starting in mid-1991, and began analyzing helioseismology data, the study of five-minute acoustic oscillations in the interior of the sun. By mid-1994 I had moved to Tucson, Arizona; I was writing my fourth paper in solar astrophysics; and I considered it a good time to again seek a potentially permanent position. I knew by reading the *Young Scientists' Network Digest* that the academic market had become extremely tight, but I still felt that teaching was the right field for me, combined with some solar astrophysics research. I was not satisfied with temporary contracts anymore—existing as a second-class citizen to the administrative and faculty bureaucrats at any national lab or state university, who spend the majority of their time traveling the world and lobbying federal government departments with suspicious promises and results. I was tired of nonscientists and former scientists splurging and junketing from my work.

I told my supervisor that I would be seeking a teaching position, and he agreed to provide references for me. I arranged three more references among former colleagues and supervisors. My source of job advertisements was primarily *Physics Today*, and I applied to undergraduate teaching positions located essentially everywhere in the United States, plus one position in Australia. I estimated that if I applied to sixty jobs and if three hundred other people were sending applications everywhere, like me, I would have a one in five chance of securing a position. I reasoned that my experience in two fields, physics and astronomy research, plus my five years' teaching expertise should increase those chances greatly.

I also reasoned that I must put my primary concentration on preparing cover letters, teaching and research statements, résumés, curricula vitae, and other information carefully tailored to each institution. It would do me little good to push for a fifth publication; my time would best be spent enhancing my public image, sharpening my interaction skills with people, and attempting to become an independent scientist. Therefore, I decided to propose a National Science Foundation Grant related to the work I was doing, to become more active in the Young Scientists' Network by becoming the editor of the *Moderated Digest*, and to run for councilor of the American Astronomical Society (AAS). My political platform was for scientific societies like AAS to help emerging scientists like myself gain lasting employment and to encourage graduate programs to limit the number of graduate students admitted. Luckily, I could keep my job until July 1995, so I would have time to pursue these goals.

As the weeks rolled by, I applied to every appropriate teaching professorial job available, about three-quarters tenure-track and one-quarter replacement. These jobs ranged from Maine to Southern California, Florida to Washington, and beyond. As mentioned above, one advertised position was in Perth, Australia. I provided all information requested by each school, including a teaching portfolio in one case and a ''multicultural statement'' in another. I preferred colleges that deferred request of letters of recommendation until after their initial pass through the applicants, but I carefully sent addresses to my references whenever necessary. I had four references—two research and two teaching. In most cases I provided two teaching and one research recommendation, but in cases of prestigious schools with explicit research-presence requirements, I requested letters from both of my research references.

I thought I had done my best to offer compensation to three of my four references in a way that I have never heard of before—a way that is certainly not standard in my field. I mailed checks for $100 of my own money to them for their hard work of writing, altering, addressing, and mailing so many letters in a timely manner. Only one of them actually accepted this money, but I considered it a necessary offer. Gone are the days when an advisor, employer, or colleague must send recommendations to only a few prospective employers, and I felt uneasy about casting such a large imposition on people whom I consider to be friends. Also, I had this naive impression that spending a little money on my job search would somehow make interviews come my way.

Instead, my telephone remained quiet. By February my application count was over fifty, and I received a strong message that I should have heeded. In three cases, schools that had requested letters of recommendation after an initial pass through the applications rejected me soon after receipt of the letters.

Soon it was March, and my situation was no better. After over sixty applications, I had nothing but a growing folder of rejection letters. By the end of my search, I had heard from all but three of the seventy-one schools. Two colleges in eastern Pennsylvania told me explicitly that each had received over 350 applications for a single tenure-track faculty position. One college in North Carolina sent a very elaborate, apologetic discourse on their selection procedure. A few schools actually told me the name of the selected new faculty member. Three schools canceled their searches due to changes in budgetary situations, and even the school from Australia sent me two letters—one of receipt for the application and one of rejection. A few schools sent very terse, copied signature form letters; but only the "if you don't here from us by April 15" receipt/rejection postcard from a university in New York City was noticeably insulting. I also learned that my bid for the AAS Council was unsuccessful, although the AAS secretary said that I made a strong showing.

By April I was in dire straits, facing the fact that I might not receive a college teaching position while my existing job would definitely expire at the end of July. I still wanted to be in education, so I decided to pursue a high-school teaching certificate. In Arizona I needed ten college courses, the U.S. and Arizona State Constitution exams, and a teachers' proficiency exam—a political device ensuring that I could read, write, and do simple arithmetic. I started this procedure on April 22, 1995, by taking both the U.S. and Arizona Constitution exams. I ended up passing both of these tests easily, but it dawned on me in the middle of the second test that neither had been updated in over four years! During that time the 27th Amendment to the U.S. Constitution concerning congressional pay raises had been ratified and several portions of the Arizona Constitution had been changed. These changes affected answers to several of the questions. I immediately sent letters to the testing board and to the Arizona superintendent of public instruction asking if the questions with errors could be counted correct for me if I did not pass. Sure enough, the superintendent sent me an acknowledgment letter two months later, vowing to bring the exams up to date.

By that time I had taken and passed with A's two education courses at the University of Phoenix. This private commuter college teaches weekend education courses such that students can receive a semester of credit for a Friday evening, Saturday, and Sunday class plus a ten-page paper and answering some questions. Each course cost approximately $350; so, since I had plenty of money saved, I put myself on track to finish my requirements by August. My plan was to gain Arizona high-school certification and to try to get a job in Kentucky or southern Indiana, where I had grown up. I heard through the grapevine that there were very few high-school science openings in southern Arizona, but I could conceivably teach with an out-of-state certificate if I could find a school anywhere that needed me. I actually called a principal of a public school in North Carolina from an advertisement I found at the University of Arizona School of Education, and she said to wait until after I had my Arizona certification, just before the new academic year, before searching for a job. My cousin, who had recently obtained a junior high teaching job in mathematics with her B.S. in math and her Ph.D. in German, agreed. She had difficulties because unlike me she was tied down to her family and was not willing to teach anywhere.

In mid-April a miracle occurred. I was offered an interview at a small Augustinian school near Boston, Massachusetts. The school wanted me to purchase my own ticket and get reimbursed, and I found that staying over a weekend offered tremendous savings over the normal, during-the-week price. I therefore arranged to stay over the weekend before my Monday interview. My visit lasted from Saturday afternoon until Tuesday afternoon the last weekend of April. I was dismayed that no leaves had even begun to grow on the trees by that late date, but that's New England. I spent a lot of time with the department chair, showing him copies of pages from college guides and other information I had found about his school. He drove me around the area while I did my best to display the proper emotions of marvel as he spoke French with his wife: the proper concern as he expressed his dissatisfaction with the Augustinian college administrators who were educated as priests, not as managers; and the proper commitment to improve when he exclaimed that I did not pronounce "Boston" correctly and when the department secretary called me a Southerner. I dressed in a suit and tie for my interview, and I brought a slide projector with me so that I could present slides with my talk without a hitch. I reiterated during my interview the teaching experiences I described in my application, notably science courses for non-science majors: astronomy, conceptual physics, the physics of music, and meteorology. I described my commitment toward instilling within science majors the need for vocational training such as computer programming, due to the difficult job situation. I described my ability to be involved in solar astrophysics research and my recent proposal writing. All in all the interview went very well, and I wrote a thank-you note to the department chair immediately upon returning to work.

A few days later another miracle occurred. I got a telephone interview with Birmingham-Southern College, my current employer. Again I reiterated my teaching and research strengths, emphasizing that I was born in Louisville, Kentucky, which is somewhat south, and that my aunt, uncle, and cousins live in Knoxville, Tennessee. They then told me something very important, which I should have suspected long before. One of my reference had written, along with several very good things about me, one comment that was just plain awful. I tried to explain this as backlash from my running for AAS Council, and of course I thanked them heartily for this valuable information. Needless to say, I did not expect to hear from them again, but I sent them a carefully worded thank-you note that same afternoon.

I immediately called my former supervisor and explained that I had learned about his comment. I found that we lived in different worlds. He had no real gripes about me, and he simply thought that he should write the "problem comment" in order to provide a balanced judgment about me and to protect himself from the management of his national lab—where I had gotten into a political confrontation two years previously. His uneducated opinion was that what he wrote would not adversely affect my employment chances. However, even though my referee was not even forty-five years old, he had no idea that over 350 people could apply for one faculty position or even that he should tell me about any comments that might get my application thrown out immediately. After all, he had received his tenure during the 1980s, when government money

57

flowed like water, and he had no idea that the world had changed. Of course, the main problem was my failure to either ask my references for their letters up front or name a bogus college with either my brother's or my parents' address so I could secretly see the letters with my own eyes. I trusted blindly, and I got burned.

Luckily, still another miracle soon occurred. Birmingham-Southern College (BSC) awarded me an interview. In this case they provided the airplane ticket and they told me when to show up. I again studied the college guides and other standard references, and I prepared the same research talk and sales pitches about my experience and abilities. This was a different part of the country from Boston, and I almost blew the interview within five minutes of the initial breakfast meeting at 7:30 A.M. The cafeteria line contained pancakes, scrambled eggs, biscuits, and what looked like gravy for the biscuits. When I asked what this fourth item was, my future boss yelled, "Why, you Yankee—that's grits!" I immediately ordered two heaping ladlefuls, realizing that I must be much more careful about what I say.

I did well the rest of the day by being polite and courteous, by saying "Good morning," "Good afternoon," "Please," and "Thank you." They told me that my interview with the president of the college was most important because he had final say in everything, which I took as a sign of interest in me. My meeting with the president went well, and I even flattered him, noting that the faculty said that he had really turned the school around during his twenty-year tenure. The only unexpected question he asked me was whether I was United Methodist, the charter religion of BSC. I simply said no, feeling that a discussion of religious affiliation might not benefit my chances of being selected for the job.

My research presentation audience was the biggest I had ever seen during the eight interviews of my professional life, and I thanked the faculty members profusely for requiring their premedical students to attend. Again, I gave my talk without a hitch, using the slide projector that I had brought with me, as before. All in all, I felt very good about my interview performance, despite the grits gaffe, and I was much more excited by the possibility of living in the Birmingham area than the idea of locating near Boston. My girlfriend in Tucson said that she too felt that I was more excited about the second interview.

Nevertheless, the day after I returned to work, the provost of the Boston-area school called to offer me their job. Although I acted very pleased over the phone, the salary was dismal, especially given the astronomical living expenses of the Boston area. The provost said that pay was uniform for all faculty and not negotiable. At this point I was happy to have a job, even though I was still considering continuing to pursue my teaching certificate. I really wanted the Birmingham-Southern job, but I had only a week and a half to see if BSC wanted me.

I needed some negotiating assistance. Luckily, there were many administrators where I worked, so I told one of them my story and he seemed to burst with enthusiasm about all the possibilities. He told me to call BSC immediately, to tell them about my existing offer, to find out if they were interested in me, and to ask if they could put together an offer in a week. I did as he suggested, and yes they were interested in me. The BSC administration agreed to prepare a contract within a few days, so I asked the Boston-area school to give me a week to decide. My negotiator told me to refrain from telling them anything about my dealings with Birmingham-Southern unless they asked directly. He indicated that a week is typical, adding that if an applicant does not accept a job within that time, the assumption is that he or she does not really want it badly enough. He also said that accepting an offer and then resigning after getting a better position is something a person can do maybe once in a career.

Sure enough, the BSC dean called to make me an offer. Unfortunately, this offer—although higher than my existing offer—was a significant drop from my salary at the national lab, something I expected when moving from a government job to the private sector, but disappointing nonetheless. I remained very congenial on the phone, and the dean did not ask for a verbal yes or no. He only advised me that the written contract was in the mail. I immediately sought out my administrator again, and he told me to call the dean back and ask for more money, using my first offer as a threat. I told the dean that I really would like to choose BSC, if they could up the salary. After some talking, the dean agreed to a $2,000 per year increase, but no more. This was getting closer to my government salary and I thought I could also do some summer teaching, so I accepted verbally, and he agreed to put this second, updated contract in the mail. I waited until receiving this contract before telling the Boston-area school about my acceptance, only one day before our agreed deadline.

So, I finally have a job with which I am happy. Believe it or not, I received phone calls of interest from two other schools after that. Apparently, my general level of perceived quality was being sought at this late time in the academic year. All the real hotshots had been chosen already, so I was glad to have continued to persevere in my search till the end. In my present job, I see that many faculty members who gained tenure in the 1980s and before do not always appreciate how lucky they are to have an academic job these days, as they battle over trifles with their administrations. I also see that it is difficult for a small private college to compete with the almost free ride offered by state-funded colleges and universities. Private colleges must demonstrate a higher-quality product through small classes and personalized attention to all students. Currently, my work efforts involve teaching, curriculum development, and locating money to fund research equipment for a small, on-campus research program. I believe that the lessons I learned during my long job search about planning, persistence, and politics are helping me with these projects and will continue to benefit me in the future.

T_{wo}

Cattle Call:

The Academic Conference and Interview

Introduction

Daniel Born
Department of English, Marietta College

am not sure about cattle, but it is well known that lab rats literally smell fear emanating from the bodies of stymied comrades—no metaphor this—and will avoid that portion of the maze where frustration runs highest, where rewards and reinforcement are sought but little or none found. Consider, then, the world of the academic conference: a behavioral sink of equally strange disturbances, where young scholars instinctively seek cover but must—if they are to harbor any hope of employment—perform. And more than that: perform fully conscious of statistical odds for newly minted Ph.D.'s which make a whirl on a riverboat casino look attractive.

Performing in this particular arena, as O'Donovan-Anderson, Wachtel, and Gruner indicate in the section ahead, can be cruel and unusual punishment. Every candidate who has been through the ordeal once has favorite horror stories to share. Yet such honest reflection has value, beside the usual therapeutic effect of transforming pain into comedy. Listen to enough anecdotes about Attack Interviews and you might avoid being blindsided by one yourself. And while none of these writers subscribes to the mantras of creative visualization, they each offer behind the guise of anecdote some respectable helpings of utilitarian wisdom, touching on, among other things, the necessity of mock interviews and rehearsal; the importance of honing your "specialty" for different audiences; and the twilight zone of the on-campus "teaching demonstration" which more often than not is a performance done for the benefit of administrators and faculty.

Nothing really prepares you for this first encounter, the interview at the academic conference. Whether conducted in the stuffy confines of a hotel suite, hotel room ("Would you care to sit on the couch or on the bed?"), or in a garish hangarlike chamber crowded with hundreds of numbered tables, the event is daunting. Nothing has prepared you for it. Not the intellectual juice and *jouissance* of seminars, not the monkish hours reading in the stacks, not the marathon of the dissertation you have lived and breathed for years. If you are fortunate, an interview will lead to a campus visit—or in the jargon of the jaded, a "fly-out." And absolutely nothing has prepared you for the perverse vagaries of a process in which what you say about Paul de Man may actually matter less than the color of your shoes.

Yet from the other side of the interviewing table, the process seems considerably less random. First, the importance of flawlessly written c.v.'s and letters cannot be overstated. As a professor at a small liberal arts college, I've had opportunity to serve on a variety of departmental search committees and I've been stunned by the high incidence of writing errors in materials received from Ph.D.'s around the country. Hiring committees tend toward ruthlessness on these basic matters. One service your graduate department should provide besides mock interviews is thorough proofreading of your outgoing letter and résumé by professors on the job placement committee. Elisabeth Rose Gruner's remarks about a department's responsibilities to its job seekers are absolutely on the mark.

Such blistering rigor, like the stimulation and sparring in mock interviews, may leave you feeling bruised, but it is worth it if you are competing with one hundred, two hundred, or seven hundred other candidates for a position. I recall well the searching questions

raised during my mock interview, queries more difficult than anything I faced in the actual MLA cattle call. Is there an element of
sadism here, the opportunity to let our graduate know one more time
how little he or she actually knows? Perhaps. Not to sound too
Maileresque, but the tougher your handlers in the months preceding
the conference interviews, the better you will be in the ring. And no
longer, given the paucity of jobs, can an interview be treated as a
rehearsal or "warm-up." You must go fully primed.

Being prepared means also knowing thoroughly the department
that is about to interview you. Familiarity with the teaching faculty
and course curriculum allows you to ask probing questions too. Take
a look at their catalog before you head to the conference interview,
and most definitely before a campus visit.

Getting a read on potential future colleagues is crucial. We have
all at one time or another—usually at conferences on the eve of an
interview—grasped shreds of professional gossip as if they were
holy relics. And there is good reason for this. But picking up the
phone and calling the chair of the interviewing department is a tactic
sometimes forgotten. If you want to know the exact nature of your
audience for the teaching "demonstration," ask! To be sure, as
Wachtel points out, you can't always predict how the teaching demonstration will be set up. A campus visit provides the hiring committee with an opportunity to view the candidate's energy level, as
well as general adaptability to shifting conditions. But I've seen
candidates fumble such teaching demos precisely because they
didn't request clarification prior to the visit.

A final word about "lying," which O'Donovan-Anderson
briefly discusses. A good interviewing committee will ask follow-
up questions to ascertain exactly how big a fish story you are feeding
them about your half dozen areas of expertise. It is all relative, of
course, and small liberal arts colleges with departments of five define
"specialties" differently from universities with departments of fifty.
Still, be prepared to back up your claims with demonstrable course
work, as well as judiciously produced syllabus material in progress.
Lying varies in quality.

The Cattle Call without a doubt comprises the most demoralizing phase of the job search, especially because you may have to repeat it more than once. Anxiety hangs heavy in the air and in your heart. The sound of so many thundering hooves beside your own, heading for the same chute, can produce exquisite angst. Yet to know the situation as fully as possible, as the following writers indicate, may constitute the very foundation for shifting the odds in your favor. You'll want to feel the Force—and think twice about wearing brown shoes.

Scenes from the APA, or Odysseus Looks for a Job

Michael O'Donovan-Anderson

What follows is the true story (in the artistic sense of "true," which means a particularly edifying sort of lie) of my trip to the annual job conference of the American Philosophical Association. Any resemblance to persons living or dead is probably intentional, except in those cases where this could involve libel or prove a hindrance to my job prospects. Then it is a regrettable coincidence. Many of the characters' lines are actual quotes from the APA conference. But my lawyer says I can't tell you which ones. One final note: the character "I" is entirely a fictional construct. No such person exists.

As the reader may not be familiar with the intricacies of the academic job conference, and with philosophy in particular, I have compiled the following glossary.

analytic philosophy a redundancy
continental philosophy an oxymoron
DGS that faculty member of each department in charge of demoralizing graduate students
dissertation completion schedule the first lie on the c.v.
Eminence, an famous living academic whose work is relevant but sloppy

hack a person to whom the following criteria apply: (1) wrote a paper accepted by the APA selection committee; (2) has a full-time job; (3) is published in the *Journal of Philosophy*; (4) is not an Eminence

interviewer a worshipped and feared subset of hack; a hack with power

irrelevant an argument that addresses more than one sub-sub-field, but is not written by an Eminence

job candidate all of the following must apply: (1) an individual so convinced of his/her own superiority to the members of the search committee that their rejection is further proof of his/her philosophical integrity (and intimidating presence); (2) an individual so convinced of his/her superiority to all other candidates that their selection for an interview or job is further proof of his/her philosophical integrity, and their status as hacks; (3) an individual who proudly declares his/her distance from hack sellouts—unless offered a job

relevant anything written by an Eminence

sloppy missing the subtle distinctions between sub-sub-fields which protect the arguments of hacks from the criticisms of an Eminence

specialty the second lie on the c.v.

sub-sub field (1) covering an area of philosophy slightly broader than the space required for forty-seven dancing angels; (2) invented by advanced graduate students so they can write an "original" dissertation; (3) the largest set of problems or issues that one is permitted to master prior to becoming an Eminence; (4) the smallest permissible area of philosophy to which an APA paper session can be dedicated

white male applicant (1) the distinguished gentleman who, in the face of the fact that 80 percent of all jobs go to fellow WMA's, resolutely, politely, and with the proper amount of courtly embarrassment reveals that his job was stolen by a black feminist; (2) thinks that "avoiding PC" requires this announcement

Arrival

As we rode up the multiple layers of escalator, past each successive circle of lounges and meeting rooms, one could differentiate profs from graduate students by their reaction to the painful opulence of the Marriott Marquis. Indeed, a sense of entitlement surrounded certain philosophers like a smug aura, allowing them to blend in with the regular guests in a way which was, for the soon-to-be unemployed graduate student, impossible. Of course, there was sufficient tweed and facial hair to mark even the comfortable as "other" in the swank midtown motel. The women didn't need any particular fabric to achieve this effect.

The APA had arranged to accommodate poor graduate students (another redundancy) four-to-a-room; it was a gracious but breathtakingly inauspicious offer. For, of course, the ratio of jobs to candidates was about 1:4, and one could easily imagine the following scene playing itself out many times over, with some well-meaning (read: clueless and full of "tough love") DGS playing the role of drill sergeant:

"All right, men [still, in 1996, mostly men] take a look around. I won't kid you. It's a tough mission and even with your extensive training, odds are only one of you makes it out . . ." Each eyes the other with both a camaraderie born of shared circumstances and a competitiveness born of, well, shared circumstances. Still, they are soothed by the thought that, unlike the less fortunate souls who had to hear this speech from a real drill sergeant, they will make it through this ordeal alive if not victorious. And then they remember they are in New York.

We burst upon the main lobby, which looks like nothing so much as the nerve center of the Death Star, with a great black obelisk of silent elevators dominating the soaring atrium, at once immense and menacing and, thanks to the many thousands of small white light bulbs that cover the edges of anything with an edge, as

69

comfortably kitschy as an (eponymous) Times Square marquis. Although I am not a novelist, or (thankfully) a literary theorist, I was tempted to see in those elevators a symbol of the upward mobility mockingly out of reach of the down-and-out Ph.D.-to-be, a reification of the institutional hierarchy that denied us entrance to any level higher than the registration circle. Ironic, that: here we were asked to present credentials to secure further access to the elevated academic obelisk, to which we needed access in order to have the credentials to present. But it turned out the nice people at the desk really only wanted money, and later I went all the way to the top floor in one of those laconic glass elevators. All the way to the top. So much for analogies. I resolved to stick with the Dante-esque circle imagery and *Star Wars* motif.

As I moved across the lobby to the job candidates' registration room, I felt lucky to sense that sickening knot in my intestines that signaled the imminent appearance of a pit of existential despair. Because of this unique early-warning device, I was able to skirt the void when it appeared a few seconds later, feeling only a momentary doubt about the uncommon brilliance of my dissertation. This creeping insecurity was an old friend, so I knew just how to get rid of him: "If anyone had liked my dissertation," I intoned, "then it would only be because they recognized themselves in it, and this would prove that the work was conventional and unoriginal. Who wants to be a hack?" There was no arguing with such logic. But judging by the drop-jawed stares and shaking cigarettes, many less agile than I were caught in the swirling angst. I grimly set my jaw and moved onward, trying to ignore the silent cries that filled the windless lobby.

The gate stopped me cold. Cracked and peeling paint covered the doorway, managing by its decay to issue the following warning: "Abandon All Hope Ye Who Enter Here." Although impressed by the literary acuity of the door frame, I knew I had to do something fast, what with that existential pit whirling at my back. Reaching into my standard-issue black grad-student shoulder bag, I found just the thing: Incantation 103 from the APA Eastern Division Meeting Program.

If It Is to Mean It May Not Just Be

In the service of the proposition that naturally occurring phenomena have no semantic content (that linguistic significance and meaning require the intention of a language user), I argue against the apparent counterexample posed by such thought experiments as Putnam's Anglophile Ant (who inadvertently draws a pattern in the sand with an uncommon resemblance to Churchill), or the case of the sidewalk whose cracks apparently spell "Hello," by showing how the three most widely cited arguments (Goodwin 1987, Marin 1988b, Simpson 1988), which allow referential connections to obtain in these cases, fail to distinguish between the semantically active position of the "reader" and the semantically inert status of the accidentally formed proposition per se. This distinction raises a problem for the semantic status of written language in general, which it is beyond the scope of this paper to address. I hope to show only that by invoking this distinction we can avoid the otherwise plausible conclusions of Goodwin, Marin, and Simpson.

It was an arcane spell, which took months to master, but luckily it proved potent enough for the current purpose. When I looked again at the door frame, I saw the same pattern of peeling paint ("Abandon All Hope Ye Who Enter Here") shorn of its semantic content. I had sufficiently adjusted my intuitions to see that the proposition was meaningless. Thus reassured (and deeply thankful for my philosophical training), I entered the room.

I was immediately met at the door by a woman with such immense spectacles that she gave the impression of having only a single eye, bloated and distended and hovering four inches before her head.

"Specialty."

"What?"

"Specialty." No change of tone from the first, and still no indication that this was a question.

"Uh. Metaphysics?"

"In what category does your school lie?" She handed me a sheet of paper, split into three categories: "Big Name Schools," "Little Name Schools," "No Name Schools."

"Um. One."

"Publications?"

"Yes, I . . ."

"Board one please."

"But, I . . ."

"Board one please."

I went for board one, the first of several in the room. It listed four jobs. Harvard, Princeton, UCLA, Penn State. Right. I went back to the woman.

"Specialty."

"No, you see, I was just here and . . ."

"Specialty."

"Um, history of philosophy."

"What century?"

"Nineteenth?"

"Which half?"

"What?!"

"Which half?" I walked away, and she moved to block my path.

"Specialty."

"We've been through this."

"Specialty."

"None." The single eye blinked. Then blinked again. Soon the blinking grew more rapid, and the convulsions began to spread to the rest of the face. I quickly stepped aside as she blindly wandered out the doorway and landed right in the middle of the pit of existential despair (it is amazing how long those things last around gatherings of graduate students). I still don't know what became of her.

I began to canvass the job boards, trying to make sense of their arrangement. There were nine boards, arranged in groups of three, and it was clear that each of the individual boards in each group represented one of the great triumvirate of philosophy: Logic, Epistemology, and Metaphysics; Ethics and Political Theory; History of Philosophy. But the three groups themselves seemed to represent no significant sequence, except, maybe, increasing teaching duties, which ranged from 2/2 in Group I to 5/6 in Group III. Group III also included ads from schools looking for adjunct faculty ("Wanted: Candidates whose DGS has been so effective that you will allow us to treat you somewhat worse than you were treated as graduate students. Low pay! No benefits! No guarantee of teaching! Extend the bohemian glamour of grad student life! You know you want to! It's better than selling insurance [although we make no guarantees]! Our staff is sublimely disgruntled! Free cathartic gripe sessions! Act Now!!"). It was very puzzling, indeed. Why would the jobs be grouped this way, and why would we be directed to specific boards? It took some digging, but I finally uncovered the following clue, typed in a small font at the bottom of the ad for Southeast Central Louisiana State Community Technical College: "We are primarily interested in an applicant who will be happy with the atmosphere at SCLSCTC (Slick-el-suck-tick, as we affectionately call her) and not run off for greener pastures at the drop of the proverbial hat. Besides, we hate New York City and don't want to have to hire again until someone else dies. And, anyway, anyone with a Ph.D. from a good school scares us. Candidates prone to exploitative power relations are encouraged to apply. SCLSCTC is an AA/EEOC employer."

Question and Answer Period
(people actually said these things!)

"Ah, yes, Dr. Johnson. I like his book. I read it every time he writes it."

"In the end I cannot agree, but it's hard to see where you go wrong."

"Yes. This is very interesting, but I wonder why you didn't write about Hegel instead."

"I'm sorry. That cannot be right, for I have been studying Descartes for a long time and I never thought of it."

The Book Fair (those damn sirens, again)

I stood before the great gates of the book fair as people streamed past me in both directions. Slowly, methodically, I lashed my wallet to my body with material so strong and knots so clever that even the Great Houdini couldn't have escaped. If he had been in my pocket, I mean. A withered old man crouched unsteadily by the gate, and he cackled as I strode past.

"Wise fool. Wise fool," he spoke with the sound of a homeless parrot. "Those are truly wise who know they are fools." Being too sophisticated to even pretend to grasp the meaning of this, I bestowed upon him that smile reserved by Easterners for the lost souls of Midwest colleges, and passed over the threshold.

There before me was a garden of delights-with-the-added-advantage-of-seeming-spiritual, even while available here on earth. I was blinded by color and font, and I walked the corridors in a gossamer haze of potential pleasure, just thinking how lovely these books would look on my shelves as they waited to be read, and waited and waited (nevertheless providing me with the right to say that I "knew" a certain book the next time it was mentioned by someone in that you-must-know-this-to-be-competent tone). Many was the time I reached for my wallet, but here my cleverness saved me, for each time I touched the ropes and chains (Oh, what a sight I must have been, could any have seen beyond the stacks of books they carried!) surrounding my pockets I smiled an apologetic smile and walked on.

But slowly, painfully, surely, a realization crept from the nether reaches of my mind: I was not enjoying this! Without the consumerist titillation of the potential purchase, the capacity to cease deferring my gratification, the danger of stranding my household on the rocks of financial ruin, academic books were just, just, well, badly written prose on dead trees! The spines I thought so beautiful held no more allure than modernist painting. And so few of the colors went with my apartment! My despair was so deep there was nothing to do but exit. Past the fixed, noncommittal grimaces of assistant editors ("Sure, we'll take a look at the proposal and get back to you") and the manic assertiveness of the young and untenured ("Of course my book on the origins of postmodernism in the corset rebellion of 1211 is suitable for the undergraduate classroom. It's really all about Economic Globalization and the Culture Industry. 'Think globally, write locally.' Yup, made that up myself. Oh, no. Intro level. Of course I'm sure."), I moved heavily into the main lobby and sighed, somewhat cheered by the dawning thought that I wouldn't have much time to read working for Yellow Cab, anyway. And always one to look forward, I turned my attention to a more pressing problem: how to get all this crap off my wallet so I could eat.

The Smoker
(an anthropologist's report)

The philosophical tribes have gathered under one tent, and although there is very little tobacco, there is plenty of smoky obfuscation to cloud the room.

"I understand you are interested in Rousseau."

"Mmm-hmmm." Speaker2 looks over the shoulder of the first speaker, to assure him that this conversation will last only so long as no one more important appears on the horizon.

"Which Discourse? I specialize in the first." The linguistic emphasis is designed to reassert the speaker's existence. The conversation is in its early, Cartesian stage and revolves around that all-important cogito—the aggressive "I think"—which grounds one's sense of being and self-importance, while simultaneously permitting rational doubt about the existence and importance of the other. To complete his answer to the dismissive body-language challenge of speaker2, speaker1 picks at random a silver-haired person in the vicinity and executes a well-timed smile and nod. If successful, this maneuver will cause speaker2 to reevaluate the importance of speaker1: could talking to speaker1, who knows eminent old philosophers, increase my prestige? The maneuver appears successful, for the conversation continues. But if the encounter is to progress past its early-stage solipsism, dominance must be established.

"The first, hmmm? Very popular in 1749, I hear. I specialize in the letter of March 11, which is the absolute key to Chapter IX of the second."

"I understand Chapter IX is very in vogue." Speaker1's sarcasm is très heavy. Speaker2 repeats his search for a more important interlocutor, just so speaker1 doesn't suspect speaker2's suspicion that speaker1 is well connected. It is an elegant and complicated dance of micromovements, as each glances over the alternate shoulder of the other in ritual dismissiveness, punctuating their conversation with the "I" of self-importance. The encounter has now reached a crucial juncture. For speaker2 has won the "limited specialty" contest, opening speaker1 to charges of vague superficiality. But speaker1 has an edge in the "appears better known" category, making speaker2 vulnerable to marginalization. The conversation has reached its Hegelian stage; self-identity is displaced from the cogito, and now depends on intersubjective recognition. The two interlocutors, all the while keeping up their dismissive head dance, must struggle for the following admission from the other: you are essential to my work/career/reputation, I am inessential to yours.

Speaker1 feints left—"March 11. Huh."—and then moves hard right. "So. Any job prospects?" It is a risky move, for if the candidate with the narrower specialty has more interviews, the contest is lost. But it proves a good choice, for speaker2, already suspecting that speaker1 may have connections, immediately deflates.

"Um. No. You know." By the time speaker2 remembers the "integrity and originality defense," it is too late to employ it. His admission has cost him the battle and the "I" drops from his speech. "What about you?"

"Sure. A few good leads. Maybe I could introduce you to some second discourse people."

"Yeah? That would be great." But speaker1 has already broken off the exchange, having spotted a potential prestige enhancer. Speaker2 looks speculatively at his glass of wine, adopting a pose of Socratic contemplation. But he is saved from further humiliation by the entrance of an Eminence, one so exalted that the artificial light reflecting from his silvery, respectable-evangelist hair leaves a glow in the wake of his careful movements. The tribes part for his passage, and many braver souls try the "familiarity" maneuver to enhance their prestige in the eyes of their currently dismissive interlocutors, but such moves are doomed to failure: an Eminence is beyond familiarity. As he works his way through the sea of onlookers, water-skiers gather in his wake, mostly DGS types with students to sell, and powerful hacks with books in need of review. A long night ensues.

Parting Advice

Because of the apparent mismatch between my credentials and marketplace demand, there had been arranged a meeting with an Eminence. He sat down as I nodded my thanks at being granted an audience. His smile was gracious and his eyes sage as he took my c.v., and, lowering his glasses to the edge of his nose, began the diagnostic. I was sitting suspended in silent anxiety, when the Eminence, having turned to the page containing my dissertation abstract, quickly moved his hand to stroke his perfectly placed beard.

His fingers rested lightly on his throat, taking a quick check of his pulse to confirm his judgment.

"Ah. Your dissertation is irrelevant to the central concerns of analytic philosophy." So simple and elegant it was almost worth applauding. Except, given my training, the contents of the dissertation, and the opinions of my advisors, it couldn't possibly be true. I indicated as much.

"Yes. You do seem like someone interested in analytic philosophy. But perhaps you could change the abstract so it doesn't reflect the breadth of your interest. To treat Davidson, Putnam, Frege, Dummett, and even more in the same dissertation seems, how shall I say, implausible." I suspected he meant "impermissible," and I was gauche enough to protest once more. My work is concerned with the role of our physical, active embodiment (and not just our senses) in establishing our epistemic connection to the world, a theme which threads its often inexplicit way through many works (and several fields). To present a full picture it is necessary to treat all these figures (and even more). To indicate otherwise would be, how shall I say, dishonest. At this he looked at me squarely and, as if addressing a class of overly earnest fifteen-year-olds about to make a field trip to Madison Avenue, said,

"Ah. Perhaps you are the victim of a basic misunderstanding." He gestured with my c.v. "This is a sales document."

My Journey Through the Job Market in Mathematics

Howard Wachtel

At the 1996 Joint Mathematics Meetings in Orlando, Florida, I heard a new mathematics professor at a small college offer the following memorable words: "Getting a [math faculty] job is like surviving a plane crash. Everybody wants to know why and how you did it, and then you're afraid of ever taking another one."

My own route to the doctorate was neither the most traditional nor the most direct. First I spent five years in one university's doctoral program, studying the branch of mathematics known as abstract algebra (more specifically, ring theory and homological algebra). Like many young mathematicians, I was enthralled by the beauty of abstract mathematics and did not seem to care much about its applicability; in fact, the closer a piece of mathematics came to real-world application, the less I liked it. Years later, after I found that I had lost interest in the subject matter and cared mainly about effective teaching, I left that program, and four years later enrolled in another university's doctoral program, ultimately spending another six years there. With virtually no help from my thesis advisor, I wrote a dissertation on a highly unusual topic which is somewhere between math education and educational psychology, and finally received my doctorate in mathematics in the fall of 1994, having done at least enough work for two doctoral degrees.

My latest search for a faculty position (i.e., my first job search since obtaining my doctorate) took place in the 1994–95 academic year. Ironically the tightening of the job market has been so severe that this search was more difficult than my previous searches, when I had no doctorate and fewer qualifications. I knew that many talented doctorates were and are still being forced out of the academic profession due to the shortage of faculty positions. I had sixteen interviews for faculty positions across the United States during the summer of 1995, including two second interviews. However, I managed to procure only one job offer, coming near the end of the summer, on August 14, after which I had to begin working in a new city three days later on August 17. Four of my interviews were in the Midwest, including only one in Chicago, where I had completed my degree and hoped to remain, but I had come to accept the fact that in the academic profession one cannot expect to choose one's city of residence. The remaining twelve interviews were on the two coasts, four on the West Coast and the remainder on the East Coast. Toward the end of the search period, I was becoming so desperate I considered applying for private high-school teaching positions, although I did not think I would be prepared to handle the discipline problems I would face there. Another difficulty is that private high schools require the same state certification as public schools, which I did not possess. I also did not seem to have the right qualifications for a position in industry or government, having studied pure (theoretical) rather than applied mathematics.

Like many other new doctorates, before the offer of a full-time position came, I was working at whatever part-time positions I could find, making very meager wages which were not nearly enough to pay for my living expenses. A typical part-time position pays approximately $1,200–$1,500 for teaching one course, so one cannot come close to making a full-time salary even with several courses. At one point, I was teaching three classes at three different institutions in Chicago (I have heard anecdotes about part-time faculty who have done even more than that), which is tantamount to having a full-time workload and getting paid next to nothing. The hardships resulting from having so little income included having no social life, no vacations, worrying about saving pennies on grocery items, and putting off obtaining medical examinations or treatment. (It goes without saying that most part-time faculty do not have any health or dental insurance.)

The members of my doctoral dissertation committee could not or would not offer any assistance in the job search process, and some of them would not even agree to serve as references on my behalf, saying that they knew only of my research and not of my teaching. However, I knew of no one individual who was familiar with both my research and my teaching. Even though I had other references for my teaching, I knew that this might not be adequate, since some employers will not consider references which are more than, say, three years old. (My latest reference from institutions other than the one that granted my doctorate was about three years old, and most were older than that.)

Graduate school, which prepares one to devote one's life to research, certainly did not prepare me for the process of filling out employment applications, which was not a trivial matter in many cases. Some of the applications for employment, particularly at community colleges, were lengthy and contained difficult essay questions. Some of the essay questions I encountered most often were the following:

1. List all developmental mathematics courses you have taught in the last five years.
2. List all nondevelopmental mathematics courses you have taught in the last five years. (There were too many to remember!)
3. Discuss your teaching philosophy.
4. Discuss your experience with culturally diverse and multi-ethnic populations.
5. List all professional meetings and papers presented in the last three years. (Professional meetings? I never had

81

time for such meetings—I was too busy either working on my dissertation or looking for a job, or too poor to afford to travel.)

6. Discuss how you have used technology in your teaching of collegiate mathematics. (I had some experience teaching with graphing calculators, but did not have either the time or the resources to keep up with the latest developments in the use of technology in the mathematics classroom, as faculty would be expected to do.)

7. Discuss your experience in course development. (Fortunately, I had had enough of that kind of experience in my full-time positions prior to earning my doctorate.)

8. Discuss your experience with alternative or nontraditional modes of learning. (I had very little of that kind of experience.)

Even though I had had six years of experience teaching full-time at four-year institutions (as well as much part-time experience), the vast majority of my interviews were at two-year colleges. Ironically, most of the people interviewing me did not have doctorates, and some had only bachelor's degrees. Interviews were generally of a formal, impersonal nature. Sometimes they would be no longer than forty-five minutes. I would be asked a set of questions that were carefully prepared in advance by the committee members, who would dutifully write down each of my answers. In a few cases, the institution actually sent me the questions ahead of time. My understanding of the nature of interviews in higher education is that it has been greatly constrained by legal considerations; institutions normally take great pains to avoid a question that may approach the brink of illegality (although I have indeed heard anecdotes of candidates who experienced interview questions that were blatantly illegal, such as questions regarding age or marital status, and wondered whether to answer them anyway), and therefore administrators will insist at least on approving in advance the questions to be asked of candidates, if not also on having the interviewing committee record all of the candidate's responses. Often the interview questions were similar to those listed above as typical essay questions for application forms, and indeed when the interview was short I wondered why they had made me travel such a great distance when they could have had me mail in or fax my answers, or at least have conducted the interview by conference call.

At the end of the interview, I was always asked to give a brief teaching demonstration—except for just one institution that did not require such a demonstration. (Coincidentally, or perhaps not, that was the institution that ultimately offered me a position.) In most cases I was assigned a topic for the teaching presentation, for example: "You will give a ten-minute lesson on conic sections." In only a few cases was I permitted to choose a topic for the demonstration from any low-level mathematics course. In those cases, I usually gave a presentation on a topic that had been required at an earlier interview. Sometimes the teaching demonstration did not even take place in a real classroom, but in a conference room that happened to have a blackboard or dry-erase board. In any case, the demonstration was done only for the interviewing faculty and administrators, not with real students. In that sense, it was really not teaching, but could be more accurately described as pretending to teach, acting, or role-playing. Since the audience was not students but faculty, who themselves knew thoroughly the subject matter being "taught," their questions on the lesson (they do ask questions!) were necessarily artificial and not questions real students would ask. I have serious doubts about the validity of using a role-playing exercise to assess someone's teaching effectiveness. A true teaching demonstration should be done only with real students. If no actual students are available, I believe that it would be better to have the candidate give a presentation on some mathematical topic that is not a "standard" topic in the low-level math curriculum, so that the interviewing faculty could learn a new topic and thus experience the presentation in a manner closer to that of actual students.

Second interviews were somewhat less formal, and, naturally, the questions were tougher. At one community college on the West Coast, I was informed by the institution's president during my second interview about a "multicultural" program called "math for

Latinas'' which had met with some resistance from the institution's faculty, and asked what I thought about the idea. As on a few other occasions, I was careful to give the politically correct answer, irrespective of my own views on the subject. My answer to that question seemed to be satisfactory, but I ran into trouble later in the interview when the president asked me to demonstrate how I would assume leadership in coordinating with K–12 teachers in the area, and I had no idea how to answer that question, particularly since I have no K–12 experience. Later on, at an institution on the East Coast, the president assailed me with long-winded questions which asked me to address teaching, research, and service all at once. The questions ran on at such a great length that by the time each was over with, I had already forgotten most of what had been asked. Now I wonder if that was just one person's idiosyncrasy or a standard interviewing practice.

I often wondered why I should have to fly across the country for a forty-five-minute interview, especially when I learned that (in most cases) a few successful candidates would have to return for a second interview. In the majority of instances, the school does not pay for the candidates' interview expenses; in some cases they do not even pay the expenses for the second interview. A few schools will pay one-half or some other fraction of the candidate's travel expenses. Some have still more complex arrangements; for example, in one case I made a plane reservation on a discount airline on the last day on which I could procure a certain low but nonrefundable fare. Only after doing so did I discover that the institution interviewing me had decided they would reimburse candidates' travel expenses only if the arrangements were made through their travel agency!

Even worse than having to pay for my own travel expenses (while earning very little income) was the knowledge that the schools were interviewing a very large number of candidates. One community college told me that there were twenty-two candidates being invited to interview for the mathematics position (all at the candidate's own expense), in part because the college's affirmative action office demanded a large pool of candidates. This practice seems unnecessary and wasteful, and I even wonder whether it is counterproductive—members of underrepresented groups being particularly sought by the institution may be even less willing or able to pay their own travel expenses under such circumstances. Another community college told me that they received 120 applications and roughly half of them were invited to interview! Also I would wonder whether it paid to fly to an interview for a temporary one-year position, knowing that if I accepted the position and signed a contract, I might miss out on an opportunity for a tenure-track position that might come along later in the summer, unless I wanted to risk violating a signed contract.

The process of arranging and scheduling interviews was unlike anything I had experienced previously—I really needed to take a course in juggling. One school would call and tell me that the interviews were scheduled on a day when I already had an interview scheduled in another city a long distance away. Should I call the first school and ask them if they would change my interview to a different date? In many cases I had to change plane reservations I had already made (and pay whatever penalty applied) for one interview in order to accommodate another, particularly if the second school would schedule interviews on short notice. Some schools gave a choice of two days on which I could have the interview, while others prescribed a specific day and left me with no choice. One even gave me an assigned day and time right away with no consideration of my schedule: "Your interview will be on July 10 at 2:15 P.M." Another, very tiny college went to the other extreme, saying, "We'll work around your schedule." There were many other inconveniences, such as getting home from a trip to a distant city only to receive an interview offer from another school in that same city and having to plan another trip there right away; taking flights at 6 or 7 A.M. so that I could fly in and out of a city on the same day and save the cost of a hotel room, and returning phone calls from a college on one coast from a motel room on the other coast. During one particular week in July I had seven interviews, three on the West Coast and four on the East Coast. That week I rented cars at both ends of the country and drove between San Diego and Los Angeles, and between northern Virginia and southern New Jersey.

In view of the current climate for postsecondary faculty positions in mathematics, admittedly I should consider myself fortunate to have landed a position anywhere. As the quote at the beginning of this article suggests, I would not want to go through this experience again. This strongly underscores the importance of working hard in the tenure process at my current institution, which amounts to jumping through many more hoops, a process which could be the subject of another article.

Feminists Face the Job Market: Q & A (Questions & Anecdotes)

Elisabeth Rose Gruner

S ometime in the early spring of 1993, I saw a call for papers that interested me: "Equipment for Survival: Getting a Job," the panel was called, and it was sponsored by the Women's Caucus of the Modern Language Association.[1] Flush with my first success on the job market (I'd just been offered and accepted a tenure-track position after two years on the market), I still wasn't quite sure how I'd done it. Thinking back over my two years of looking for a job, I recalled advice (much of it contradictory), encouragement, discouragement, elation, and depression. But no pattern emerged. Curious, I proposed a paper for the panel: I would survey women like myself who had been on the job market recently—"successfully" and "unsuccessfully"—and I would find the pattern, locate the clues that would help me tell others how to do it right. Or at least what to expect.

I started by collecting stories. I designed a questionnaire to be filled out by women who had recently been on the job market. I hoped to develop a magic formula—twelve writing sample requests divided by three interviews multiplied by two publications equals an 87 percent chance of getting a job, for example. But I had trouble developing the formula. Indeed, at first I had trouble even gathering data, as questionnaire after questionnaire went unanswered. So I began to reconceive my project. Perhaps rather than developing a formula, I could demonstrate that there wasn't one. If I couldn't help people succeed in the job process, perhaps I could help them understand it—because it embodies all that is best and worst about our profession, from the sense of collegiality and spirit of common inquiry to the ritual humiliation and hierarchization. Step one was learning—relearning, actually—that we don't *really* like to talk about the job market. It's too scary—or, as one recalcitrant respondent acknowledged, it was "so unpleasant that I wanted to forget it as soon as possible." This, by the way, was from a woman happily placed in a good job!

I do believe, however, that talking about the job market—and talking about it early and often—is the *only* thing that will help us demystify it, which is an important first step in empowering women candidates to take control of an often out-of-control process.[2] As Paula Caplan notes in *Lifting a Ton of Feathers*,[3] women may be more likely than men to take what she calls the myth of meritocracy seriously—we believe, then, that our failures are our own and the exceptions to the rule. Perhaps if we hear how often the same unpleasant (and pleasant!) things happen to others, we can get beyond blaming ourselves and begin to focus on change. Indeed, part of the unpleasantness of the process seems to have to do with its mysteriousness—even successful candidates can rarely point to what they did right or deny doing anything "wrong."

Finally I was able to collect some stories, and I offer them here in the spirit of demystification. My first group of anecdotes has to do with preparing for the job market; here, as one respondent noted, we come directly into contact with the whole notion of "worth," and how it is defined and measured in the academy:

> It has occurred to me that one hard thing about being a feminist on the market has to do with all the traditions of "worth." Part of identifying myself as a feminist has involved wanting to challenge the traditional hierarchies of

"merit" that have been constructed to serve the interests of a tiny portion of the population. But being on the market put me right in the thick of these hierarchies—trying to represent myself on paper so as to look sufficiently worthy to merit an interview, and then in person so as to merit a campus visit, and so on. And creating the in-person appearance of worth involved more shopping and hysteria about clothes and hair than I engaged in even when I was a teenager.

I should like to consider, as all of my respondents have, the issue of "worth"—and what we can do to succeed in a system that defines it so narrowly—and so secretly. As another candidate remarked, "Knowing what to do 'differently' involves, in part, having a precedent for doing something 'properly.' " For most of us, "properly" is still an undefined or nebulous term when it comes to many aspects of academic life, including especially the job market itself.

In preparing to go on the job market, many of my respondents received confusing and even careless advice. One wrote to me:

My MLA experience is memorable—and, I'm sure, by no means extraordinary—for its series of small humiliations, many of which were connected to my status as a woman, on the one hand, and my commitment to feminist scholarship and teaching practice, on the other. From the time I entered the job market, I was made aware—by the job placement officer at my school (who was presumably supposed to encourage me)—that my work was passé. If I had been a feminist in the seventies, I would have been "hot," but women's studies, he claimed, particularly in my field, was no longer the rage. Taking his advice seriously was my first mistake, because I found myself attempting to write a job letter which downplayed and apologized for my research.

Another candidate wrote:

> Principally, I would wish that there were some meaningful
> mentoring available in English departments, for, at present,
> lesbian and gay graduate students are largely self-taught
> people whose inquiries (particularly at the beginning
> stages) into the sexuality of authors or texts are met with
> skepticism by people not well acquainted with the critical
> tools for conducting such investigations, and, to boot, often
> uncomfortable with the topic itself.

Advising and comments from colleagues often bleed into each
other, and many of us have had the experience outlined for me by
another candidate:

> One thing . . . that bugged me over the course of the whole,
> long, dragged out ordeal of being ''on the market'' was
> having other people, mostly white men, tell me how lucky
> I was not to be a white male. Of the four people from [my
> institution] who got jobs last year, three were white males.
> This statistic really means nothing (except perhaps for serv-
> ing my sense of self-righteous indignation), but it does
> seem to me that there is no ''lucky'' position to be in when
> it comes to the market.

Candidates at larger schools, particularly, have felt abandoned
by their placement counselors when on the second year of a search
(although Paula Caplan quotes Phyllis Bronstein as suggesting that
an academic job search will probably take four years),[4] when not
doing a national search, or when not doing the ''hottest'' or ''latest''
thing—but, as the lesbian critic above noted, sometimes the ''hottest'' thing is something that makes counselors and advisors personally uncomfortable. So we need mentors, advisors, who take some
care to understand our work and its relationship to other work in
the field, so they can help us present and articulate it as well as
possible to hiring committees, journals, conference organizers, etc.

This advising process needs to begin as soon as a student enters graduate school, if not before.

A recent discussion of the job market which took place on a Women's Studies electronic listserv I had earlier mined for anecdotes turned up many postings offering advice, anecdotes, support, and complaints, in stark contrast to the relative quiet that had met my original request for help. Such discussions, indeed, may supplement or even foster the mentoring that seems so crucial to me; women without mentors in their own graduate programs may find them elsewhere—through professional conferences, through dissertation support groups, through Internet discussion groups. I find recently placed Ph.D.'s to be uniformly generous of their time in helping junior colleagues at local graduate schools or at their alma maters; if more people asked, perhaps even more such contacts could be developed.

The most useful anecdote I received came from a job candidate who, noting that her department had no formal structure for advising students on preparing for the job market, organized one. She pulled together students, faculty, the department chair, and the dean for a marathon afternoon workshop which went from working up a c.v. to how to talk and eat at the same time in a luncheon interview. While the advice they offered was sometimes contradictory, it still helped, she said, to hear the range of responses and—again—simply to raise the issues. Of course, some mentors already do this kind of advising on an individual basis, as well as making the secondary calls and writing the extra letters that are now becoming the norm in many people's job searches. One of my respondents offers the following advice to advisors:

> Realize that in this market *all* job seekers—regardless of brilliance, experience, or "hot" scholarship—are going to have a great deal of difficulty finding a job. Given this, it's important not to undermine the confidence of any job seeker by suggesting that they are responsible for any lack of success—the job search itself will do nicely in the confidence-sapping department.

One final comment about advising. While the woman candidate who organized her own workshop is to be commended for her initiative and perseverance, some people have found even this step difficult; some have even had their confidence undermined by simply asking for such help from their departments.

One respondent told this story:

> A year or so before I expected to go out on the market, I and a (male) fellow graduate student asked our (female) grad chair if the department would consider providing a series of what we called "professional development" seminars—how to turn a seminar paper into an article, to prepare for MLA, to interview, etc. She demurred, claiming that she didn't like to make academia seem so "professionalized," and further claiming that "cream rises" anyway. While I agree that one can't expect that such a series of workshops would actually have guaranteed jobs to the participants (which seemed to be part of her concern about professionalizing), I began to feel that perhaps I wasn't "cream," as I hadn't yet felt myself "rising" in the manner she seemed to be suggesting.

This was, I hasten to add, not everyone's experience—many of my respondents participated in "professional development" seminars; many of them had feminist mentors and felt well advised. The process often seems so capricious and secretive that even the best advice can't guarantee a job, but it can help a candidate feel that "failure" is not necessarily due to some oversight or lack on her part. In the current job market, "failure" can simply be a function of oversupply,[5] and no amount of advising or effort can change that.

My other set of anecdotes is about interviewing, mostly MLA interviewing. Here I got more responses, and more varied responses, than to any other set of questions I asked about the job process. People who wanted to "vent" had a lot to say here, but there are encouraging stories as well. First, though, a point I don't think gets made enough: screening only through MLA interviews may in and of itself be to some extent discriminatory and biased, as one of my respondents pointed out:

> This is my third year and I am really torn about going to MLA. Frankly, I resent the class discrimination that is involved; candidates are *expected* to spend $700–$800 to travel to the MLA, regardless of where it is held. When one is a graduate student from the working class or an exploited part-time faculty member who makes less money than a graduate student, how can this amount be scraped together for what is essentially a screening interview?

I might add to this comment my observation that while some departments cover airfare for a job search visit to the MLA, they usually do so only once per graduate student; those who search twice or more must hope to be supported for delivering papers, or must go into debt. The issue of the MLA as a screening mechanism deserves more attention than I can give it here, but I did want to raise the question before moving on to specific tales of the convention and its aftermath.

Now for the good news: many candidates find the interview process quite positive. I have heard more than once in conversations and from my questionnaires responses like the following:

> When I first went to MLA, I didn't know what to expect and was, consequently, a nervous wreck. In fact, I don't think I kept a meal down during the whole three days, nor did I sleep well . . . the nerve factor was overwhelming. Add to this the fact that by the time I got to MLA for my three measly interviews I was really beginning to second-guess my right to be in the academy—I'd been turned down for so many jobs already, I couldn't imagine that I was worthy of the ones I was interviewing for. Oddly, the interview process itself laid that fear to rest. I found my interviewers for the most part cordial, interesting, interested people—they treated me with respect, courtesy, and best of

all, curiosity—as if, indeed, they could imagine me as a future colleague. While I didn't get a job that first year, I felt much better about myself as an academic, a teacher, and a scholar, because I'd been to some extent validated in these interviews.

Again, then, the issue of "worth" keeps coming up. Many of us, of course, share the values of those who interview us, to a greater or lesser extent, and many other respondents reported similarly pleasant experiences at their MLA interviews. Finding common cause with future colleagues is an important first step in thinking about the kind of "worth" or "merit" that we want to reward, even as we realize that other "worthy" candidates may not even be interviewed.

The worst thing many feminist candidates could say about the interview process was that they felt that they were too often quizzed on whether they could "handle" the canonical male authors, especially if their dissertations and/or research interest lay with women authors or non-canonical authors. This becomes, as one of my earlier respondents noted, a kind of apologizing that no one wants to do; and many wondered whether men working on non-canonicals were similarly quizzed on this topic. Can we make equations of "worth" here? Is one Tennyson worth three Felicia Hemans, for example?

But beyond the rather simple issues of canonicity—most of us *do* manage to convince interviewers that we know the "great ones"—there are still some very unpleasant interviewing experiences, and most of them have to do with illegal or at least distasteful questioning. Here are some examples to mull over:

Two years ago I had an interview with a small prestigious liberal arts college. . . . The interview was to take place in the convention hotel's restaurant which, due to the hotel's layout, was difficult to find the entrance to. My husband, wearing his MLA name tag, stepped out of the elevator with me, with plans to make sure I found the place for the interview and then to make his way to the lobby to wait for me. One of my interviewers, standing outside the restaurant, happened to see us together. My first interview question: "Was that your husband I saw you with?" I admitted as much. Then, "Is he in literature too?" "Does he have a job, and would he mind your moving cross-country?" I hastened to assure both interviewers that, in fact, I was further along in my graduate program than he was, that I was the only one of us "on the market," and that he would certainly go wherever my job took us. One interviewer—male—then persisted with "Well, but will he be willing and/or able to commute to a job in . . . [the closest source of other schools who might employ a spouse]?" At this point, I felt as though I ought to be objecting to the sexist tone of the interviewer, but I was too anxious to get the position to risk offending my interviewers.

Most such stories have to do with academic spouses, although the questioning can work two ways. One interviewer asked a candidate

when I could move. . . . After telling him that I would need two weeks notice for my current employer and one week to pack up and relocate, he looked at me puzzled and said, "What, no attachments?" Perhaps I'm being sensitive about being a non-coupled woman, but . . . I thought this question was illegal to ask on an interview.

One candidate, asked if she had children, responded brightly, "No, do you?" Treating the question as if it were a conversational tactic rather than a substantive issue may work for some, but for others the issues are more subtle and more difficult to parry. For example: "I am applying for a post-doc at [an Irish university] and was told by a current fellow (female, Catholic) to say I was Catholic (I'm not) as the university is rather anxious to redress its Protestant bias." Or:

Over drinks [after a somewhat awkward MLA interview] they asked me some illegal questions—whether I had someone who would be moving with me who would need help finding a job. I told them that my husband was applying to [professional] schools and that several of them were in commuting distance of [their city]. They suggested two other schools he might consider. . . . [On the campus visit] the faculty seemed very uncomfortable with our ambitions of being a two-career family. They kept telling me how difficult it would be, and seemed to think that [my husband] should make career decisions that would commit him to [their city] for life. (Specifically, they expected him to go to [a local] law school, which has open admissions and couldn't actually take him for two years. . . .) This was a real change from the MLA discussion, when they were positive about commutes to [several other cities]. But when they found out that *I* might be commuting at first, rather than [my husband], they were less sanguine about it. And at our final discussion during the campus visit, the chair told me that she wasn't sure that I could be as committed to the department as she thought I'd need to be. This pissed me off, partially because they had changed tunes so abruptly, and partly because I thought that they were being unreasonable. [My husband] and I were considering coming to a different part of the country altogether, and while we were certainly open to settling there, we weren't ready after two days to promise to spend the rest of our lives there. This, I had a feeling, was what she wanted me to promise. But it was an interesting spin on the two-career thing— suggesting that my husband should immediately declare himself career-secondary and surrender any aspirations of his own.[6]

These unpleasant questions, raised of a female candidate by a female chair, implicitly measure the husband's "worth" against his wife's. Whose career is primary? Whose should be? Is a spouse or partner's career an impediment to one's own, or vice versa? Few of us can avoid this balancing act or similar ones, but shouldn't we at least be allowed to negotiate it on our own?

These stories, which came both from MLA interview and campus visits, raise for me one of the crucial questions of the job search: what are the sanctions against illegal questions, and what can we do about them? Paula Caplan suggests that women politely redirect them and then document them, but she doesn't say to whom such documentation might ultimately go. To whom might a candidate report such questions? A lawyer? The MLA? Other interested women professors who might be in a position to speak to the questioners? It can be a useful and reassuring experience for candidates to keep an interview diary of sorts in which experiences like this are noted; if nothing else, they can be referred to later as a reminder that the candidate herself has not "failed:" the interviewers have. But candidates who have supportive mentors should also provide this documentation to them; often an advisor has contacts at a hiring institution who can be alerted to such problems.

One last two-career story: one respondent had the interesting experience of going on the market as half of a couple; the two of them applied for jobs separately but—at different appropriate times—tried to negotiate for two jobs in the same department. On one occasion, my respondent reports:

> We were invited to a cocktail party so that the search committee could meet me. At the party, the head of the search committee, when he was introduced to me, said, "So, you're the encumbrance on [your husband's] career." Honestly, I'm quoting.

> After MLA, this same man called the house to speak to [my husband]. I told him [he] was on his way home and would be there in fifteen minutes. He said it would be fine to leave a message. After I told him that I'd prefer he speak to [him] directly, he continued to insist I take a message. The message was that they would have brought him to cam-

pus, but I was "an encumbrance" and they were not going to be considering him further. This was the message *I* had to give my husband.

That story does actually have a happy ending, with two jobs—but many others may not.[7] One respondent thus suggests that advisors help empower their students with awareness:

[They should] prepare women candidates for the sexism that is still likely to exist in interviews and campus visits by helping them to think out appropriate—and "safe"—responses to likely questions. If sexism in the profession can be acknowledged by advisors, beyond the abstract "deploring" of it, it might give women candidates the courage to respond to it.

I seem to have come full circle back to advising, perhaps the best place to close. The key to the process, from beginning to end, is advising; good advising should be realistic (keep track of the numbers and kinds of jobs filled over the last few years in each candidate's field, for example), focused, and consistent. As I said earlier, this alone cannot guarantee a job, but it can at least provide a sense of control and perhaps ward off a sense of personal failure in the case of an unsuccessful first search. Increasingly, I believe, departments and/or universities must also provide some sort of counseling on non-academic career choices for Ph.D.'s. Departments must provide, and job seekers must demand, the kind of help they need to face the difficult process of looking for a job.

Postscript

As I said at the beginning, I began work on this topic flush with success and hoping to be able to share it with my colleagues, known and unknown, who would soon be facing the same process I'd just successfully navigated. Having now spent over three years in an academic job, and seen more than one job search conducted in that time, I'm less sanguine about my ability to "advise." But when I titled this paper I purposely redefined the initials "Q&A" to stand for "Questions and *Anecdotes*," not "Answers." Anecdotes may not be sufficient evidence to construct a logical proof, but as students and teachers we must all be aware of their power to persuade, enlighten, and even shape our experience as we negotiate our own similar passages. The more stories we tell, the more we know; the more we know, the better equipped we are to face the often disheartening, but potentially rewarding, process of navigating the academic job market.

Notes

[1.] An early version of this paper first appeared in the Modern Language Association's Women's Caucus journal, *Concerns* (Vol. 24, No. 1).

[2.] I want to thank those women who were willing to share their stories; their articulate responses were invaluable to me in shaping this paper.

[3.] Paula Caplan's book *Lifting a Ton of Feathers: A Woman's Guide to Surviving in the Academic World* (Toronto: University of Toronto Press, 1993), which came out after I was on the job market, is essential reading for women considering—or beginning—academic careers.

[4.] While a four-year job search may sound unthinkable, Bronstein and Caplan may derive their estimate from the sciences, in which postdoctoral fellowships and research positions antedate academic jobs yet figure in the time line of the job search. Nonetheless, my (admittedly unscientific) survey suggests that up to three years is not at all uncommon, and some of my respondents did take up to four years to land tenure-track positions in English and foreign languages. Often they spent some of this time in one- or two-year positions or in part-time work, some of it perhaps before completing their dissertations. See Caplan (op. cit.) and Phyllis Bronstein, "Applying for Academic Jobs: Strategies for Success," in *Career Guide for Women Scholars*, ed. Suzanna Rose (New York: Springer, 1986), pp. 3–26.

[5.] While the term "oversupply" here implies some politically neutral process—as if, accidentally, all the seeds in the garden germinated—there are of course large political issues involved in the question of the academic job market. While it is not my intention to get into those questions here, one important one which I hope others will begin to address seriously is the use of adjunct and contract labor in place of tenure-track professors.

[6.] Along the same lines, a friend recently likened a campus visit to a "blind date, but when it's over you have to decide if you want to get married."

[7.] For an extended discussion of a different solution to the two-career problem, see Elizabeth J. Deis and Lowell T. Frye, "Balancing the Personal and the Professional: A Shared Appointment, the 50–50 Solution," *Written Communication*, Vol. 10, No. 3 (July 1993), pp. 420–37.

Three

The Aftermath and Beyond

Introduction

Barbara Louise Ungar
Department of English, College of Saint Rose

I am one of the lucky ones. I have a job. A tenure-track job in my field. So my colleagues and I repeat to one another, staggering under our 4:4 load. We live in exile in the provinces (I know there are some Latin poets I should be reading, but who has time?), working much harder but making less money than a secretary. In my interview, I confidently answered that I could handle four classes a term, having adjuncted that many while writing my dissertation and applying for jobs. But full-time responsibilities—committee work, advisement, and community participation—really do make a profound difference. And guess what—I'm still (re)writing my dissertation and applying for jobs. It doesn't get any easier across the finish line, it gets harder; or, perhaps "the finish line" is the wrong metaphor. My first year, I didn't feel I'd won a race—I felt as if I'd been shot out of a fire hose. Eight classes, seven new preparations. Hundreds of new names and faces. My other favorite metaphor is juggling: I can juggle three balls and walk, but add that fourth ball, and it's all I can do to stay on my feet and keep them in the air.

But I am one of the lucky ones: I have actually had a paid

103

summer off to write! I have health insurance and a retirement plan! And my grad school debt is much smaller than that of most of my friends, who are not academically employed. So what if I live in Albania? (My first day teaching here, I asked the class hopefully, "What do you call people from Albany, Albanians?" A guy in back answered dryly, "We call them People from Albany." Sigh.) It could have been Taipei, or Laredo. Did you know that the original name of New York State's capital was Beverwyck, Town o' the Beaver, from Dutch trapping days, when New York's legal tender was beaverskins? (After one winter here, you know why.)

Throughout my three-year job search, I had not one MLA interview. (Like Joe Aimone, I went on the job market too early, wasting time and energy on hundreds of letters before my dissertation was complete.) I did have interviews in New York City, where I wanted to stay. The first year especially, my hopes rose and fell precipitously with each nibble and jolt: rejection by community colleges for remedial English-teaching jobs was particularly depressing. I enviously watched peers receive dossier requests and MLA interviews, but usually no job resulted, so all that anticipation, anxiety, and envy was in vain. None of it mattered. By the second year, we'd grown more sanguine and fatalistic. Being a poet was excellent preparation, as I have been one acquainted with the night of perpetual rejection. My calluses are thick. I had already spent years obsessively collecting, analyzing, and finally discarding rejection letters, as both Anahid Kassabian and Daniel Brownstein describe so beautifully in this section. (Note that Martha Hollander, also a poet, doesn't mention rejection letters in her moving account of her four-year job search. So being a poet is good for something, after all, if not necessarily getting a job.) My mailbox was never empty: scattered among the bills and junk mail were poem rejections, manuscript rejections, job rejections, and terse exchanges with my husband of fifteen years, who was rejecting me for a younger, less hyper-educated model.

"I'm Nobody! Who are you?" became a mantra. Writing my dissertation on Emily Dickinson helped: I figured I could always retreat to my old upstairs bedroom in Minneapolis, wear white, bake, and write poems all night. Though I never discussed this fallback plan with my parents, I don't think they would have minded . . . "How dreary—to be—Somebody!/ How public—like a Frog—/ To tell one's name—the livelong June—/To an admiring Bog!" I recited inwardly when classmates who had admired my brilliance in grad school walked off with jobs I was better qualified for. I recommend carrying the pocket edition of Stephen Mitchell's essential translation of Lao Tzu's *Tao Te Ching*, and committing #44 (among others) to memory: "Fame or integrity, which is more important? Money or happiness, which is more valuable? Success or failure, which is more destructive? . . . Be content with what you have; rejoice in the way things are. When you realize there is nothing lacking the whole world belongs to you." Mitchell quotes another fine mantra from an enlightened Japanese woman named Sono: "Every morning and every evening, and whenever anything happens to you, keep on saying, 'Thanks for everything. I have no complaint whatsoever.'" It may not get you a job, or enlightenment, but it helps keep the bitterness at bay. During my worst winter, Les Visible, the Woodstock poet who turned me on to the *Tao*, kept reassuring me, "Your job is out there." He was right, though not exactly the job I'd hoped for.

E-mail was (and is) a lifeline. The summer after my divorce, I did go home to finish my diss (as I affectionately truncated it) in the garage converted into my father's painting studio. Like Martha Hollander, I was a faculty brat who could imagine no future but teaching college; as a child, I planned to earn a series of Ph.D.'s. That summer I helped my father clear out his old office at the University of Minnesota, and he gave me the scarred, honey-colored briefcase he'd brought home from a conference in Florence years ago (way too heavy for me, the refurbished briefcase doubles as heirloom and talisman on interviews). I began every diss-day by e-mailing my grad school friends, scattered by then across the country, to warm up before easing myself back down into the Augean stables. Throughout the job search, and after, e-mail support from friends has been crucial. No one else could possibly understand the angst. (Hence, this book.) Joe Aimone's comic poems on rejection are perfect examples of the way cyber-camaraderie can keep us afloat, alive, and even laughing.

Everyone's story is different. Mine? After an ego-crushing year—not one dossier request, let alone interview—with my entire extended Hungarian-Jewish family in town for commencement, I landed two last-minute job interviews: Juilliard and a small Catholic liberal arts college I'd never heard of in Albany, three hours upstate. The Juilliard interview was the best I'd had so far, though, in retrospect, I erred on the side of caution, because I wanted the job so badly. I was so exhausted by the time I got to the second interview in Albany, what with commencement, family, Ellis Island, etc., that all my adrenaline had been used up. Besides, I didn't really want the job, so I was myself, and got it. Two truisms: when I read the Albanian job description, it fit me to a T—no stretching necessary; and the interview was a warm, relaxed conversation, as with friends.

How to negotiate salary? High twenties, low thirties, they offered; low thirties, at least, I said. I could hold out as long as I had another possibility. But by the time they made their final offer, Juilliard had turned me down. What can one do? $32,500 is a pitiful salary after seven and one-half years of graduate school, but also a 50 percent raise from adjuncting full-time. The best bargaining technique, I'd learned in Mexico as a child, is to walk away. But in today's climate, without another offer, who can afford to? (I did learn afterward, off the record, that although all new humanities hires got the same amount, new business hires came in at $10,000 more. But they have Ph.D.'s in making money, while mine is in "I'm Nobody—") There was ugly talk about "right-sizing" and other new business-speak when I arrived, causing such hostility between faculty and administration that after my first two days of orientation and meetings, I dreamed of Jesus climbing down off the cross. Luckily, a new administration has come in, and my department is as warm and simpatico as the interview promised, although the larger financial picture remains bleak.

It amazes me to hear legislators blather about our easy life: we professors work more hours for less money after more preparation than anyone I know (except adjuncts, of course). For a creative writer, trained to steal every spare moment to write, committee work and face-time are perhaps the cruelest exigencies of the job. I have thought about retooling (for what: social work? massage therapy?) but teaching is my vocation: I love it, and my students. After my adjunct years at City College in Harlem, the students here all seemed to be blondes named Jennifer and Jessica. I couldn't tell them apart. By the end of my first year, having heard their tales of anorexia, divorce, date rape, and suicide, I realized that the mall-lands of America need poetry just as badly as the ghettos, if not worse.

So I don't plan to change professions. Though I do keep applying for jobs, hoping for a human course load. No one can think or write teaching four classes a semester, except insomniacs with no life. At least now I can apply only to select jobs, without that unmistakable aura of desperation. I can walk away. But the precious time put into the job search is stolen from my own work—from my writing or research (never from teaching).

The teaching goes fine, as always, but I seem to have time for little more than teaching and preparing to teach. Now, my question is, having begun this Ph.D. business in order to earn a living and have time to write, when is the time to write? A vicious circle: how will I publish while teaching 4:4? and how will I escape teaching 4:4 without publishing? I've barely been able to look at my dissertation, not to mention write poetry, in this harried state. And I am one of the lucky ones.

Thanks for everything. I have no complaint whatsoever.

Grape Expectations

Joseph O. Aimone

started looking for work too early. I started when I decided to go to graduate school. I had returned to college as what we called a "non-traditional" student, to finish my B.A. and start looking into a career with a living wage. When I found that I loved the English classroom, which I hadn't when I left school some years before, I determined to become a college English teacher.

In the years since, as I finished my dissertation, I've had interviews and campus visits, but I haven't yet landed an assistant professorship. In 1995 I came close, but it turns out the fix was in one way or another beforehand. Ah, well, I thought, I have to do something.

As president of the Modern Language Association's Graduate Student Caucus, I frequently contribute to the electronic mailing list we maintain, called e-grad. I sent the following posting to that list:

> Announcing the first annual e-grad Sour Grapes Poetry contest: Designed to vent both specifically job-search-related frustrations and general mean-spiritedness, this contest will allow anyone to participate. No entry fee. No publication

beyond e-grad guaranteed or even likely. Winners will be declared by universal acclamation. Failing that, everybody—appropriately enough—loses. No prizes will be given, and winning will not be something to list on your c.v. under publications, if you have any sense.

So, just to get the ball rolling, here's a little ditty I wrote because I was feeling . . . well, you know, after that letter explaining what I already knew about how I wasn't the obviously most perfect of all possible candidates for that one little job . . .

A Fish Story for Ph.D.'s

> Do not let our refusal be
> Discouraging. We all had fun.
> The best of luck to you. Feel free
> To think yourself the lucky one
> Who got away, interviewee.

Others began to contribute. (There are several hundred members. I do not reproduce any of their entries here, since I do not have their permission to do so.) I began to feel the heat of competition, so I made another attempt to sweep the field, with this posting:

Applying for Work in Sin City

> The University of Mammon glows
> With neon in the desert. In their ad
> They asked among the perfect just for those
> Who have a sense of style in English prose
> That their rejection letters never had:
> Their commas were misplaced, their grammar bad.

109

The Consolation Prize (If You Get It)

I picked the phone up. Said, "What is it?"
"We've called you back to let you know
We would like you to come and visit."
"I thought you said the market forces
Would give you God to teach your courses,
And leave near full your empty coffers."
"We did. But then He didn't show.
It seems He got some Better Offers."

The first of these, "Sin City," came out of a common experience: I talked with someone else to whom the same thing happened. The second is strictly secondhand: I haven't received a call from anyone like that. Yet. (Though I hope to.)

There's No Place Like Home

Martha Hollander

When I was six years old, I drew a picture of a large family—mommy, daddy, brother, sister, toddler, and crawling little baby—all smiling and waving, with the schematic hilarity of characters in Archie comics. They all wore glasses and were dressed in academic caps and gowns; above their heads I wrote, "Be smart. Be a Prof."

I come from an academic family. Many of my baby-sitters were college students; I remember trips to my father's office at Yale, an intriguing cluster of Gothic buildings, where students and professors bent down to say hi. (Now I often find myself in the oddly pleasurable situation of interacting with faculty who first met me as a three-year-old.) Our family life was linked to the rhythm of the school calendar: we often spent whole summers in rural retreats or in Europe, where my father could write and research. The harmonious, small-town continuum between campus and home and even my nearby elementary school, and the contact with a perpetually changing group of eighteen-to-twenty-two-year-olds, have been familiar to me since my earliest childhood. In fact, this early experience left me with an unshakable attraction to the romance of academic life. "Being smart" clearly meant living that life. Ironically, while making me instantly at home in that life, this ideal view of the academy has made my progress through professional training and the job market exceptionally difficult.

While many former faculty brats would rather do anything than enter the family business, I felt it was the most natural thing in the world to become a professor. Once I graduated from college, I spent a few years in publishing, and made a brief stab at film criticism. It was all new and interesting, but once the initial relief at finally being out of school was past, I realized that I missed academic life. Although my publishing job was quite pleasant, I allowed myself to exaggerate the clichéd differences between office life (bureaucratic, tedious, intellectually sterile) and the life of a student (stimulating, sexy, surrounded by books and talk, lots of free time).

While I was still working in publishing, I moved uptown to be near my younger sister, who was at Columbia. I spent as much time as I could around the university. I shared an apartment with a graduate student and his wife, and spent time with my sister and her student friends. I participated in a graduate readings group in contemporary poetry. Soon afterward, I decided to go to graduate school in art history. I had already known that seventeenth-century Dutch painting was my singular love; now it would become my field of expertise. Though I chose Berkeley, farther away from home than I'd ever been, going there seemed potentially like returning home.

I started at Berkeley in 1983, during what was probably the last phase of optimism about the academic profession. The famous—by now, infamous—predictions about the great new boom in hirings around 1990 seemed timed just for me. Armed with this assumption, I never worried about the question of future employment, assuming that I'd get a teaching job as easily as I'd found work in publishing. No one said to me, when I entered, that I might not find a job. Rather, I was assured that with a degree from such a prestigious institution I would have no problem.

From early on in our student careers at Berkeley, most of us were more or less insulated from thoughts about the job market; a job was an abstraction, to be considered at some indeterminate point in the future. Instead, we focused on the more immediately compelling issues of graduate education: how to think, how to write, what relationship to form with the de facto authorities of source material as well as our teachers. Those days our struggles to survive centered on negotiating the university's numbing bureaucracy and the problems of securing financial and administrative support as we made our way through the program. It struck me how unlike a professional school this was. The program never offered any kind of general advice about finding a job; we never had workshops on job applications, were never given tips on what kinds of jobs to apply for. (The one exception was a terrific workshop on grant writing, one of the few official acknowledgments that a professional academic world existed in our futures.) These were, I should add, my own experiences, and may not have been shared by all the other students; experiences varied according to one's advisor and even one's field. Yet the general emphasis of a Berkeley graduate education in art history did appear to be on "internal" training, that is, developing intellectual rigor in our writing and thinking, rather than negotiating the context of a profession.

The only concrete instruction we were all exposed to was in the form of teaching assistantships, which offered priceless on-the-spot training to those of us lucky enough to get them, and giving oral presentations at conferences, which we all practiced in a yearly graduate symposium run jointly with Stanford. In fact, these two aspects of school formed the best professional training I received. But in the main, I sensed that actual job hunting strategies were virtually ignored. This was in part because the average time for finishing a Ph.D. was seven to ten years, and by the time students were ready to go on the market, they had long since left Berkeley. But perhaps the faculty's neglect of practical job hunting was also based on a prevailing attitude about the function of graduate school, which would make us thinkers, while the nuts-and-bolts professional stuff we could easily enough figure out on our own. Independence, after all, was an important priority for us.

In any case, it was easier not to think about the remote issue of job hunting. Progressing even up to one's exams was challenge

enough. Besides, much of school was an enormous, if anxious, pleasure. I found teaching, as I turned on the slide projectors for my
first freshman discussion section, to be a joy. I learned how to write
about art; I learned how to approach it through history, economics,
and anthropology; I discovered the esoteric pleasures and perplexi-
ties of critical theory. After five years of profound delight in learning
mingled, inevitably, with great uncertainty about how to process it
into well-formed scholarship, I was eager to write my dissertation
in a hurry. In fact, once I passed my exams, I worked furiously. My
art-historical training was somewhat unusual: instead of the canonical two or three years in the Netherlands, studying the language,
culture, art, and archives, I completed all my on-site research in a
few months. This was partly due to the theoretical nature of my
dissertation, and also due to necessity. I was never granted a research
fellowship despite my many applications, and couldn't support myself abroad for longer than two months. I felt that the faster I wrote,
the sooner I'd get out there and wow them in spite of my shortcom-
ings as a researcher and my failure to embark on the traditional
Grand Tour. I felt both marginalized and defiant: if I couldn't spend
all that time doing research, I'd finish my dissertation in record time.
This mingling of insecurity and arrogance was a typical response to
the pressures of school; indeed, I think it would be difficult to design
a degree program that did not foster these feelings in its students.

I took only two years to research, write, and file the dissertation.
During the course of writing, I relocated to New York, worked at a
part-time publishing job, and taught adjunct courses at several city
art schools. It was relatively easy to work fast. Being single and
childless, I had no pressing domestic commitments. I also had a
generous advisor and group of readers. Far from being the perfec-
tionist zealots some of my fellow students had to contend with, they
were eager to push me through the bureaucracy, responding to my
scholarly potential rather than to my ability to produce a gleaming
product. (And it wasn't anywhere near gleaming: there are numerous
hasty, ill-thought-out passages that still make me cringe.) They were
understandably eager to streamline the process, and were pleased to
use me as an example of how a student could move through the

entire program, from entering school to filing the dissertation, in just seven years.

While I was still finishing the dissertation, I finally picked up a copy of the College Art Association job list. This was the year I presented my first CAA conference paper; the time was ripe to apply for a job. Yet I deliberately refrained from going on the market. Looking back, I'm a little appalled at my shortsightedness—here I was, giving a paper in a popular session at a national conference, and blowing the chance to show off in front of potential interviewers—but I felt, at the time, that I wasn't ready. Not only did I still have a chunk of dissertation to write, but I felt emotionally and intellectually unprepared. I was haunted by various accounts (some first-person, others hearsay) of people being hired while still in mid-dissertation, and being so overwhelmed with professorial duties that they had to struggle to finish their dissertations by the third-year review. And despite my efficiency and hard work, I was almost superstitiously afraid the same thing would happen to me.

In fact, the actual process of Getting A Job had become so mysterious and demonized for me that it was hard to take seriously. I'd been giving talks at conferences for a couple of years already, but presenting a lecture was sheer pleasure and seemed oddly divorced from actually being hired by an institution. I didn't have a clue how to write a job application letter: what tone to take, what to say, what to include. I didn't understand the jargon and abbreviations of the job descriptions, didn't know how to read between the lines, didn't know which jobs would be better than others.

An admittedly self-imposed aspect of my isolation from the system was that in relocating across the country, and focusing so relentlessly on the dissertation, I'd effectively cut myself off from whatever support and advice my department might have offered. I was very much on my own. My advisor was traveling abroad; my relations with other professors in the department were minimal. Most of my friends from school were either installed at jobs (only a couple, in fact), had fallen out of touch with me, or had quit the field altogether. My father and stepfather, who'd both spent over thirty years helping their graduate students get jobs, were of some help.

But the situations in their fields, English and philosophy, were sufficiently different from art history that their advice was of the most general sort.

By the fall of 1990, I'd filed my dissertation; finally, I was ready for the next step. It was perhaps typical of my naïveté about the market that I felt it was essential to have a degree in hand—that is, to do everything according to some canonical script—before moving on. After some panicked, rather sheepish phone calls to a couple of school friends, I figured out how to write an application letter. I was happy and excited. I'd done everything properly. In innocent good faith, I assumed that with dissertation in hand—so speedily dispatched!—my job was waiting for me.

Instead, to my utter astonishment, puzzlement, shame, and finally despair, I spent the next four years perpetually looking for a job. I haunted each CAA conference like a starving person at a banquet. Altogether I had about ten interviews, three campus visits, a couple of cliff-hanging near misses, and always ended up by midsummer without a foreseeable future. Every apartment I lived in during these years was a sublet, since I was always prepared for the contingency of having to relocate. During this time, I scraped together a living out of adjunct teaching at art schools and continuing to work for the nonprofit publishing company I'd started out with while still writing the dissertation. The people there were enormously sympathetic and gave me the flexible schedule I needed for teaching and conference travel. Not a bad life in some ways, but I was constantly broke, and constantly trying to carve out time for research. I lived with the catch-22 of needing to publish to augment my slender record, yet not having the time or resources to do the research properly.

As a babe in these particular woods, I quickly became familiar with the usual horror stories among academic hopefuls in the humanities. Most of my application letters were rejected on the first round—which I soon realized was normal—and I managed to get only a few interviews. Over the next few years I participated in just a handful of these encounters: they ranged from enjoyable to embarrassing to dull to scary to incomprehensible. Certain isolated moments still stand out for me. I got embroiled in an argument with a department chair about a passage describing my research I'd included in my application letter. One person tried to engage me in a serious discussion of pedagogy while her colleague asked me if I could read Dutch. (If I were a Michelangelo scholar, would I have been asked if I could read Italian?) A group of graduate students asked me what my political agenda was. During a lull in one interview, I was offered a sumptuous plate of muffins. Once I was barely able to stammer out answers during a cross-continental phone interview with poor reception. There were evasions, thinly veiled hostilities, even flirtations.

For the most part, though, I enjoyed the interviews. I hadn't had the opportunity to talk about my work since my Ph.D. orals. The people involved seemed genuine; they seemed to care about their school and about their students. Those rare moments when I felt that things were clicking, that these people and I clearly saw eye-to-eye, gave me an enormous charge. More than anything I wanted to belong somewhere, to be part of a department, to have colleagues, to work hard for our students and for the institution. And yet I was never hired.

I was, ironically, lucky enough to be a finalist for three different jobs. These sought-after "callbacks" were a delight, and for the first time I felt a sense of reality about the job hunting process. Here were offices, slide libraries, art studios, real students—a professional life rather than just a bunch of people in a hotel room. In one case at least, the place seemed so perfect—intimate, serious, with smart, engaged, excited students—that I realized I'd accepted an institution before it had accepted me. I knew how it felt to consider being *happy* at a place, not just relieved and grateful.

And yet I still wasn't hired. In fact, in two cases I was in the odd position of being *almost* hired, as the chairs would go out of their way to explain to me: I *would* have been their choice if it hadn't been for . . . etc., etc. At one place, the question of my hiring came down to a departmental battle; at another, there was apparently a misunderstanding about the nature of the job. I was disappointed and angry. Not just that I didn't get the job, but that the reasons for my not getting it seemed so incomprehensible. That is, the decision wasn't just based on practical notions of who would be best for the department, which were completely understandable, but on miscommunications or conflicts that had nothing to do with me. I would have preferred not getting a job because they didn't like me or didn't think I could cut it; instead, I seemed to be not getting jobs because of other relationships, other contingencies. More than anything else, I was floored by the overall arbitrariness of these decisions, by the murky waters of departmental relations, of dealings with deans and presidents, of conflicting personal and political agendas. Second-guessing, I quickly realized, was a waste of time. Given the necessary secrecy surrounding much of the motivation of a department, I was always surprised at being vouchsafed their feelings. Clearly, I was being informed of these "almost" decisions to make me—and themselves—feel better. For my part, I preferred not to know.

Even though I had few opportunities for real research, I tried to compensate by getting the dissertation published. I let it alone for a year, and then sent it out to several presses in its unrevised state. The three readers' responses were confusingly mixed: one was guardedly praising, one generously damning, one bizarrely malicious. Ultimately no press felt sufficiently confident to publish it without extensive revision. I was disappointed; publishing would have meant validation and perhaps even a ticket to a job. On the other hand, I couldn't envision when and where to do the necessary research and revision if I *didn't* get a job on the strength of a publishing contract.

Things looked so bad that for a couple of years I tried to diversify. Since I had published a book of poems, I was also eligible for jobs in creative writing, and I began applying to English departments. This proved to be an interesting study in contrasts between the two fields, and between the needs of a creative writing program and an art history department. To my astonishment, I actually had an interview with a distinguished English department. While I wasn't hired there either, I was secretly relieved. It seems incredible to me now that I considered giving up my years of work in art history to "cross the line" and become a creative writing teacher. It would have meant abandoning a whole way of thinking and teaching, my ideas for articles, my lovingly tended (and expensive) collection of slides, my piles of bibliography, my studies of Dutch. Would I really have wanted to sully my work in poetry by turning it into an academic career? I may have been coolly pragmatic to consider switching disciplines, but perhaps this move was only one of desperation.

I also applied for every post-doc I could think of, everywhere and anywhere, if for nothing else than to pay the rent for nine months. My sense of a "project" was limited to revising my troublesome dissertation; I polished and fretted over my proposal essays with greater care than I'd ever lavished on the dissertation itself. I continually had to ask for letters of recommendation for a project I felt less and less confident about. In any event, I never received a fellowship. Even my steadily growing experience writing grant proposals at my publishing job never seemed to pay off. My inability to secure my own research funding seemed inexorably bound to my failure at getting published, at getting hired, at being able to advance at all.

I also applied for creative writing grants. The application process was blessedly easy, just selecting poems, and seemed like a professional advantage. Nonetheless, it ended up being an even greater source of anxiety. Sure, I'd love to spend time at a writing retreat, but how would it help my art history career? Writing more poetry would make me happy, and perhaps garner me a second book, but how could I make a living? I couldn't even "cheat" and bring research to a retreat; where would I find an extensive library with periodicals in Dutch? In any case, these applications were never successful either.

Meanwhile I kept working, hustling for adjunct teaching jobs, changing apartments three times, going broke to pay for rent and therapy, and wondering where I'd be by the following September of a given year. I couldn't concentrate on poetry. I was both infantilized and independent, stuck in a position of perpetual supplication (as well as being financially dependent on my parents), yet working without a net, going it entirely alone. Most of the people I saw were

non-academics who listened to my war stories. I was glumly grati-
fied by how aghast they were.

There was one rock-bottom year when my application letters
were all rejected, when I didn't get a single interview or a single
call. I actually gave a talk at the CAA conference that year, spending
a month's salary to install myself in Chicago. Apart from the usual
excitement I felt at speaking in public, I was precariously close to
being engulfed in ignoble self-pity, great gobs of it. That night, I
couldn't sleep, but paced up and down in my incongruously luxu-
rious hotel room, weeping, in a kind of ecstasy of despair. I really
believed that I could do good, could open students to an awareness
of art, of the past, of approaches to history, of their own minds and
visual capabilities. I couldn't wait to get involved, to work hard in
a department, to go to meetings and initiate projects, to work with
students and colleagues, to help expand the slide library, to interact
with the art teachers and the arts community. All this quite aside
from getting a real salary and benefits, an institutional affiliation so
I could finally gain admittance to good libraries, have summers off
for research and writing, not to mention some professional status,
and an office of my own.

And everywhere I was blocked. I had failed; wasn't this obviously somehow my fault? I was thirty-three years old. I had been
training since I was twenty-four. I had no prospects, no money, no
husband, no children. (These absences from my life had been liberating while I was a student; now they felt like pure failure.) If I
was to be shut out of academia, the only life I felt comfortable in,
then hadn't I been wasting my time? And yet what else would I do?
Certainly I was skilled for a number of jobs, and had spent more
time outside of academia than many of my peers in the profession,
but I had no ambition for anything else. I could never bring myself
to give up an academic career entirely; yet whenever I heard that
someone else in my position had done so, I was envious. Not for
that person's finding a better profession, but for his or her having
the guts to give up the previous one. I would never be able to give
up what I felt to be my home.

Throughout this experience I tried to escape the encroaching bitterness and resentment that I feared would alter my character. Since I was clearly in the middle of a professional horror story, clearly a statistic, I tried to take a step back from my own situation— after all, what was my critical training good for?—and deconstruct it. In those rare, calm periods of genuine curiosity, I considered the job process almost as a philosophical problem. Take the interview. These well-intentioned people were obviously doing their best, and in many cases didn't know what they wanted, and were taking their cue from me. Or, conversely, they knew exactly what they wanted, and were waiting to see if I was it. In this situation, could I even afford to consider whether they were what I was looking for? What about my appearance, my carriage, my clothes, my rhetoric? Did it matter whether or not I accepted that muffin I was offered? Why did this process feel so much like dating (a common but intriguing metaphor), and what were the ramifications of this similarity?

Other questions came to mind. What did it mean to be qualified? Did it mean having intelligence and passion and charm, an inventive approach to teaching, a devotion to scholarship, and a good-looking résumé? What else could it mean? Even though I knew it was use-less, I tried to assess the qualifications of the people who'd gotten the jobs I applied for. What did they have that I didn't? In a rela-tively narrow scholarly field like Northern baroque art, most appli-cants for jobs, myself included, position themselves along a Renaissance-Baroque axis, covering about four hundred years of art history in several European countries; experience or even expertise in a given field is essentially a non-issue. So what else could it be? Had they published more? Was it because they were men? Once I found myself in the humiliating position of losing a job possibility to one of my undergraduate students from Berkeley.

And what about the less mysterious issue of publications? Was it quantity or quality that mattered? Was it significant that my first (and for a while only) two published articles had been solicited by the magazine's editors? Did anyone ever read the offprints I sent? And if they did, what kind of effect could I expect my writing style to have? And what about those mysterious letters of recommenda-tion, which I felt so guilty about having to solicit over and over again from the same patient people? Were they read, or was their value merely as an edifice of impressive names on which my identity and reputation would rest?

I also thought, as "objectively" as I could, about the kind of person I was becoming. The effect of my four-year job search on my relationships was subtle but powerful. When I wasn't getting a grim satisfaction from the horror stories I told my non-academic friends, I struggled to keep from envying them for their relative comfort with their jobs and personal lives. Many of them were making comfortable salaries, marrying, and having children; they bought lovely, spacious apartments and houses, tended their gardens, made plans for the future. My envy was profound, well nourished, and had very little relation to reality. My bitterness about the few friends I had who were becoming successful academics was even worse. One friend of mine, with whom I had been quite close during my last years at Berkeley, spent several years abroad on a fellowship. I was so resentful of her luck and her progress that without realizing it, I alienated her completely; we have never been as intimate since then.

Ultimately, my life seemed to be ruled by a wearying ambivalence. On the one hand, there was all that fear, anxiety, and insecurity. On the other, I still felt an enormous sense of accomplishment. I was proud of being a survivor, having finished the dissertation, given three talks, and published two articles all while working multiple jobs, without support for research, either from a post-doc or a spouse, and without free time except what I stole from weekends, nights, and, occasionally, my job. This constant shuttling between accomplishment and failure, between lousy self-esteem and a wildly exaggerated sense of entitlement, all without a real frame of reference, was perhaps the most exhausting aspect of the whole four-year period. As well as making me frustrated and angry and self-pitying and difficult to be around, being on the market made me *tired*.

All this exaggerated anguish came from something more than just job hunting. I was not only striving to get somewhere in my profession, but pining for a way of life. The day-to-day circumstances of academia are unique. The cyclical progression of the school calendar, with its regular periods of stress and renewal; the summer, with its potential for intense scholarly concentration in an atmosphere of pleasure and ease; the perpetual shifts in the content of classes and makeup of students as opposed to the far slower-moving processes of writing and professional advancement; the relative lack of immediate supervision; the possibility of variation offered by dividing one's energies among teaching, writing, and administrative tasks; and the ideal of a college or university as a community.

Nonetheless, I had few illusions about the unalloyed pleasures of the job itself. I was quite prepared for the frustrations, the politics, the bureaucratic tangles, the constant struggle against budget cuts and mediocrity, the urgent demands of teaching on the one hand and publishing on the other. In a sense, I *wanted* these problems. They seemed more meaningful and worth worrying about than being stuck in the groove of the perpetual suppliant. The singular interaction I perceived in academic life, among the intellectual, the moral, and the social, was absent from the other working environments I'd known over the years. This was what I felt barred from experiencing, in effect a recapitulation of my childhood circumstances, only from an adult's perspective.

Ultimately, unexpectedly, I did find a job. Ironically, it came my way through word of mouth rather than an advertised search. A friend suggested my name to the dean of a small interdisciplinary program where he teaches, and after an hour-long interview I was hired, one of only five candidates. I spent my first summer of real employment joyfully getting back into research, spending long weekday hours at the library. In the following year or two, I developed new courses, and I gave more talks. I encountered eager, frustrated, angry, funny, adorable students. I worked on committees, went to meetings, argued and laughed with colleagues. I turned my dissertation into a book. I got married. Freed from that wildly exaggerated cycle of hope and resentment, I'm now trying to pursue my work, and take stock of the profession, in a more measured way. Of course, this still isn't easy to do. Many of the problems inherent to academia are still with me: the isolation, the lack of mentoring, the bizarre discrepancies between my authority and ease as a teacher and my insecurity about publishing, the difficulty of finding a critical and scholarly identity within my discipline. Indeed, writing this essay has been agitating, embarrassing, even painful; yet it seems essential never to forget my four-year job search, and at the same time, to recall why I entered this beleaguered profession in the first place. As I write, just as I've heard it since getting my doctorate, a voice at the back of my mind whispers at me to stop whining and get on with it. On the wall in my office, I still keep a photocopy of "Be smart. Be a Prof."

The Sound of the Mail Truck, or How I Learned to Stop Worrying and Read Rejection Letters

Anahid Kassabian

When I began graduate school in 1986, there was little reason to predict the academic job market as we know it today. Almost all of my friends received offers in their first year "on the market," and many had multiple offers among which to choose. By 1990, when I began applying for tenure-track positions, our expectations had changed dramatically.

Since my degrees are all interdisciplinary, I varied my strategies for job seeking from year to year, much as a lab rat might design her own experiments for keeping alive. Over the five-year period during which I was applying for permanent positions while also working as a part- or full-time instructor, I collected my rejection letters. Many of my friends and colleagues made convincing cases for the ritual destruction of such painful bad news, but I organized and filed my demons with an almost obsessive desire to control them. Perhaps my choice to write about them for this volume is a continuation of that impulse, or perhaps it is simply a way to justify my files. In either case, it is my sincere hope that some good will come of revisiting them, both for writers and receivers of such letters.

125

The first important point to make about academic rejection letters is that they dominate the lives and thoughts of their recipients, both before and after their arrival, both specifically and generically. That is to say, one of my most vivid recollections of those five years is listening for the sound of the mail carrier's truck. There was a part of me that began to hope for rejections simply on the grounds that some information is better than none. Waiting for information became a structuring feature of my life.

But the arrival of a rejection letter often brought a different kind of uncertainty. Some phrases will always stay with me: "As our search has proceeded, it has become evident that your work is less competitive than a number of other applicants"; "We have narrowed our choice to a short list of persons whose qualifications and background clearly place them at the head of our list, and we must now regretfully eliminate all of the other applications, including yours, from further consideration for this position." It is not difficult to imagine that the authors of such statements did not mean to suggest that the letters' recipients were in some irreparable way less worthy of a permanent academic position. It is nonetheless impossible for any applicant to read them any other way. Each letter becomes the occasion for scrutiny and self-doubt, requiring an entire series of life decisions to be made anew.

And even beyond such unfortunate phrasing, the standard disclaimers produce similar anxieties. Here is an example of a very routine rejection letter:

On behalf of the search committee of this department, I regret to inform you that we are no longer considering your candidacy for an assistant professorship. We received more than 250 applications for this position and have concluded that there are other candidates whose qualifications are more suited to our needs.

Thank you for your patience in awaiting a response, as well as for your interest in our university.

On a completely rational level, it is not difficult to understand how a search committee might find a candidate qualified and desirable, yet not suited to its department's needs. But for recipients of the above letter, it is nearly impossible to imagine that the outcome of this particular search does not reflect on their general chances for employment.

This may sound like an argument that rejection letters will always be read by applicants as a generalized rejection of their work. To some extent, this may be true. And each applicant's reading of each letter will, no doubt, vary according to many factors. For the purposes of this brief essay, I want to focus on just one of those, which we might call the rhetoric of rejection.

During the same year, 1994–95, that I received the above letter, I also applied to another department at the same university. I was not chosen for that position either, but the letter they sent seemed to me then, as it does now, exemplary in its careful and thoughtful wording.

> I am writing to inform you of the status of your application for the assistant professor position in our department. The search committee is presently selecting one or two candidates for interviews. Your application is not among those being considered for interview at this time.
>
> There were 190 applications for the position. Your application was among the top 20% of this number. Let me assure you that your application was given very careful consideration, and that you were perceived as a potentially very desirable colleague. Obviously, only a few of these applications could be advanced for final consideration. It is unlikely that we will not be able to select from our list of finalists, but I will inform you should the status of your application change.
>
> On behalf of the search committee and the department, I would like to express sincere appreciation for your interest and your effort in applying to our program. We wish you

the best in your job search and in your future career pursuits. We invite you to apply to our program should we have a suitable opening.

This letter does not do anything that the previous letter avoided: it makes no promises, leaks no confidential information, puts the department at no risk. It did, however, leave me with a good feeling about the department and the search chair. Just as I remember some of the difficult letters and their authors, so too do I remember the more encouraging ones.

At the end of this search, I got a letter from the committee's chair informing me of their hire. As it turned out, they chose someone whom I both like and respect, and I was genuinely happy for him. The following year, I ended up with two permanent offers, either of which would have made me perfectly happy. The position I chose is closer to my extended family, and matches quite closely the kind of teaching I have always imagined for myself. I am in many ways grateful both to the department that hired me and to those that didn't. But it will be a long time before I forget the sound of that mail truck or the sound of those thoughtless phrases in my head.

"Cadences of Rejection"

Daniel Brownstein

A letter arrived from a large, northeastern Ivy League university on stationery of a wonderfully elegant sort, so I held it up to the light to admire the filament-thin filigrain, and I numbed myself to the sound of its words, which I had already read several times. The paper was the sort that, when I was in high school, cost fifteen to twenty cents per page to copy onto at the corner Xerox shop in New York, and it was a kind of paper that my own university never used in its correspondence with me, not for my diploma, not even for the faux-elegant letter of congratulations that the secretary in the graduate division gave me, with a butterscotch lollipop, when I handed in the two white cardboard boxes, each of which held copies of my nearly five-hundred-page thesis. This was a more solemn moment, in its way; this was contact with a voice of academic venerability.

I admired the filaments and the fine penmanship of the signature, the fully formed, Waterman light-blue ink signature of the chair drawn by him or a skilled secretary, the sort of secretary who probably had a degree in library sciences and may have almost decided to write a thesis on eighteenth-century orthographic styles. I had been receiving similar letters all year; the letter of rejection was a recent sort of tradition for me, and I quickly forgot about its actual content. The signature, loose but distinguished, was a bit dated, as one would expect from a chair, but gracefully Boston, belying the fact that it had been repeated hundreds of times. It probably was a secretary's, but there was no reason to think so. It seemed to scream Ivy League, Kennedy administration, vintage early 1960s, I thought, since that was before I was born; even if it was tossed off into a bulk-rate envelope, it had clear historical resonance.

The more I contemplated the paper's elegant stock, the farther away it seemed to be from me culturally, however—the farther away it seemed to be declaring itself to be from the mottled brown wall-to-wall carpeting of the one-bedroom where I lived and where I had only recently finished printing the last chapters of my dissertation. The letter was a sign of just how far off I was to think I would fit in as a lecturer at this sort of an institution anyway; it was asking me by its grace whether I had even realized what sort of an institution I was applying to, or if I had realized who I was dealing with when I tossed off my letter of interest on Xerographic Hammerhill.

I wasn't, I noticed, addressed as "Daniel." I had been in the first-name-basis rejection letter from the chair of the Early Modern Search Committee at another, slightly less venerable, elite school, who was still thoughtful enough to respect the proxemics of rejection letters alive by signing a formal Anglo-Saxon "Wm. E." in front of his family name; to do so set the letter apart from those beginning with an almost interchangeable (do they really care?) "Dr.," "Mr.," or "Professor," which I get from other places, one of which went so far as to type "Professor" on the envelope itself. The first-name address felt like more of a compensation (we'll treat you as a colleague anyway), and it made me want to write back to "Bill," thanking him for reading the application anyway, asking him to play doubles in a few weekends on a nearby grass court. On the other hand, it seemed fitting to acknowledge that by this point I had become on familiar terms with the nice people in Vancouver, Washington, whose long, friendly letter of rejection described how many applications they had read, only to have the funding pulled from under them, and had the strong, empathic undertones of "we know it's hell out there"—in contrast to the crisp, single-paragraphs from rejection letter–writers at other schools. Then again, they probably had more fun up in the Pacific Northwest.

Of all the salutatory codas, I liked best the somewhat Homeric dactyls from one university which read, "I want to thank you for your application and wish you good luck in your career. " This was a huge expansion on the "thanks for your interest," and the letter even went on to include an apology that they didn't get a chance to meet me. "Good luck in your efforts to find academic employment" was pretty snide of one of them, I thought, as if they had developed a pretty good idea of how slim those chances were while flipping through many applicants' dossiers. I didn't know what to make of the "Sincerely yours" with which yet another university closed its "thanks-but-we-regret-to-say . . . ," but it was cute.

How different from the letter I was still holding in my hands as if it were the document of another culture. I wondered for a bit about how much the guy who penned these signatures got paid. I folded the letter back up, put it in the light gray (mauve?) envelope, and placed it in the stack. They were only looking for the sort of person who wouldn't be impressed by the paper they used anyway, who wouldn't pause to consider the extra cost of the letters they knew were their due. I kept this letter along with the other rejection letters I'd received, as a confirmation of my insufficiency, and thought for a while about what I was to make of the fact that it was on almost archival bond. It was later, out of some perversity, that I threw that one out, keeping all the others in the piles of old correspondence I stored in my closet or on one of the two crowded tables I had been using as my desks.

My friends used to collect these sorts of letters too, perhaps as mementos or out of a sort of pride, but stopped after a year or two. I let my letters pile up; though I doubt they will ever become collectors' items, or be as valuable as the tersely dismissive missives T. S. Eliot issued from his desk at Saber. But they are nonetheless dying for careful analysis—who signed them, what salutation was employed, what tropes of distancing they used to acknowledge the job candidate that they turned down all seemed worthy of study. As the job market narrows, it seems that these letters have become marked by an almost existential anxiety on the part of the letter writer him- or herself ("It is, therefore, with great regret that we inform you that the position has been filled") and by the department's suggestion of the difficulty in undertaking that particular job search, implicitly reminding you that you're really on the same side of the fence, even if they get paychecks. What are the motivations for the appearance of such changes in tone? Are the decisions in how to express formal regrets driven by the marketplace, by an attempt to maintain a sense of moral economy, by chance? How, indeed, did what might have been a simple one-line rejection note come to be elaborated into a three-to-four-paragraph explanation of the hardships created by the market that we're all too familiar with, as if to create a false empathy between rejected applicant and school?

In part, rejection letters subtly suggest the amount of time the search committee members have devoted to the whole affair, and give you the distinct sense that they find the whole job search almost as unpleasant as you. Perhaps, the choice of first-person address (is this new, or was it always the case?) creates a solidarity across discrepancies of income, rank, or class: you have all paid your dues, albeit at varying rates, to the same professional umbrella group, which might inspire some guild-like confraternity. The dates these letters are sent offer a whole other area for analysis which surely corresponds to the vagaries of the marketplace, the increased insecurity of obtaining funding for posts, and the rise of one-year replacement jobs: sometimes these letters come over the summer, when the next year's schedule of classes must have been long past due to the registrar, and the proper names of certain instructors for certain courses have been plugged in with that reliable capital-letter dummy, "STAFF."

But as I looked at the filigrain of the letter that had traveled across the United States from Cambridge, Mass., I felt myself staring down a tunnel of underemployment, which echoed with the unanswered cries for attention of endless résumés. My heart sank. I realized that, though I was entranced by the weft and weave, these letters were inscrutable no matter how much I was tempted to press meaning into them. But needing to feel a sense of balance for the time we invested in the search, we are so tempted to press meaning into them. I thought of a friend who had studied the AAA tour guides for the town of the university where he had given a job talk, considering the restaurants where he would eat, the nearby national parks, the community in which he and his family might finally invest their nest egg. I thought of another friend who had waited, on his toes, for a response from a state university in his city of residence, after he had interviewed with them at the national professional meeting, to which he'd traveled cross-country for a prearranged interview which, ostensibly due to poor scheduling, never occurred; he told me of the subsequent depressed if pregnant sense of frustration he'd felt when he finally called for the answer he'd never officially received, and was told without apologies that another candidate had been chosen for the post in the meantime. I had so many friends who had repeated this exercise three years running, still finding the energy to get up and try for another round, their backs against the walls; others, in a new strategy, decided to limit their applications to one or two schools, in order not to face the depression of repetition, or the realization that one might not want an acceptance from these places anyway. I thought of one particularly nice and conscientious friend, whose mild question as to what the faculty did in their spare time on an upstate campus among cornfields received the response: "We drink heavily." The paper house of application letters quickly fell down yet again.

Nothing similar had, however, so drastically collapsed for me. As I held the letter up to the light, I realized I was a neophyte and that this was still the first wave; I had only just received a doctorate that spring. But my eyes glazed as the image changed before me: I now saw myself in a maelstrom that I realized might surround me for several years and, as my depression suddenly began to take fixed form, I imagined myself being trapped in it like Pigpen's everpresent dust cloud. I tried to take in the huge swirl of papers that I was slowly being enclosed by, as I imagined the sheer volume generated by each job search, the nights slouched over revising my dissertation, making those revisions on which any hope of a future would depend. Those simple, telling words, "after giving careful consideration to a large number of highly qualified applicants," lifted a corner on a new moral universe.

Four

Identities and Politics

Introduction

Elizabeth Freeman
Department of English, Sarah Lawrence College

n the 1990s, utopian politics are the privilege of the well employed. The tenured scholars who trained my generation have published books rupturing sexist, heterosexist, racist, nationalist, classist, and disciplinary paradigms. Sometimes, their work has even exploded the tenets of the "vulgar" identity politics that characterized the nomination of Clarence Thomas. They have trained us to believe in complex categories—in short, to do the kind of work they do.

Yet as paradigms for hiring, their ideas seem to have limited influence. From year to year, there may be a mini-boom in African-American studies, gay/lesbian/queer studies, or some other minority category. But these momentary flashes do not transform the majority of job descriptions, which remain so archaic that we graduate students doing interdisciplinary work and/or work defined by gender, race, sexuality, or class must quickly "rediscipline" ourselves into exemplars of nation, genre, and period. As Brian Caterino suggests in "My Life Part-Time," hiring policies simply overlook complicated identity categories, lumping in working-class, first-generation college-educated, and socialist white men with their privileged and conservative counterparts. As Julie Vandivere's essay "Where's the Closet at the Hilton?" makes clear, gay and lesbian scholars must dissociate their scholarly work from their actual identity, which it hardly seems possible to ask scholars in gender studies or studies in race to do. And as Gene McQuillan observes in "White Men Can't Teach," the very policies that in the past twenty years or so actually redressed the imbalance in the academy between white male scholars and the rest of us are mystifying in ways that damage all candidates.

While it may seem that incorporating "identity politics" into hiring policies has primarily benefited nonwhite scholars, things are not so simple. While queer scholars are forced to dissociate their identities and their work, in "Of Job Trails and Holy Grails for Feminists Out There" Sivagami Subbaraman points out that scholars of color are frequently pushed into doing work "within" their racial category. There are other stories from minority candidates missing here too: the young minority candidate hired with one dissertation chapter, who is expected to participate in so many campus political brouhahas, curriculum development projects, and student identity crises that she cannot finish her dissertation and is not granted tenure. The story of African-American candidates who are expected to cover Asian-American and gay/lesbian studies too (as if all categories of "otherness" are interchangeable). The story, in numbers, of exactly what category of people have benefited most from "affirmative action": I suspect the answer would be straight white women hired in the 1980s. The story of a "special interest hire" dismissed as a disposable departmental frill, and yet paradoxically asked to be the only one responsible for material by and about "otherness." In short, the crude taxonomies of "affirmative action" have been used by conservative *and* progressive members of hiring committees to further a regressive status quo.

At this point, white male or otherwise, we are all "damaged goods." Our damage comes as much from the cognitive dissonance and material hardship that we have experienced in the 1990s as from the traditional axes of gender, race, class, and sexuality. The academy has managed, somehow, to use identity categories in ways that *obfuscate* the class exploitation that it perpetuates as a matter of course. While hiring committees typecast us in ways that set us against one another and ourselves, their very members continue to receive low teaching loads, opportunities to teach interesting self-designed courses, and research and travel funds *because* we exist as a labor force. Without us, their well-paid jobs, intellectual freedom, and "star" status would disappear. And we, in our despair, internalize the academy's misrecognitions and misrepresentations. As McQuillan shows, our rage at the way affirmative action is practiced slides dangerously into negative feelings about affirmative action itself. Like Caterino, we see that education is no longer the way out of poverty, but a route toward it. Like Subbaraman and Vandivere, we wonder if we should have capitulated to other people's expectations about the relationship between our identity and our work.

This does not mean that the traditional forms of oppression have ceased to exist, for Vandivere, Caterino, and Subbaraman's essays all reflect the experience of being shut out of networks of power for being queer, working class, or a person of color. It only means, as these essays powerfully show, that "traditional" forms of oppression have compounded an exploitative job market, for which nobody seems to want to take responsibility. In the 1960s, the students who now mentor us recognized the university's perpetuation of class oppression and demanded that academics take more than a rhetorical stand against the university operating as a power tool for what they quaintly called "the establishment." Now that this oppression is in their midst, now that it is called "downsizing," are they blind to it? With tenure and job safety, can they not take the risk of alienating their conservative colleagues? How many administrators or "stars" would sacrifice their perks for our generation's livelihood?

I suspect that we must depend on ourselves—but not in individualistic ways that foster isolation, rage, and despair. As far as I can see, the only good reasons to stay in the academy are my students and my own generational cohort. We must hang in there, work together, fight with our mentors and colleagues for the things these essays call for. And in the meantime, for those still in the midst of things, some (cynical?) advice about identity politics, and the job market, from one who did things wrong.

First, as Vandivere also suggests, never underestimate the sexism, racism, classism, and homophobia that go on behind closed doors, in committee meetings. But rather than living in fear of these prejudices, arm yourself to negotiate them in terms familiar to your detractors as well as your allies. The trick is to make your work (and yourself, if you can swallow it) "pass" well enough to get you a job: it's difficult to challenge academia without one, and you can't eat radical chic. So in graduate school, take some courses with one or two older, traditional scholars. Angle to teach survey courses as well as specialized courses in your field. Get at least one older, more traditional scholar on your dissertation committee, perhaps as a second reader. This person can help you frame your project so that it's still legible within the most traditional terms of your discipline. Ask this person to write recommendations for you as well. In your dissertation and publications, write about what is most important and urgent to you: that's *not* the thing to sell out. But practice describing your scholarship and teaching in terms of traditional as well as progressive paradigms, so that when interview and job-letter time comes you can talk to more than one person on a committee.

Within your field, find your intellectual and political allies quickly. On the other hand, don't assume that your primary detractors will be traditional scholars instead of "progressive" ones: power is power, and progressive scholars are just as capable of misusing it. Most importantly, foster good working relationships with peers whose work and outlook you respect, especially those a couple of years farther along in the rat race, even if they (or you) end up jobless. Consider whether the academy is the best, or the only, place to further the politics that have animated your work—many of your brightest peers will not survive this process or will choose to save themselves from it, and they may have valuable resources or insights for you. Until senior academics stop wringing their tenured, star-studded hands and commit to some major restructuring of their profession, their former students have very little to survive on but what we can offer one another. Let these essays be a beginning.

White Men Can't Teach: Affirmative Action and the Academic Job Search

Gene McQuillan

> "We should read the Job Information List as we would any text."
> —Gordon Hutner, from "What We Talk About When We Talk About Hiring"

> "The official line varies so much from the word on the street that graduate students have only gossip to rely on as a guide."
> —Erik D. Curren, from "No Openings at This Time"

I admit it—I sometimes listen to Rush Limbaugh.

I am an assistant professor of English at Kingsborough Community College (City University of New York) in Brooklyn; the position is a full-time, tenure-track line. Perhaps the most annoying part of my job is the commute. I drive roughly thirty miles each way from northeast Queens to southwest Brooklyn four days a week during semesters. Most of this is on the Belt Parkway, and the best one can say about the Belt is that the Brooklyn-Queens Expressway is even worse. The only manageable way for me to commute is to leave home at roughly 6:00 A.M., which allows me to get to my school office by 6:45. I do my paperwork, review my lessons, and meet students until my first class, at 9:10, and when my classes end, at 1:40, I will sometimes try to beat the rush-hour traffic home. However, "rush hour" in Brooklyn basically means anytime during daylight, so I've gotten used to ninety-minute drives home. That's where Rush Limbaugh comes in.

I used to do a lot of truck driving during college and graduate school, and while doing so I learned a simple trick of long-distance drivers. When you are behind the wheel and feeling tired, do *not* put on your favorite music. Instead, put on something you intensely dislike: some really awful country music, a rude advertisement for something you would never buy, or even a program in a language that you don't understand. Soon you'll be gritting your teeth, perhaps even yelling at the console, but you will at least be wide awake. (Not a good method for one's long-term health, but perhaps no worse than potent coffee.) In simple terms, when the Mill Basin drawbridge goes up, and people can actually park their cars and stroll on the Parkway for a few minutes, I've been known to turn on Rush Limbaugh on WABC. It was a January day in 1996 when Rush was rambling through a long monologue about, of all things, job advertisements for college professors. It seemed that a full-time tenure-track position had become available at a college, and the job listing included some basic requirements of applicants: a Ph.D. in the field, some scholarly publications, and evidence of dynamic classroom teaching. Yet a controversy had developed at the school regarding one word in this ad—''dynamic.''

It seems that the ad had originally asked for evidence of ''excellent'' teaching, but this criteria was thought to be either vague or obvious, so the word ''dynamic'' was chosen for its greater specificity. One professor at the school filed an official objection to this editorial decision, claiming that the word was culturally coded. Various arguments against the term were explained. The ad would attract men rather than women, since ''dynamic'' was more often associated with certain ''male'' qualities—a booming voice, perhaps. The ad was seen to discourage members of certain ethnic/racial groups, specifically Asian-Americans, whose cultures have not placed a premium on highly expressive teaching methods. Also, ''dynamic'' could imply some degree of motion or movement around a classroom; would a wheelchair-bound scholar meet this criteria? Having expounded at length about what he saw as the absurdity of the situation, Rush then tried something truly unexpected and far less successful: he tried to explain "phallocentric and logocentric" to the afternoon audience of WABC!

I can't say with any certainty that my story is fully accurate. I am relying strictly on my memory of what Rush Limbaugh said; he in turn was relying on a news account of what happened at the college. It can be inferred that different people at the college would give varying accounts of this debate. I don't have a copy of the actual job listing in front of me. However, Limbaugh's point was clear: as he saw it, the word "dynamic" was not some insurmountable obstacle to a job, since no well-qualified applicant was going to be turned away simply because of that one word. (Only the "undynamic" need not apply.)

I was wide awake, and angry as hell. But I wasn't really angry at Rush Limbaugh, although he was so wrong in his assumptions that I could barely begin to explain how. I was angry because I had lost my first full-time, tenure-track job two years earlier, and I had lost it precisely because of a protest about the job listing.

I received my Ph.D. in American Studies in 1991 at the age of twenty-nine. My first two years on the market were, in a word, painful. I had made a tactical decision during graduate school to focus all—and I mean all—of my efforts on finishing the dissertation before it finished me. In retrospect, I sense how lopsided my c.v. must have looked. I had finished the dissertation in less than two years, but I had only a few conference presentations and no articles to my credit. (As my chairperson said back then, "If you don't get an article out this year, you're dead meat.") I began piling up the usual listings on my c.v., and I considered myself a reasonably good, but certainly not spectacular, candidate. The University of New Mexico was considering my book manuscript, and though they didn't accept it, that prospect was enough to interest a few schools. My search for a job included two more possible problems. First, my fianceé had a very good job in New York City, and since she had been my source of financial and emotional support during graduate school, I was not about to ask her to move across state lines for my chance at a $25–30,000 job. The second problem was this phrase, one which was appearing (in various forms) in some job listings: "Women and minorities are especially encouraged to apply." The first problem led to some serious discussions with Linda: what options did we have if I received a good job offer at a school one hundred or three hundred or five hundred miles from New York? I knew other couples who had juggled commitments, plane schedules, used cars, second apartments, and epic phone bills in order to seize that first tenure-track job. We hardly looked forward to such situations, but at least we could find out some clear information about them. Yet when it came to the second problem, I was at a loss.

What was the corollary of this statement? How would one complete the sentence, "White middle-class males _____?" I knew at least a few ways to complete it:

1. White middle-class males have generally formed the majority of most English departments in America.
2. White middle-class males have continued to hold major positions of influence—such as being on a hiring committee—on almost all college campuses.
3. White middle-class males are still getting hired for substantial positions as teachers and/or administrators.
4. White middle-class males should recognize that English departments, like other work forces in America, have to become more diverse.

In spirit, I agreed strongly with *all* of these statements. I could hardly look around the campuses where I taught and claim that white middle-class men were under-represented. I knew that my ESL students came from at least twenty different countries and spoke at least ten different languages, and I knew that English departments needed teachers who could understand and represent these myriad cultural backgrounds. But in practice, I was becoming less interested in "white men" and much more concerned about this one white male Ph.D. who could barely meet his rent and who could not contribute his share of the money for his own upcoming wedding. I must also say that graduate school in the humanities had not exactly been realistic training for this scenario. We all knew that an M.B.A. program was "the shark tank," but we often deluded ourselves into believing that we could *all* do well. I was in American studies, while my closest friends were studying the lives of medieval saints, the political poetry of Yeats, the lesser-known novels of Willa Cather, and the prose of John Milton. At times it seemed that competition was not only unlikely and unnecessary—it was *impossible*! But on my thirtieth birthday I came to a humiliating recognition: I had seriously underestimated the requirements of my profession, and it might be too late to change that.

I come from a close and wonderful family. My parents are both teachers, and they were very understanding about my situation. My two younger brothers, however, expressed their sympathies in a more sardonic manner. I don't know if it's a male thing, an Irish thing, or a McQuillan thing, but in my family, friendly insults pepper all conversations. At my thirtieth birthday party, my brother—a twenty-eight-year-old M.B.A. with a $90,000 salary—thought he was being appreciative when he compared me to my favorite writer, Thoreau: "Here's to my older brother, Gene, who made it to thirty without ever holding a full-time job!" When I was twenty-seven, I had enjoyed the life of a gypsy scholar; I enjoyed unstable schedules, different schools, odd teaching assignments (a carpentry factory, a psychiatric hospital, a nighttime adult education program in the South Bronx). But I now had a longing for a "real job."

By the time the October 1992 MLA Job List came out, I was beginning to read phrases such as "Women and minorities are especially encouraged to apply" as something between a clue and a warning, one far more imposing than the word "dynamic," for it had the potential to exclude roughly 50 percent of the applicants for certain jobs. (That ratio would vary, of course, depending on the field of study and other factors.) Many of my white male friends on the job market had their own interpretations of what that sentence actually meant. Optimistic readings were along the lines of "White men are still encouraged to apply"—we were just a little less appreciated; we were not "especially" welcome, but qualified applicants would be fairly considered. The more ominous reading, which became increasing prevalent with each successive poor job market, was "White men are especially encouraged *not* to apply." We realized that this reading was both petulant and paranoid, but during our calmer moments we did seriously wonder about the expectations which such a phrase created or reflected. If a search committee specifically stated that they eagerly awaited applications from women and minorities, did that not make it unlikely that they would choose a white male as their final candidate to present to the P-and-B (Personnel and Budget Committee)? If the race and gender of applicants didn't matter, then why would such a statement be included in the job listing?

Some male colleagues hesitated to apply for such positions. Of course, Rush Limbaugh—and the placement officers at my school—suggested that any good worker would just apply, regardless of the minute details of an ad, but it wasn't always so simple. What if the "application" was not just the standard cover letter, c.v., and dossier? What if the school wanted transcripts, a writing sample, last year's syllabus, or next year's plans for research? Few graduate students had the time or resources to file such complex applications, and the thought that such applications would receive less than full (or fair) attention led some to look elsewhere, even if they were otherwise well qualified. Rumors—later confirmed—began to spread about "fixed" job searches in which final candidates would be picked long before the MLA interviews (see Caminero-Santangelo's "The Ethics of Hiring"). The mood in the "bullpen" where the adjuncts had their cubicles was getting strained and even strange. Highly trained and articulate professionals were acting like poorly prepared freshmen who wandered around asking "What do they really want from us?" Yes, we knew that job committees wanted degrees, publications, and teaching experience, and we did our best to produce, produce, produce. But what else did they want? We honestly didn't know, and if anyone did, they weren't speaking openly about it.

I don't know if these comments seem accurate, overstated, or downright reactionary; I admit that some are part guesswork, and in retrospect I see that bitterness is both a cause and an effect of failed job searches. However, I will also say that confused bitterness had become a sort of common tongue for part-time instructors, especially those with Ph.D.s and publications and serious teaching experience, and the dismal developments in the 1990s job market have only increased this sense of conflict. From such anger came rumors and then accusations, and as often happens, the rumors had no clear source and the accusations had no helpful purpose. Yet they proliferated. For example, in 1991 and 1992, I began to hear stories about the "chances" a white male would have when applying for an "affirmative action" line. You could get an interview, even a second interview, perhaps even a campus visit, but you wouldn't get the final job offer. I heard so many rumors that I finally began to ask senior professors about this prospect—and to this day I have yet to receive a straight answer. I believe that the lack of reliable information about affirmative action, rather than affirmative action policies per se, is what fuels these rumors and conflicts. The reluctance to address such questions in open, candid terms may even represent an ethical failing by hiring committees who feature such "preferences" in their job listings.

After one rejection letter which informed me that I had been one of the better prospects among 920 applicants, I went to apply for a New York State high school teacher's license. I was told that my six years of college-level teaching would not count toward the license because I had taught part-time. I would have to do a year of student teaching to get the license. Back to the "bullpen."

Several adjunct positions later—the fall of 1992—I was on the job market again, but this time I had an enticing prospect: an MLA interview with a four-year college located thirty minutes from my home in New York City. I had passed the first major hurdle; there had been over four hundred applicants, including a few from Europe. I was further reassured by the fact that they wanted someone who could teach American Literature and ESL and education theory. I had ample experience in all three areas, and had written articles in each field. To prepare for the interview, I made three campus visits, during which I spoke to anyone who would spare me five minutes. (I mean anyone. It was the electrician who told me about the computer network for the new Writing Center.) I reviewed the English Department course listing and wrote a mock syllabus and a book list for numerous courses; I also learned about the demographics of the ESL population for the school and spoke at length with the chair of the Education Department, who was trying to jump-start a teacher training course for the humanities. (As my wife said, I didn't practice for my interview, I *trained*.) The MLA interview room at the New York Sheraton was quite intimidating, but the interview went well. Early in January, I received the call—I was the one and only final candidate! I was told that the Office of the College President would rubber-stamp the committee's selection, provide the contract of employment, and I would have a full-time, tenure-track line. What can I say—I partied for a week!

One month later, I was still waiting for the contract. Three months later things got weird.

During the previous three months I had called the department every few weeks or so to check on the progress of my situation, although to be honest there wasn't a damn thing I could do about it. The chair of the department would say that I was still the candidate of choice, but he didn't—or probably couldn't—say much else. (I still believe that he did the best he could to be honest with me, but I also realize that he had to be circumspect about certain matters.) One day he left me a message to call him, and I was ecstatic until I heard the tone of his voice as he answered. He was very direct. The money was still available for the job line; there were no problems with my qualifications or application; however, a group on campus had objected to my hiring. The objections had been sent to the affirmative action officer at the school, and after a review of the search it was determined that the search would be reopened. The original job listing had been sent to the MLA Job Information List, *The Chronicle of Higher Education*, and *The New York Times*. However, it was argued that the listing had not led to a sufficiently diverse applicant pool, nor had it targeted the sort of candidates that this group supported. The stated objective of the new search would be to find a more diverse pool of applicants, and the new listing would be sent to a carefully selected range of professional newsletters and periodicals. My own position was not quite clear. It seemed that I had not *lost* the line yet, and if no better applicant were found, I would get the job at last. I was told that the process would take at least three more months. I cannot say that I was reassured when I was given free rein "to pursue opportunities at other schools," but I quickly did.

I began applying to community colleges, which were still hiring in April and May, and I was pleasantly surprised to get three interviews. Two months later, I was hired for my current position at Kingsborough Community College. In many ways the loss of the other job was a blessed fall, since I have thoroughly enjoyed working in the English Department at K.C.C. and I'll most likely go up for tenure in 1998. I have spoken only once with the other school since their search "reopened." The last I heard, the controversy over the position had led the college president to terminate the line—no one was hired for that position, although the line may have been transferred to another program within the school. I should also add that two of my male colleagues from graduate school also achieved "the impossible" by landing tenure-track jobs in the New York area. Yet a person who climbs into a lifeboat also holds the memory of being in the water.

Affirmative action generates strong responses during the best of times, and during periods of layoffs and job insecurity, these responses often veer into racist and sexist accusations, oversimplifications, and distortions of the actual workings of this policy. (I will admit that I've settled for a few oversimplifications myself in trying to reconstruct my own job search.) I have not written this article because I have any expectation or even a desire that it will change or confirm someone's political stance toward affirmative action. I would not argue that my situation has been typical, and for that reason I am not sure what clear lessons may be drawn from it. I would, however, argue that affirmative action policies represent a crucial ethical issue for the American higher education system. I lean on the word "ethical" because it has become a key term in debates about hiring practices at colleges. When the "Statement of Professional Ethics" appeared in *Profession '92*, it somehow managed to avoid discussing hiring practices. However, by the time *Profession '94* was published, the editors felt it necessary to feature eight articles on the issue of hiring, and one recurring theme was that the job market crisis is not just a serious economic problem but a complex moral issue. I include some key quotes from this series of articles:

> We are not lost; we were left on a hillside and devoured by wolves. (Lemiesz 68)

> Is it morally responsible to continue to train people for the Ph.D. when their future likely holds only marginal academic employment? (Curren 59)

> What are our ethical commitments to the graduate students we train? (Holub 82)

> Departments need to consider the ethical and practical dimensions of their hiring practices for applicants facing seriously diminished job opportunities. (Caminero-Santangelo 63)

> Yet if these fears were in everyone's mind the climate in the department was not one in which such heresies could be openly debated. (Lemiesz 67)

Article after article suggested that ethical problems arose not from some evil set of decisions, but from a continual exchange of vague, incomplete, or deceptive information which left graduate students frustrated and also exploited. In the words of Erik D. Curren, the president of the MLA Graduate Student Caucus, "*We need more candid information*" (60; emphasis added).

I wish to make it clear that this article does not propose to place affirmative action policies on either side of some ethical line. The crucial issue is their inclusion, without clear explanation and without consistent intent, in job information lists. It may be that such policies do not need to be changed, yet at the very least they must be clearly articulated. Unlike Rush Limbaugh, I believe that words such as "dynamic" do matter. It is both naive and self-serving to think that one can "encourage" some groups in a tight job market without discouraging others. Those who defend the inclusion of such statements or phrases as "Women and minorities are especially encouraged to apply" surely have their own valid reasons, and I recognize that in some cases these phrases are legally mandated. However, in this case, following the letter of the law may compromise the spirit of a fair and impartial job search; if nothing else, it dampens the hopes of certain applicants, some of whom may not even apply for such positions. If such phrases do in fact ensure a more reliable and impartial search, then it should be possible to explain their meaning, their intent, and their effects in a coherent manner. In simple terms, one should be able to offer a clear, unapologetic, and *written* explanation to *all* graduate students—certainly not just the white males—who come to professors for advice about the job market in general and the job listings in particular. If such phrases cannot be clearly explained, or if the answers become no more than tailored responses for each particular category of applicant (the Italian-American woman, the West Indian man, etc.), then their eventual removal from job listings might need to be considered.

In simple terms, what advice should I give the following potential candidate? Assume for the moment that a graduate student earns a Ph.D. from a reputable university, publishes a dissertation chapter in a substantial journal, teaches a solid range of courses during this period, and plans to apply to a school at which "Women and minorities are especially encouraged to apply." I would be the first to agree that scholars argue at length about the reputation of schools, the quality of journals, and the subjective nature of teaching evaluations—yet I am not asking that these criteria be removed from the listings, although all of these criteria have appeared in vague or perhaps even misleading ways. An inconsistency in my logic? Consider that the last criteria is the only one that could possibly be used to reject *qualified* candidates for something that is permanently beyond their control. In simple terms, an average candidate who wishes to improve the odds can attend a Dartmouth Theory Seminar, submit something to *PMLA*, or design a cyberspace classroom linking students in New York and the West Indies to discuss *The Tempest*— and then what? What else should this candidate, regardless of identity, be told about hiring practices? If we do not answer this question openly, Rush Limbaugh, Newt Gingrich, and Roger Kimball would be glad to try.

I can think of many reasons why such an answer might not be given; I can also think of reasons why such questions have not been asked. However, there is a good deal of honest confusion as well as vicious rumor about affirmative action policies, and in the current political climate of open hostility to such policies, colleges cannot afford to be less than candid. It can be argued that colleges in general and hiring committees in particular need a certain degree of independence and even secrecy to work effectively, and this is a valid request. Yet the articles in *Profession '94* make it clear that hiring committees have lost the trust of many of the people they might hire. I consider this sense of distrust to be far more problematic than the accusations of the Rush Limbaughs of America. Any profession that manages to alienate many of its junior members needs to take a serious look at itself.

In simple terms, I hope to receive some candid responses to my questions, for I still believe that the academy is *the* place where "such heresies could be openly debated."

Works Cited

Caminero-Santangelo, Marta. "The Ethics of Hiring." *Profession '94*, pp. 62–63.

Curren, Erik D. "No Openings at This Time: Job Market Collapse and Graduate Education." *Profession '94*, pp. 57–61.

Holub, Robert C. "Professional Responsibility: On Graduate Education and Hiring Practices." *Profession '94*, pp. 79–86.

Hutner, Gordon. "What we Talk About When We Talk About Hiring." *Profession '94*, pp. 75–78.

Lemiesz, Linda M. "And the Lost Shall Be Found." *Profession '94*, pp. 67–69.

Where's the Closet at the Hilton?
In or Out While You're On

Julie Vandivere

In many ways, my discussion could, unfortunately, be very short. I could simply say, "Being 'out' on the job market will hurt you more than it will help you." Still, although that might be the bottom line, the process of marketing our queer selves is both necessary for our own professional survival and a positive political act. And the marketing process reveals more than a few of the quirks within contemporary academia. I want, consequently, to highlight some insights I came to as a lesbian on the job market, and to suggest strategies for doing something short of simply locking oneself into the closet at the MLA convention.

First, I think we need to be aware, however we try to finesse it, that despite the occasional ad that says a school would like someone with an interest in queer theory, most universities are still driven by a homophobia that would prevent departments from hiring an openly self-identified queer. Although some institutions—primarily Ivy League and very good state schools—feel that their faculty

"Where's the Closet at the Hilton" will appear in a forthcoming issue of *Concerns*, the Journal of the Women's Caucus for the Modern Languages.

would benefit from the diversity created by lesbian, gay, bisexual, and transgendered individuals, the vast majority of schools give little conscious thought to queerness when narrowing a job pool. And, unfortunately, their unconscious thought is shaped by the messages from society that inform all our psyches—those messages that cause most queers a crisis of identity when coming to terms with sexual diversity, those that drive a frightening proportion of queer teens to attempt suicide (all too often, successfully).

I don't mean to suggest that a small group of men and women in cardboardlike sport coats will bludgeon you with file folders in an MLA interview room just after their question about your dissertation and just before the one about how you handle a classroom. But the history of hiring shows that, despite their best social intentions, people like to hang out with (i.e., hire) those people who feel comfortable—who seem familiar and nonthreatening; and, despite our 10 percent status, the majority of members in university departments are not queer. A queer anywhere in a heterosexist society just does not create, for most people, that warm, familiar feeling. Now, these days few members of a hiring committee would say in public, "Let's not hire her because she is not clearly heterosexual"—though they still do so out of harm's (and in some cases, affirmative action's) way. But, both I and others have sat in hiring meetings where faculty raise thinly veiled objections to self-identified lesbians: "She wasn't very nice to the men," "She seemed hard," or, my personal favorite, "She sure didn't look comfortable in heels."

Now, my second point is almost contradictory to my first. For, although scared to death to hire someone who might not be heterosexual, many hiring committees erase homosexuality more quickly than you can say (or they would understand) *Tender Buttons.* Often, in fact, they'll refuse to read a candidate as queer despite substantial, sometimes even overwhelming, evidence. Since hiring committees usually don't *want* to read you as queer, they are capable of going to great lengths to "normalize" your deviant sexuality, whether or not you feel you can easily, or would even want to, "pass." I have tried both self-identifying as a lesbian and not doing so during MLA interviews. Whether or not I have stated directly, "I'm a lesbian," to MLA committees, I've always been pretty clearly out: i.e., my teaching interests include a number of queer topics, my research involves queerness and modernism, and in most interviews I discuss my commitment to making campuses more comfortable for people of different self-named sexual identities. Although it may be coincidental, I've had a number of on-campus invitations from schools where I *skirted* lesbian issues in the MLA interview. Never once have I received a single invitation from an MLA interview where I out and out (so to speak) self-identified as a lesbian.

I've concluded that hiring committees, like society, prefer (and it's no surprise, though they'd probably not be pleased by the connection) the military policy of "don't ask, don't tell." Regretfully, I believe it's still the case, even long after the advent of queer studies, that unless you're applying specifically for a queer theory position, using words like "gay," "lesbian," "queer," or "homosexual" about yourself will work against you on the market.

If you get to the campus visit stage, the masking/unmasking question becomes more pressured. For on-campus visits you will find yourself talking about the job and living conditions in its area in more specific, and more numerous, conversations. In that situation, I have generally been even more out—for my current position, for example, I discussed my lesbianism directly with the chair and the dean, though not with the committee or other faculty.

Nonetheless, I think you will still be read as straight whenever possible. Let me give you a couple of illustrations. One university I know of invited a well-known local woman to an on-campus interview. Unusually masculinized, she wore men's clothes and sported very, very short hair. It was common knowledge that she had lived with a woman (a gym teacher no less) for fifteen years. Although I knew this woman was a lesbian, I heard a straight faculty member (in oddly Cleaver-esque tones) talk of how difficult it would be for the candidate to find likely male romantic mates in a noncosmopolitan setting.

Second, on the campus visit at the school where I'm presently employed, not only did I talk about my work on lesbian writers, but I mentioned my partner and followed with a reference to "her." Yet the faculty didn't get it (and the dean and chair didn't out me). "We thought you misspoke when you called your partner a 'she,' " one of my colleagues told me later. Another said he thought it was strange that I'd referred to a lover as a partner, but it never crossed his mind that the partner was female or that my research on lesbian writers might be related in any way to my own life. Now securely hired (but not securely tenured), I'm the only out, but of course not the only practicing, homosexual faculty member on campus. My colleagues, when I have asked, have told me privately that, especially since the applicant pool was so competitive (as are all pools these days), if the department had "gotten the clues," hiring me would have met with direct and indirect opposition from some parts of the department.

I can see that. Although most of my colleagues are amazingly supportive, one warns female students not to take classes from me, lest they become (and we might only wish) "radical dyke feminists." Another stormed out of a department meeting to object to the department's support of one of my syllabi that included "perversions." While in the minority, these voices still exist in many, many departments and can become quite loud in the crucial stages of hiring. If the department had been more astute about the language of outness and recognized my sexual preference, I believe there would have been enough debate that, in a field of qualified candidates, I would have been moved down a notch or two at some stage and not received the job.

Regardless, I want to finish with a third point on a much more positive note. The floating—at once masked and unmasked—nature of queerness in our society can help professionally. The queer studies field is a promising one these days. A couple of years ago on a queer theory e-mail list, newly minted Ph.D.'s discussed the job market jubilantly: they knew some of the most exciting scholarship in the field was presently in queer theory; out lesbians, gays, and bisexuals were now peppered through the academy like seasoning on a seriously underspiced piece of meat; and a number of schools indicated in their ads that they were looking for people who had, among other things, an interest in queer theory (the way one would have an interest in the ballad or Goethe's theory of color). One graduate student posted that, in the past, his advisor had once told him that doing a dissertation on a queer topic would prevent him from ever getting a job. Now, it seemed to this graduate student, his queer topic was the very thing that *could* get him a job. Indeed. A contagious intellectual excitement permeates contemporary queer studies, making for exciting, stimulating work.

In addition, the work, and the identity, links queer theorists together. Somewhat of a network forms. Let's face it, being ostracized by family, fired by employers, outlawed by governments, beaten by gangs, and condemned by the religious right has its up side: if the gas station attendant wears rainbow rings and you do too, she'll be a bit nicer to you. She might even wash your windshield. In a world where they're reviled, queers tend to be especially courteous to other queers, and eager for their presence in the academy generally and in their own schools particularly.

An applicant's allusion to work on a queer theorist or to the importance of being aware of sexual orientation issues in the classroom beneficially flags her as queer to many queer readers. A subtle reference is not enough indisputably to identify someone as queer, but I have seen it work more than once to prompt a queer faculty member to make a couple of phone calls in this small academic world of ours to find out if an interesting applicant happens to be "a sister."

When my partner applied for a position, she was not aggressively out, nor does she work directly on queer topics. But she also had no interest in being carefully closeted. We both knew, for instance, that members of the department at the school that ultimately hired her, near my own university, would have knowledge of her lesbianism because of our relationship. Not only, then, did we allow academic gossip to take its course unimpeded—and it did—but she also sprinkled references to queer theorists during her on-campus interview for those who could to pick up on. And they did. Several people let others who would be sympathetic know that we were partners. But no one let anyone who might have been less sympathetic in on her queerness.

Now, when all is said and done, and we are hired or not, a question remains: is this masking and unmasking, playing close to the in/out line . . . well, moral? Perhaps it isn't, finally. Does this closeting hurt me as a person? Contribute to the killing myth of virtually universal heterosexuality? I'm afraid the answer is yes, it does both. Hiding that I'm a dyke does not enhance my own integrity, self-esteem, or sense of self, nor does it help destroy others' illusions of our scarcity. But, alas, my morality (that nontransparent, power-inflected something that all "morality" is) can be bought for a tenure-track job in a world where heterosexuality still stacks the deck. Now that I have that tenure-track job, I don't closet myself when I'm on the market for "better" positions. My partner and I are both fully, clearly out (sometimes against the "better judgment" of our peers) to administrators, students, and colleagues. Whatever challenge our queerness poses to our tenurability doesn't seem sufficient to silence us. But the bottom line of employment did.

My justification has been that I can't make a difference until given the chance to do so. Perhaps you can be better and stronger than I, and declare yourself even more loudly and earlier. I'm not convinced, though, that it would be either worth the possible price, or wise strategy amid the still potent and pervasive onslaught against us.

My Life Part-Time:
Reflections on Damaged Goods

Brian Caterino

"And they wandered in from the city of St. John's without a dime."[1]

My grandparents came to this country to find an opportunity for a better life. They were among the laborers who built your buildings, ran small shops, or worked in sweatshops making clothes. They did not always find the opportunity they sought. In Rochester, New York, where both branches of my family settled, Italians could not get jobs at Eastman Kodak, the paternalistic overlord of Smugtown. I know of children sent out of town to relatives on the farm when there was no money to feed them during the Depression. Houses were almost lost during the Depression, saved only thanks to today's hated government programs. Underneath the facile mythology of a smooth assimilation, another story lies untold. Like others, I am of the first generation of my family to have made it to college (in my case further), yet we often found a reality more hostile and less just than we hoped for.

For those from working-class backgrounds, education was the golden road to advancement. While the reality of upward mobility was always a far cry from the myth of equal opportunity, education still represented the best chance to improve our lot. Now many of us find that even the gains our parents achieved—a house, the opportunity to have a decent, not extravagant, life—are increasingly difficult to achieve no matter what our education. Staying afloat is a struggle, having health insurance a luxury. Will I have a pension or will I end up literally on the street in my old age? Marginal once, we are marginal once again.

Today I am consigned to another group of marginals: adjunct faculty. Trained to be educators, researchers, critics, and writers, we are dispersed from centers of learning throughout the country, a permanent class of underlings who populate the colleges and universities of our nation. It has become hard to imagine the academic world today without this vast reserve army of cheap labor. I worked for three years (one year full-time) as a contract instructor in the State University of New York (SUNY) system, one of the largest in the nation. The university system has a high proportion of part-time workers, upward of 40 percent, perhaps higher. Yet, in spite of their numbers, part-time workers have little clout and even less security. They are paid wages far below the level that their skills and training warrant. They have little if any security. They have only a second-class status, both with their colleagues and with their union.

The notion of equity, applied with such rigor to other areas, is in eclipse for adjuncts. While I cannot quote you rigorous statistics, I would estimate that at best part-timers get less than a third of the pay of the lowest-paid full-time faculty member, and many part-timers of course have as much experience as those who get paid much more. They teach the same courses, sometimes have even more demanding teaching assignments, including high-enrollment lower-division courses. The only difference between adjunct and tenure-stream faculty involves committee work.

Yet part-time work can represent a real cash cow for many colleges and universities. A part-time teacher who teaches introductory courses can generate at least $30,000 worth of revenue for the university while costing much less. At elite schools with high tuition, this would mean even more revenue, as much as twenty times more. In reality academia is a two-tier labor market with one set of standards for tenured faculty and one for part-timers. Like many on the downsizing merry-go-round, part-timers are told the fault is theirs. We made bad career choices, or simply lost in the lottery of life. The plethora of adjuncts is not due to cyclical forces—to excessive demand and limited supply. The use of adjuncts is integral to the restructuring and downsizing of higher education.

What kind of pay can one expect as an adjunct? I received $1,800 per course. At other schools, the pay can be lower. One year, counting summer courses, I taught five courses. I made $9,000. Well below the poverty level. Minimum wage for maximum work.[2] Yet, the system is flexible in a rather cynical way. Some are able to get more money from the system without others knowing about it.

Part One: I get the news—bad shoes

I can't even count how many times I've been told I lack the "right stuff." It's never said because I lack ability; it always boils down to the same things: I lack the proper respect for authority or the proper work attitudes. I raise a lot of hackles and opposition. It may be the sign of a good mind, but in a narrow-minded world, the worst thing you can do is make waves. When I came out of graduate school, my career was already dead in the water. Despite the fact that I had good recommendations, a publishable thesis, and was acknowledged to know my stuff, I did not get a job interview for years. Academic hiring is shrouded in mystery and one never gets the real dope, but the reasons were many: a weak advisor, a bad rap due to student activism and union activities (I once took the university to arbitration, always a good way to get blacklisted), the wrong intellectual leanings, definitely not a schmoozer, and being a left-wing male of the wrong class. You should not fool yourself on this point: in the academic world class still tells. The resurgence of such status markers has increased as times get tougher.[3] But you quickly get the news that whatever your qualifications, you're not even in the ball game. This is especially galling when you see people not especially bright or well qualified get jobs. A good friend of mine, who had just returned from the MLA, once shared with me her cynicism about hiring practices: the same teachers we thought were mediocre were the ones doing the hiring. Best, she reminded me, not to expect much better.

It should not be a surprise that when I received a call from SUNY-Brockport, I approached it with a foreboding reserved for the Inquisition. My expectations were not disappointed. The department needed someone to teach some courses because a minority candidate that they had hired took a job somewhere else. I was not offered a full-time position, however, even though it was in my field. Instead it was made clear that I was the second-class citizen here. Straight out they told me I would never (emphasis on the never) be hired permanently because I did not fall into any acceptable hiring category. The outgoing chair, a male, had an explanation for my dilemma. As a leftist and a male, I was stuck with a double whammy. Politically sensitive jobs, i.e. leftist ones, were reserved for women or minorities.

Don't mistake my position here. I believe in affirmative action. I'm no friend of the boys' network (not always composed of just old boys), and they don't accept people like me in their club. I have seen enough discrimination in my time to make my stomach turn, and it's certainly the case that the disciplines I work in (philosophy and political science) have done a poor job in recruiting minorities and women. But I've also seen plenty of other forms of exclusion and discrimination not covered by legally recognized categories. We need a wider net to capture these subtler forms as well. Much of the problem stems from an economic system that pits one group against another. Instead of building an inclusive educational system, the current downsizing means your gain is my loss. Moreover, affirmative action can be used hypocritically and strategically (does the name Clarence Thomas ring a bell?). On the other hand, affirmative action considerations are often abandoned when expedient. In fact, the first person hired permanently at Brockport after I left was a white man, and a very conservative one at that. What that says about what was told to me, or the depth of the department's commitment to affirmative action, readers can judge for themselves.

If the circumstances of my hiring were discouraging, the interview was more disturbing. I was interviewed by the outgoing chair and the incoming chair. While the outgoing chair was pleasant if distracted (the type of person who cannot organize the next five minutes of his own life, not to mention the whole department), the incoming chair was vaguely hostile. Subtle innuendos followed, provided mostly by the incoming chair. "You seem to have excellent recommendations and credentials, why don't you have a job?" she asked. It's not always easy to convey the tone of such questions in an essay, but there's a palpable difference you can hear between shocked surprise at how something could be and the skeptical surprise that indicates a more negative judgment ("that really couldn't be"). I was presented with the latter. I decided to preempt the next question. No, there is nothing wrong with me, I averred. It was then I knew for sure I was damaged goods.

Perhaps in retrospect I should have refused the job right then and there. I certainly would not take a job under those circumstances today. When presented with such distrust, you are put at a disadvantage that you can rarely overcome. However, I needed a job. I figured that if I didn't take the job, it would continue to look like I was unemployable. But I accepted conditions that were self-defeating.

When you are damaged goods, it is extremely difficult to prove otherwise. This is a lesson I learned after attending graduate programs in two different disciplines: philosophy and political science. Most graduate programs size up and stream their students within a few weeks. It doesn't matter that those judgments are often wildly inaccurate, based on conformity to the particular group norms of the department, or function as self-fulfilling prophesies (those who are viewed as second tier are then treated as second tier), they operate just the same. It was pretty clear from my interview that in spite of the lip service paid to my abilities, I would be just the sanitary engineer of the department. I would get to pick up what was needed to fill out the department's core requirements, but never what I was most competent or most interested in. I managed to fashion courses in environmental politics and the politics of human rights. However in my three years plus summer courses, I only taught one course in my field, political theory.

Of course I wasn't the only one in that position. There was another political theorist, teaching out of her field, who was teaching part-time. She was also slotted into excess courses. She commuted over fifty miles to teach these courses, often in extremely poor winter weather. I could see her spirit visibly sag by the second year, and the pressure of the long commute, long hours, and unresponsive students got to her. From what I could tell, she was treated as excess baggage as well. The next year she was simply gone, on the road west to seek a better opportunity.

The chair of the department had a curious and to my mind hypocritical response to her treatment of part-timers. While well off and secure herself, her knee-jerk response to any query about part-time salaries was that we were "fortunate" to have this opportunity. Since she exclusively controlled hiring, it was her view that counted. Yet this was too typical of the complacent attitudes of faculty toward part-timers. The vast majority in my department could not be bothered to step out of the veneer of their cold collegiality toward other faculty to think about the implications of policies toward adjuncts.

Part 2: The author tours smugtown and becomes a full-timer—temporarily

I had been teaching at SUNY-Brockport more or less straight through for almost two years. I had a brief break between the spring term and the summer courses and again after the summer course, but really no time to recharge my batteries. In the interlude, I would try to write some essays and do research both for my own writing and for my course preparation. In addition to the constant drain of the job search, I had a number of personal obligations as well. As far as I can see, I was more active in the discipline than most of my full-time colleagues, but, ironically, as a part-timer I did not qualify for any travel grants, which were reserved exclusively for full-timers. When I pointed out the incongruity of this policy to the administrative grant officer and to the chair, they simply said that nothing could be done. Of course such a policy only serves to further ghettoize part-timers. Ultimately I gave up and attended several conferences at my own expense. In my years at SUNY-Brockport I gave three papers. I do not think anyone gave more. I received no recognition in any sense for these efforts.

It was about two weeks before the opening of school when I got a call from a political theory professor at the University of Rochester. He was going to have surgery and would not be able to teach during the fall term. Could I cover for him? He also told me that his department's political theory job search had been reopened and that it would be a good opportunity to meet some of the members of the department. I had long ago accepted a couple of courses at SUNY-Brockport, so I thought I would have to make some arrangements. However, the department at Rochester was going to give me two courses and pay me something like $12,000, considerably more than the paltry $1,800 per course I had been getting.

Things started to get complicated. Shortly after that I got a call from SUNY-Brockport. They had a higher than expected enrollment and had come up with money for a full-time job. They offered me a decent salary, a little over $30,000. I would not have felt guilty rejecting this offer, since the department had made no commitment to me and had made it clear that this was at best a temporary appointment, somewhat grudgingly given. In the chair's words, she was "pretty sure" that the job would work out. I am "pretty sure" that I was not the first person they contacted for it. It was offered at the absolutely last minute and I know that enrollment was known before that. The attitude of full-time faculty toward teachers in temporary jobs is rather appalling. They believe that you should be happy to jump at any opportunity that arises and that you will simply drop anything to do it. If you don't, you lack the proper attitude. However, it is often stressful to have courses or new assignments dropped into your lap at the last minute. Even if you are underemployed, you have little time to organize and plan out your courses.

It also often means major rearrangement of your life and your priorities. Most permanent faculty would not stand for it. As a marginal academic you must always be on call, ready and willing to fulfill the needs of the system, or you risk losing your livelihood.

After I thought about it for a day or so, I took the full-time job and agreed to teach only one course at Rochester. However, I am sure that I did the wrong thing here for a number of reasons. I would have been a lot happier teaching a couple of courses I enjoyed, even if it was temporary and for less money. After all, the one-year job was strictly temporary too. It was not the opportunity of a lifetime.

My first term was a blur of commuting, writing lectures, and grading. I began to recognize the symptoms of burnout. After teaching summer school for two years, I had reserved most of August for a paper I had to write for the American Political Science Association meeting at the end of that month. I didn't really have the time I needed, and just barely finished the paper before the conference, then jumped directly into a round of commuting, teaching, and grading. It might not seem like much, but when you are on the road between schools half the time, teaching days and two nights a week at three different locations, then trying to prepare new material and grading essays (I still tried to assign a lot of essays), there isn't any time for a life. By Thanksgiving I was a write-off. I got a passing case of the flu, and as happens when you are overworked or exhausted, I never got the time to fully recover until the term was over. So I was ill on and off for the rest of the term. I only mention this because I was directly informed by one of Rochester's faculty that this was cited as a negative consideration on my job application for their re-opened political science search. I do not think the chair himself would have fared any better if he had followed my schedule—at the University of Rochester they only teach two courses a term and do not have huge numbers of students. I had about 150 students overall to whom I assigned at least two essays and final exams.

Part 3: Summarily seeking justice— or is it dismissal?

After a couple of years on the merry-go-round, you start to get a little dizzy. I was not very happy with my situation after my year as a full-time teacher. After all the effort, I was probably worse off than before. I was back to $1,800 per course at SUNY-Brockport. After two-plus years of teaching with a good record (my teaching evaluations were good to very good), it really did not seem to matter. I was still damaged goods. I certainly didn't feel any more secure, and subsequent events proved that any complaint on my part would lead to my dismissal.

A brief look into the treatment of part-timers in the department had led to several concerns. One was unequal salaries. It turned out that salaries were determined capriciously. One woman who had taught a course in political statistics for several years had taken a term off to have a child. I assume she had made $1,800 a course just like I did, When she returned, she found out by accident that her replacement had been paid $2,400. She only received this salary herself because she demanded it. I do not know why her replacement was paid more, nor do I know why she herself was not offered this wage. I do not, however, see that it had any merit since she had been teaching this course for a while and still taught it until recently. I do know that she was quite upset. I guess she did not appreciate the great opportunity that she had been given. I suppose it was her situation that blinded her. A young woman with a child, whose husband was working his way through school, she could not see her great fortune in taking a lesser salary.

I did not approach the problems of part-timers in a particularly offensive way. I did not even initiate the review procedure in our department, although had it not been brought up, I would have raised the matter at faculty meetings myself. But when I did raise issues in a civil and reasonable matter, I was labeled a troublemaker.[4] What was the result of my effort to raise some issues and get at least some fairer treatment? Several months later, I was coming in to teach my evening course. It wasn't a particularly good time in my life. My father had just suffered a heart attack about two weeks prior. The chair's attitude in response to this had already angered me. When I canceled one class (and only one class) because my father was in intensive care, I got the impression that my doing so was not appropriate. We must be good soldiers, and I am no such soldier. In any case, as I went into the mail room, I happened to glance at the spring schedule. I had been "disappeared." I had been told that I would be teaching two courses in the fall term; I was listed on the earlier version of the schedule to teach my usual two. No indication of difficulties had been passed on to me. I had every reason to expect to teach. However, I had simply been eliminated.

My first response was to call the union. I'm a strong union person, but I have to say that I found the union's support abysmal. They have little concern for part-timers' problems. Unions are often in a difficult position, but a union member has at least the right to expect some solidarity or support when a problem arises. I think it's fair to say that losing one's job is a serious problem. However, in my dealings with the union and especially the local union branch, I got the distinct impression that they would rather I go away and not bother them.

I was advised to contact the grievance officer. This individual came highly recommended as on the ball and willing to help. Nothing could have been further from the truth. After some effort to reach her over the course of at least a week, I had a chance to talk with her. This is the substance of our conversation: You have no case; the university only has to give you forty-five days' notice. Your previous commitment means nothing. You have no rights. End of conversation. She stayed within a confined, legalistic mentality. Other than the time I took to explain my situation—and I was almost cut off doing it—that was about the whole of our conversation. I faced an irritated silence that indicated that I was nothing more than a bother. I had to wonder: if these were the good guys, who were the bad ones?

I made another attempt, even as I was dismissed, to change hiring policies for adjunct faculty. I asked the one sympathetic faculty member I knew to propose that responsibility for hiring adjuncts be transferred from the chair to a department hiring committee. While this was no guarantee of justice, procedural justice is better than personal whimsy. At the very least, the faculty have to make up some reasons for their actions—reasons that can be put under scrutiny. Such a resolution was duly passed—and never put into practice. I was told the chair claimed it was a direct challenge to her authority.

Concluding Postscript

Are you skeptical? Am I a cynical bastard who hates the world? Or a furious fool, telling a frenzied tale out of school, that's ultimately meaningless?

Recently, one of the political theorists in the SUNY-Brockport political science department became terminally ill and had to retire. Typical of university cutbacks, there was no full-time line to replace him, only an adjunct appointment at a fraction of the cost of a full professor. Here's a job for which I was eminently qualified: I had experience, good evaluations, and the chair is on record as saying the department would hire me full-time if it could. No cutbacks here; hands untied. *Quel horreur!* I am not hired for the job. (In fact the dirty deed is done before I hear the sad news.) There is no hiring committee. The appointee is, according to faculty sources, "known" to the chair.

By now I am beginning to get mad. I write to the department, requesting information on the criteria used in filling this position. I do touch a nerve, provoking a prompt response, not from the department chair, but from the assistant to the university's president. This master of bureaucracy is blunt. We don't tell people about hiring; it's none of your business. After years of dealing with Brockport, I understand why Kafka modeled *The Castle* after the bureaucracy. It's a nightmare world: you're qualified, therefore you can't be hired; you're dismissed by necessity, but you can never be hired back; you can only have an interview when it's not a real one; our hands are tied except for friends . . . and asking for information about decisions affecting your fate labels you an intruder.

It's a royal scam.

Notes

1. For S.L., power corrupts. . . . Lyric from "Royal Scam" by Steely Dan (Donald Fagan and Walter Becker, ASCAP, 1976).

2. Just to provide a point of comparison: as graduate assistant at the university where I did my graduate work, I could make more than I could teaching four to five courses. A scholarship student receives even more. However, even there graduate students struggle to make ends meet. It's not possible even to feign making ends meet on under $10,000 per year. For the part-timer the situation is worse. One is expected to sacrifice while others prosper, to live without making enough money to get a decent place to live, to raise a family, or do much of anything.

3. As we finished graduate school, I and a number of my friends from working-class backgrounds independently made the same observation: that we were being devalued and that we were being shunted into marginal status in the new economic order. A recent opinion piece in *The Chronicle of Higher Education* also documented the resurgence of the Ivy League credential in getting jobs. See Phillip J. Cook and Robert H. Frank, "The Economic Payoff of Attending an Ivy League School," *The Chronicle of Higher Education*, January 5, 1996, p. B3.

4. Besides salaries, another issue came up at a faculty meeting that was likely central to my demise. I criticized the prevailing treatment of race at Brockport. I noted that many of my students employed tacit racial stereotypes and asked how we should address this. My discussion was suppressed with the claim that this problem had already been addressed: we should tell

students that these stereotypes were not acceptable. How helpful. The next couple of years featured some troubling racial incidents at Brockport. To me, the school's commitment to social justice is skin deep.

Of Job Trails and Holy Grails for Feminists Out There: A Postmodernist Cautionary Tale

Sivagami Subbaraman

Sketch 1: It is the last day of the Midwest Modern Language Association conference—a strange academic construct where many of us get together and talk to one another, and perhaps to ourselves, about what we have been doing the other 360 odd days of the year. I imagine that moment when I will return to my home in Maryland. My neighbor, a postal worker, will say: "So, Shiva, where have you been this past few days?" "Oh, just went to a conference in St. Louis," I answer. "A conference, eh? What did you do?" "Oh, a bunch of us just got together to talk about some stuff; I did a paper . . ." "You mean you went all the way out there to talk?" "Yeah, something like that." "You know, Shiva, you ought to get real, and get a real job like us real folks . . ." "Well, actually, I did go there to talk about how to get a real job." My neigbor was aghast at what she sees as persistent naïveté at best, and willful idiocy at worst: "Girl, when are you going to learn that talking doesn't get it?"

And that moment of *not getting it* looks back to another one:

Sketch 2: I had been "real" once, teaching American literature, African-American literature, and feminist theory classes in an English department at a large state school for over a year; in addition I served on several curriculum transformation committees, seeking to transform intransigent courses to include every conceivable "other." The following year, we hired another "Indian" woman to teach third world and postcolonial literatures, and suddenly things began to happen. Anyone who ran into me in the hallways would suddenly demand a detailed explication of Peter Brook's *Mahabarata*, which was airing on TV at that time, or say with suitable enthusiasm, "Oh, Shiva, I think it is good that you are teaching new courses in postcolonial stuff; I think it is the most exciting intellectual field right now, and you are the *right person* to do it." If I looked blank, they would hasten to assure me that they realized a new person had been hired to teach those courses; it was just that they felt I was also doing the right thing. In this world, where my identity is neatly ticked off into little geometric boxes, I had finally, to their relief, found my rightful place: who I was gelled with what I did as a scholar.

This leads to the third and final sketch. When I first began to write and to talk about my experiences in the academic marketplace, it was ironic that I had to do so in those very domains in which I had no place, namely at academic conferences. By now of course, there are a lot more like me—they call us part-timers, adjuncts, "migrant workers of academia," "living job applications" (Horwitz A6), and "temp profs" (Belatèche 64)—and all conferences now routinely genuflect to this growing "problem," in the profession. This meant that "they"—usually full professors and the tenured or to-be-tenured—had panels on the "problem," where they either wanted me to tell an "unvarnished" and "personal" tale, presumably to discomfit the powers that be, or they had panels where they wanted "varnished" tales of identity and authority to give a certain heft and weight to my academic discourse.

At a recent conference, one scholar squinted at my label and said, "Oh, you are at Maryland? Do you know X and Y?" I said, "Oh yes, I do know them; but I am not *really* there." There was a disconcerted pause of panic: "You are not there? But your badge says . . ." "Well," I responded, trying to be helpful, "I have an affiliation with them, but it is sort of a dummy affiliation; I don't really teach there and I am not an adjunct.'' ''A dummy affiliation?'' I could tell that all of this man's years in the profession had not prepared him for this tautology, and I said, just be to perverse, ''Well, think of me as a floating signifier in the profession, signifying whatever the profession desires.'' He beat a hasty retreat at this, convinced that I was an imposter, a potential Unabomber in the making. And, in a way, I was and I was not. If I had learned that who I am had to gel with what I do, I now had to learn that where I am also had to gel with what I do and who I am.

Somewhere, in those many unmarked ellipses lies the story of how I got from being a full-time real person at an ''institution'' (the word itself a telling example of the unmarked ironies of our profession) to being a part-timer at a local mall, a sometimes freelance editor, a sometimes independent scholar who is most times dependent on a better half, an immigrant non-success story among high achieving Asians—a circuitous story at best, full of slips and slides.

Fresh out of graduate school, even before I had defended, I was one of the lucky few that got a full-time tenure-track job, at a midsized, private liberal arts college in the Midwest, teaching writing and composition. Typical of a fresh graduate's angst, I was also disappointed: all my years in graduate school had been a training to expect my ''job'' and ''professional'' life to revolve around what I saw as my ''intellectual'' work, namely, American literature; and in that great pecking order composition was to literature what bologna is to meat. I took the job partly because I had the practicality to know that jobs of any kind were hard to come by, and partly because, as a foreigner, I needed a full-time job to process my visa papers.

A year later, the carrot dangled: I had an offer for a visiting position at a large state university where I would be teaching courses in American literature, African-American literature, and feminist theory. Bright-eyed, bushy-tailed, and full of the glory of the profession in me, I hit I-80 with the warning of one of my Midwestern colleagues still in my ears: ''Your charm won't help, Shiva; the big schools will make dead meat out of you." I thought he suffered from hemorrhoids; I was going to be where the "action" was.

So I arrived at this large university, unwary and unsuspecting. I was given all the appurtenances and paraphernalia of a "real" person: I had an office; I had a competitive salary; I had my mailbox; and I had the warm guarantee that my "visiting" status would be transformed to tenure-track at the very first opportunity. A very chic feminist chair told me that the department really had a great "need" for people like me to teach courses in "multicultural American" literature, and introductory courses in African-American literature, as their African-Americanist, a well-known scholar, had just left the department. I nodded, just happy that I would not have to teach Rhetoric 101´ and 105 ad infinitum, and predictably rushed in where angels would have feared to tread.

Months later, I gathered that my arrival at this department had not been innocuous; the African-Americanist had left what he/she saw as an "unfriendly" department and, more to the point, had protested my "hire" as unjustifiable, since I was not black and my primary area of scholarship was "American." I could not and did not wish to protest that my being an "Indian" (dot Indian, not feather Indian, one colleague egregiously pointed out) did raise questions both political and philosophical about my status as a "racial other" in African-American literary discourse. But surely, I told myself, questions of racial privilege, and of authority and authenticity in interpretive practices, were integral to the challenging of the consensual model of American Studies. Naively, I assumed, like many others before and since, that it was a question that could be resolved textually, although I often spoke in my own analyses of the very real political and material ramifications of texts.

As the months went by in the new job, I served on several curriculum transformation committees as we went about the job of trying to revamp many of the American literature courses to be more "diverse." I also proposed a senior seminar that specialized in African-American literature, one of the first in the department. I began to see slowly the growing fissures between the everyday running of departments and our own theoretical promulgations about pedagogy and multiculturalism. As time went by, everyone kept asking me to teach courses on third world women writers, postcolonialism, even African and Caribbean literature—we "needed" to be offering these courses, I was told. Whenever I protested and pointed out that my specialty was American, they would nod their heads wisely, and say, "but you can do it better than us." Presumably, my being "woman, native, other" (Trinh T'Minha's words[1]) in a "first world" class and department gave me some natural advantage in teaching courses about which I had not a clue.

That year, the department advertised for a tenure-track opening in feminist theory, specialization open, but preferably in American, and it was suggested that I apply for it. I would have the "insider's advantage" they told me; I was already here and everyone knew me, and I was teaching the courses the department needed. I knew the interview would be tricky: I had to walk that fine line between being an "insider" and "selling" myself to those who already knew me and had certain images of me. At the MLA interview, which went extremely well, I heard intimations of the first distant thunder: at one point, I was asked if I saw myself primarily as a feminist, an Americanist, or an African-Americanist. The question puzzled me and I said so, since I did not see them as separate or mutually exclusive areas of inquiry, and my graduate committee had repeatedly urged me to integrate all three. The question was to return to haunt me in the subsequent years I spent in that department, and this marked the first kiss of death.[2]

The second unstated push at the interview came from the constant pressure to define myself as a "third world feminist," or, later, increasingly as a "postcolonial" or "South Asian woman of color"—all of which descriptors, I tried pointing out, were Western academic constructs and not necessarily how I saw myself. I tried to resist what I saw as the continued slippage between who I was and what I did, but I was obviously not very successful. I was not hired for the position. The department chair told me with a mixture of condescension and pragmatism that I ought to get "realistic": "You ought to realize that it might be better for you to retool yourself as a postcolonial for the market." It was a stunning moment of epiphany: here was a theoretically sophisticated feminist, who in her own analyses argued against reductive and essentialist notions of identity, recommending that I "go native" for the market. It later emerged that part of the reason for not hiring me was precisely because I was "already here anyway." They also knew I could not quit either, since my visa status required me to stay in the job till the process of legalization was complete. It was now clear to whose advantage my "insider's status" accrued.

"Identity politics" had reared its ugly head. I was not considered to have the "authority" to teach American literature, African-American literature, or feminist theory (except a brand of third world feminism) and was being pushed to retool myself as a postcolonial. Of course, from an administrative point of view it is certainly most cost effective for departments to fufill their goals of both canon expansion and optic diversity[3] by having a person of color teach literature of color. The mechanics of being "repackaged" or of "re-packaging" myself as a race/postcolonial critic to meet the demands of institutional efficiency was but another way to ensure racial ghet-toization, while also forcing "others" to exploit their own "other-ness" as a saleable commodity for "Western eyes."

"Identity politics" gave focus to my pain and anger and rejec-tion. But in the years that I have spent away from the university, I have grown to realize that "identity politics" is the personal face to a problem that is far more complex and devious. And I have come to see that identity politics is a visceral explanation for what are far less visible, far more intractable institutional structures—structures by which certain areas of study are legitimated and others are not. The most urgent question that faces us is the discrepancy between our push for "multicultural American literature" and our continued hiring by the "color line." If we are in fact talking and teaching a multicultural no-one-left-out version of American litera-ture in our classrooms, it does seem to behoove us to hire faculty who can teach this version "holistically." But, in fact, we continue to advertise and to hire based on traditional divisions by century, and then separately but equally based on those immutable hyphens—African-, Asian-, Native-, etc. -American, reinforcing divisions in hiring practices that undercut our stated aims in curricula and class-room. It is crucial that we recognize that the meeting of "multicultural curricula" and "multicultural faculty" has reintroduced, in very urgent and painful ways, the old specter that William DuBois called the "problem of the twentieth century"—the problem of the color line.[4]

Nothing very much changed the next year. I continued to teach "real" courses in American literature, African-American literature, and feminist theory, but I was no longer sure about my "voice." Should I remake myself as a postcolonial scholar? I saw no legitimate way to do so: after having immersed myself and trained my mind for years to be an Americanist, how was I to be postcolonial except in my body? What then are the departmental politics that insist and require that, as a minority, I must teach multicultural, multiracial texts, preferably those of my cultural origin? What did it mean to me to both try to teach other minority texts (Native-American, African-American) and to insist on teaching non-minority or "mainstream" texts? The push to "go native" is simply another way of saying that we can only know and teach what we are. It is not entirely clear to me whether most "subalterns" have ended up speaking as ambassadors of a third world that they left behind them a long time ago because they possess the desire and the knowledge to do so, or because they are not granted the authority to speak about the majority/mainstream here.

The subsequent year the department had an opening in African-American literature, and I was asked to apply again. What followed was a bizarre and nightmarish replay of the preceding year's issues—this time focused and magnified through the lens of race, and with far more devastating results for me, personally and professionally. It marked the end of my career at any university.

When I initially resisted the idea of applying for a position that would clearly be even more sensitive and charged than a "feminist" position, I was told that this would be a "showcase" moment of sorts—what better way to combat the issues of identity and hiring than to apply for a position based on my "record" in teaching and scholarship. "There are plenty of whites being interviewed for these positions," I was told, in what was meant as a reassurance. It would be a moment of bright-eyed meritocracy at its best—free of politics, of biases, of history itself, free precisely of all of those factors that we spend enormous amounts of time and energy in our writings and in our classrooms telling others and our students that even our textual readings are not free of and cannot and should not be. And yet here we were: black and white and brown, asking ourselves and one another to free ourselves, and empty ourselves, of the historicity of race relations in this country. And here we were asking and expecting a hiring committee to walk that wavering line between diversity and democracy. It was a moment when complete idealism was matched by complete folly.

I applied. I was made to apply. I did not know anymore. Needless to say, the department itself became fairly divided along racial lines, with a few brave crossovers, about what I should do. Soon it was not even about what I should do, but about what they should be doing about this "problem." Each hire, it seems, becomes a kind of public ritual of exorcism for the department—as it confronts its ghosts, its skeletons, its absences, and its silences. This department was no different from any other across the nation in its checkered history with race. This is not to say that there are no objective criteria in the job search. It is to say that so much of who gets hired and why and where has to do with that unspecified gray area of a department's particular history and dynamic.

At the interview, the first invidious distinction was made between teaching and scholarship. Certainly, I was told, my teaching was not suspect of any contamination by my "otherness"; after all I had good class materials, and excellent evaluations even from my African-American students, who saw my presence as a positive, while challenging, anomaly. What was suspect was my scholarship. While I could concede that my "otherness" did not exempt me from the scrutiny and skepticism of critics reading my texts, I could not see how evaluation of my work could be guided simply by the cultural identity of the reader/writer. The interview itself, and all those hallway interviews, raised the specter of the "third space": U.S. race relations in general, and academic variants of it, continue to be dominated not by one, but two conceptual race hegemonies—white and black. In this world, it is not often clear where nonwhite, non-black citizens fit in. In academic politics this has often meant that "Indians" are not necessarily seen as eligible for "afffirmative action policies," but simply as fulfilling the need for "optic diversity" in departments.[5]

In the cross fire between white liberalism and black suspicion, I did not stand a chance. It was clearly imperative for the department to have more black faculty in its ranks; it was equally clear that I was being manipulated by the white liberals for purposes of their own regarding identity issues; and it was also equally patent that those few black faculty in "authority" and power owed it to themselves and their community to wield such power in their own favor. I could tell my students that it was necessary for their learning process that they be discomfited by my presence in their black-and-white world; but obviously I could not say the same to my colleagues who could not—despite their theorizings to the contrary—handle their own discomfiture at my presence. If I have learned something in this decade that I have spent in American academia, it is this: the American academic system freed me from my British colonial education only to recolonize me by American "multiculturalism," which relegates me to the outposts of a third world, but does not let me come ashore at Plymouth Rock. Or Jamestown.

I was in personal and professional shambles after this: I did not have a job; I had lost my voice and my sense of belonging in the profession; I questioned the value of my intellectual production; and after a couple of semesters of adjuncting, I finally turned my back on university teaching, though not, it seems, on academia in general. I now contribute to that increasing general pool of "migrant workers" who "now account for 38% of the nation's 800,000 faculty"[6]—a staggering number certainly, and by no means as invisible a minority as the profession or we ourselves would have us believe. While being billed as "migrant workers" may draw stark attention to the fact that capitalism works in academia too, and we may feel some intellectual solidarity with the lot of the capitalist corporate victims, it does little to address the issue of how we and our productions are viewed by the profession.

Being an adjunct takes its toll: it becomes a daily confrontation with exclusion and marginality, and is finally most inimical to the "scholar" in us. Since I quit teaching, I have mostly worked part-time at various jobs, and most continuously at a local coffee store in a retail mall. In an effort to preserve something of the scholar in me, I approached the Women's Studies Department at the University of Maryland, where I now live, which generously gave me an affiliate scholar status—this has given me a much needed "address," library privileges, and an e-mail account, and asked nothing else of me. My graduate school training has come fully apart: I started out with the premise that the job, the profession, and my intellectual work would all be located at one site; now they resemble more of a juggling act than anything else.

Creative writers, poets, and artists have always had to struggle with finding a way to support themselves while doing their "work." However, there has been no real model for the peripatetic scholar/literary critic except perhaps in the Middle Ages. It is the great achievement of the United States that in the years after World War II the country managed to give a home and address to many peripatetic scholars at institutional sites. Increasingly, such a home has become a privilege for many of its practitioners. For writers and poets the wandering ends, to some extent, when they are published and read. It is less clear where the wandering of adjunct scholars ends. Scholarship, by its very nature, is a dialogue within a community; most scholarship depends on this dialogue for its context, its meaning, and its refinement. Without belonging to a particular institution, and isolated from its hallways, our conference presentations threaten to become an isolated, somewhat lonely public gesture signaling our presence in the profession, rather than a sign of our continued scholarship. Increasingly, there is a nagging suspicion that while the profession has made some space for me, in a sense I am, and we are, irrelevant to its daily life.[7]

*   *   *

Job search narratives of the 1990s, like those old ones about the Holy Grail, tend to have a linear sequence: I was prepared; I got lost; I looked; and I found it. This "story" of mine, like all good stories, tends to be a reversal: I had it; I lost it; and I am still looking. When I first sat down to write about the job market search, I thought I would write a finely wrought tale about identity, authority, and authenticity; or a tale of personal ineptitude and naïveté. I had to confront my angers, those specific encounters that have made my life what it is today. I have paid a heavy personal price, emotionally and financially. I do ask myself every day, as I do now, why continue to write? why go to conferences? why subscribe to all those journals? why not just use all that money to go on a Caribbean cruise? Ironically, I am much too much of an academic still, despite the years away, not to see that if I have continued to write and to publish it is because like all good narratives this one is still in search of closure. Is this the story of one person who somehow got victimized by a set of circumstances and incredible amounts of näiveté and politics? Perhaps, yes; but it is also the story of how fundamentally our hiring practices have simply not caught up with, let alone kept pace with, our own rhetoric and pedagogical practices.

Do I have a career now? You tell me. I average three to four conferences a year; I send out publications; I read; I write; I think; I work in a retail mall to support myself. Is there a job for me in this profession that is not that of an eternal adjunct? Or am I better off with a job in a retail world, and a foot in the profession, the door always ajar? In the mall there is an authentic replica of the Holy Grail for sale—really. The pages of glossy retail catalogues beckon with their slick literary chic, marketing their wares in seductive language. The gleaming hallways of the upscale mall I work at seem in stark contrast to the corridors of learning. Or, perhaps they are not so far removed after all. In the mall, I am safe; at the very least, I live in a clearly defined world of consumers and commodities.

Notes

Part of this essay was presented at an MLA panel sponsored by the Committee on the Status of Women in the Profession, December 28, 1995, Chicago. This is my first "coming out" story in print, and my deepest gratitude goes to Abhijit Dasgupta, Usha Venkatesh, Emily Watts, and Laura Julier, who have continued to keep the faith; to the many friends located at universities and elsewhere who have taken me "seriously," and especially to Laura Stempel Mumford, who taught me to "dwell in possibility." Finally, this piece is for my parents, who taught me by precept to rethink the margin, but have not lived to see this in print.

[1] Refers to Minh-ha, T., *Woman, Native, Other: Writing Post-Coloniality and Feminism*. Bloomington, Indiana University Press, 1989.

[2] If, as Cary Nelson and Michael Bérubé have argued, "graduate education is losing its moral base" because we can no longer find jobs for students, I would also add that it is partly because we continue to encourage our students to train themselves in ways that are at odds with hiring practices. Recently, a colleague of mine who is on the market in English/film studies said that she was seen as having a "schizophrenic dossier"—and this, after several years of being told that it would be most to her advantage to be cross-disciplinary. We routinely ask students to be interdisciplinary and diverse—English/women's studies, TV/film studies, cultural studies/lesbian-gay theory, etc., while the mainstream marketplace continues to hire by traditional disciplines and locations of power. See Cary Nelson and Michael Bérubé, "Graduate Education Is Losing Its Moral Base," *Chronicle of Higher Education* (March 23, 1994), pp. B1–B3.

[3] Optic diversity is a term *I* have coined to refer to the usual component of racial representation and tokenism involved in hiring practices where departments hire a person of *each* racial kind.

[4] I emphatically do not wish to be misread here as a regressive Dinesh D'Souza. Historically, the various divisions—women's studies, African-

American literature, Latin-American literature, Asian-American literature—have come into place identified with their particular social, political, and cultural formations. What we need to debate is not the necessity of their continued existence, which is what the Right would have us do, but debate the aims of Americanists who would recontain radical transformations in curricula through splintered hiring practices.

[5.] The reliance on the master narrative of black and white is most evident in historical arguments over racial questions of "citizenship" for Chinese, Japanese, etc. There is plenty of analysis regarding this issue from the critical race theory group, which includes Robert Chang, Keith Aoki, and Margaret Chon, among others. And where do Indians see themselves as fitting in the "Asian" world? I am described today as "South Asian," a descriptor that reflects little of my own history. As if with the unintended humor of still being the wrong "Indian," we Asian Indians tend to see ourselves in "tribal" fashion as "Punjabis" or "Gujaritis" or "Tamilians," rather than as "Asian-American" or even as "South Asian." The terms "Punjabis," "Gujaritis," or "Tamilians" refer to social, linguistic, and cultural descriptions within India, which are also drawn along state lines. "Punjabis" refers to people from the state of "Punjab" who speak the language "Punjabi." India as a single national entity, and Indian as corresponding to that, is only one way of identification. Religious and socio-linguistic descriptions are still the primary ways we describe ourselves. These kinds of tactical blindness on the part of both the administration and the community, which sees itself as both nonblack and, sometimes, non-Asian—especially Asian as traditionally defined in the United States—bears strange fruit. Asian, traditionally defined in the United States, refers to those of Oriental origin—Chinese, Japanese. It is only recently that those from the Indian sub-continent, including Pakistan and Bangladesh, and more largely, those from Singapore, Indonesia, Thailand, etc., are being described or "classified" as South Asian in the United States. It often places me in direct conflict with white liberal politics and policies that resist essentialist versions of identity politics, as well as black politics and policies that remain necessarily conservative and wary of such white resistance.

[6.] Tony Horwitz, "Class Struggle: Young Professors Find Life in Academia Isn't What It Used to Be," *Wall Street Journal* (February 15, 1994, Midwest ed.), pp. A+. See also the speical issue of the MLA *Profession '94* that devoted a section to the "Job Market." Lydia Belatèche's essay, "Temp

Prof: Practicing the Profession Off the Tenure Track," appears on pages 64–66 of this volume. Also see Eugene Rice's "Making a Place for the New American Scholar" (AAHE New Pathways Working Paper Series, Inquiry #1), a 1996 report commissioned by the American Association for Higher Education; John Smyth, ed., *Academic Work: The Changing Labour Process in Higher Education* (Buckingham, UK: Open University Press, 1995). Cary Nelson also has a book forthcoming from the University of Minnesota Press entitled *We Will Work for Food*, which highlights the current disaster.

7. While we are justifiably concerned about the "loss of jobs" and the plight of "adjuncts," many of us who have had to "work for food" in the meantime have done so in various other ways while continuing to be active participants in the academic world. While no one could call for a cessation in the struggle to redress the profession, it is equally necessary that we find other ways to talk about intellectual production that is not located within specific institutional sites: see Laura Mumford in her essay in this volume.

Five

The Professional Meets the Personal

Introduction

Carrie Tirado Bramen
Department of English, SUNY-Buffalo

Much of what we know about the current crisis in the academic job market is in the form of statistics. Whether it is *The New York Times* reporting that 813 physicists applied for one faculty position at Amherst College, or Bettina Huber of the Modern Language Association noting that the percentage of jobs in English has declined 38 percent in five years, the quantitative language of ratios, percentages, and probability is effective in articulating the scope and severity of the academic crisis, but limited in expressing the personal consequences of underemployment.[1] The three articles in this section disclose the suppressed term of statistical discourse, namely the emotional, familial, and financial costs of underemployed or unemployed Ph.D.'s. That the three contributors are women reminds us of the historical significance of the feminist slogan of the 1960s and 1970s that "the personal is political." Due in part to the legacy of this slogan, these testimonials have found an institutional and discursive space to be published, circulated, and discussed. They force faculty members to acknowledge that the real victims of the fiscal crisis, to quote Cary Nelson and Michael Bérubé, "are new Ph.D.'s seeking jobs."[2]

191

These essays provide an important antidote to much of the discussion about the job market. Where advice about the market tends to focus on self-packaging—how to present oneself for the professional gaze—with the emphasis on making a good impression, these essays remind us that the job search is also a self-reflective process, a time to set priorities and make decisions about the significance of a career in one's life. What is one willing to sacrifice for a tenure-track position? Ingrid Steffensen-Bruce, for example, admits that her spouse's career in finance has created "geographic limitation(s)" in determining the scope of her job hunt in art history. Diana Dull similarly acknowledges that there are geographic limits to her job search in sociology. Though "single" (and told by colleagues that she is therefore not tied down by a husband and children), Dull interrogates the privileging of "families of choice" over "families of origin." Veronica Vazquez Garcia's essay provides an important contrast with the first two contributions, since the very notion of "home" is ambiguous for her. As a Mexican woman educated in Canada and searching for an academic position in sociology at a North American university, Vazquez Garcia, a transnational scholar, is not circumscribed by geographic limitations but wants to overcome them.

All three essays critique the culture of academic nomadism, where Ph.D.'s, like nineteenth-century journeymen, are expected to pack their tools of labor (i.e., a portable library, computer, and notebooks) and travel from one temporary position to the next. Given the fact that 40 percent of the nation's faculty members are part-time employees, this peripatetic lifestyle is becoming increasingly familiar, and perhaps after a few more years of budget cuts, it will become the predominant way of life within the profession.[3]

As a response to the academic imperative to relocate, it is significant that both Steffensen-Bruce and Dull refer to Jane Austen, who figures in Dull's title and in Steffensen-Bruce's explicit identification with an Austen "(anti-?) heroine," who is "isolated, intellectually frustrated, barred by her social, (or, in my case, educational) standing from any useful occupation." For them, Jane Austen signifies a woman trapped within various spheres of institutional authority, confined in an inflexible world where she is unable to realize her intellectual potential. For the contemporary academic woman, Jane Austen offers a way to criticize the rigidity of the profession, which is unable to accommodate the other commitments and relationships that academics frequently have. But the figure of Jane Austen is also limited, since it suggests that the dilemma of the unemployed or underemployed Ph.D. is a specifically female problem. Scott Heller's "Personal & Professional" section in *The Chronicle of Higher Education* (March 24, 1994) includes interviews with men from various academic disciplines, some of whom have "geographic limitations" to their job search due to their spouse's work. For graduate students of the nineties, the slogan "the personal is political" pertains to both men and women, who frequently share concerns, ranging from dual-career couples to child-rearing.

In a special issue on "The University and Private Life," the editors of *Academe* remark that with regard to "private life" issues, the university lags behind other institutions in the society. In areas such as child care and health, for example, the university lags behind the legislative process.[4] Among the three articles included in this section, Dull candidly mentions her desire to have children in a profession that too often perceives maternity as a sign of a woman's lack of intellectual seriousness. Given the increased presence of women in the profession, particularly in the humanities, it is surprising that there is a dearth of writing about motherhood and academia. Even books that profess to be a comprehensive guide for academic women, such as Paula J. Caplan's *Lifting a Ton of Feathers: A Woman's Guide to Surviving in the Academic World* (University of Toronto Press, 1993), provide remarkably little advice about starting a family, other than this caveat: "Really listen when mothers tell you that you may not get a full night's sleep for a year or more" (p. 98). Probably the most useful testimonial about pregnancy and the job search is Judith Pascoe's "What to Expect When You're Expecting," where she, in part, reviews existent research on female academics' productivity to show that women with children are not less productive at work than childless women are.[5]

A point that is not discussed in the three essays in this section, but which still deserves mention, is the dilemma of the dual-career couple. In 1996, *The Chronicle of Higher Education* featured various strategies that both straight and gay/lesbian couples have used to avoid the "commuter marriage."[6] The article is a rather optimistic overview of particular couples who have successfully managed to stay together either through job sharing or by turning down jobs at Ivy League universities in order to work together at less prestigious institutions. Then there are others who do manage to find two jobs at Harvard. By focusing on a lucky few, many of whom are rather established academics and not recent Ph.D.'s, the article does not offer advice to graduate student couples who are, given the depressed state of the current job market, not in the best position to negotiate two jobs at a time. My advice is to save the topic of a partner/spouse until you have received an offer, preferably in writing; then you can negotiate an adjunct position (with perhaps a possible chance for a permanent position) when reviewing your own contract. Make sure to have your partner's dossier and writing sample ready to send. To improve the position of your spouse, you will both more than likely have to resume the job search, ideally when the book manuscripts are near completion.

As this introduction begins with the first-wave feminist slogan "the personal is political," it seems only apt to end with the words of the contemporary feminist theorist Anne Phillips, who writes that no one is " 'just' a worker, 'just' a woman, 'just' black."[7] All three articles in this section also add: no one is "just" an academic. They invite us to recognize that the academic job search is not only about finding a job, but also about the negotiation of multiple and often conflicting desires and responsibilities that involve, among other factors, families, partners, and friendships.

Notes

[1.] Cary Nelson and Michael Bérubé, "Graduate Education Is Losing Its Moral Base," *The Chronicle of Higher Education* (March 23, 1994), p. B1;

Bettina Huber, "Recent Trends in the Modern Language Job Market," *Profession '94* (New York: Modern Language Association, 1994), p. 101.

2. Nelson and Bérubé, p. B1;

3. The figure of 40 percent is from Nelson and Bérubé, p. B2.

4. *Academe: The Bulletin of the American Association of University Professors*, Vol. 76, No. 1 (January-February 1990), p. 15.

5. Judith Pascoe, "What to Expect When You're Expecting," *Profession '94*, pp. 70–74.

6. Robin Miller, "Weary of Commuter Marriages, More Couples in Academe Make Career Sacrifices to Be Together," *The Chronicle of Higher Education* (September 30, 1996), pp. A10–A11.

7. Anne Phillips, *Divided Loyalties: Dilemmas of Sex and Class* (London: Virago Press, 1987), p. 11. Quoted in Magda Gere Lewis, *Without a Word: Teaching Beyond Women's Silence* (New York: Routledge, 1993), p. 13.

Portrait of the Ph.D. as a Young Woman

Ingrid Steffensen-Bruce

I hold a vintage 1994 Ph.D. in art history from an East Coast research university highly regarded for its art history program. I completed the process with full fellowship support, once winning a university-wide competitive fellowship; I maintained a 4.0 grade point average; and I received a prize for the best dissertation in the humanities. I therefore persist in a belief that I graduated at the top of my class. My dissertation has been accepted for publication by a small but respectable university press. The college-level teaching I have done as an adjunct netted me some very fine evaluations from my students, who I believe enjoyed me as much as I enjoyed them. I possess an agreeable personality and tend to be liked by my students, colleagues, and superiors. It turns out that I am a darn good secretary.

In the two years since I have begun searching for a position in the exalted halls of academe, I have created several bulging folders of application materials, lists, leads, and letters of rejection. I have responded to dozens of job listings, and sent out over one hundred unsolicited letters with accompanying c.v. I have not been invited to a single interview for an academic position. For the two adjunct positions I have secured, I was hired over the telephone. I have filled the interstices of time with work on my book, job hunting in various fields other than teaching but related to my training, and temporary secretarial work. The only offers of employment I have actually received—and these unsolicited!—have been for secretarial work. At the Metropolitan Museum of Art, I was invited for an interview in the human resources department. I was asked to take a typing test, but demurred; I should, therefore, have been prepared for what followed. When I entered the interviewer's office, she began the conversation with the following confidence-shattering qualifier: "Now, please don't be insulted, but . . ." I was offered a secretarial position; I left—despite the admonition, feeling insulted.

I am extremely fortunate in having a loving, supportive, and gainfully employed spouse. I do not absolutely have to do "temp" work in order to keep a roof over my head, and, in fact, have not since my most recent adjunct position ended last June. I have devoted myself to the job searching process and to the preparation of my book for publication, and teach a few SAT and GRE preparation courses for a little extra money on the side. Still, my inability to earn anything more than $10,000 in a given year during our four-year marriage has put certain crimps in our lifestyle. Every year, we decide again not to move from our ever-shrinking apartment because maybe next year I will have a longer-term job that will require another move. Tensions occasionally run high, when my business-minded husband feels he must insert himself into my job hunting process. Starting a family is so remote as to be unthinkable. Buying a house is equally so.

The complexity of the personal-professional equation is compounded by the relative values placed by a capitalistic society on bankers versus academic art historians. My husband, well trained and experienced in the world of finance and "high net worth individuals," is valued at somewhere between two and three times what I ever will be at a comparable stage in my career. It therefore becomes very difficult to contemplate uprooting our small family for an uncertain and ill-paying academic career in the wilds of Minnesota or Ohio or Indiana or Tennessee, where my husband would have to give up a secure, well-paying, promising career with which he is professionally very satisfied. The geographic limitation has made my job hunt all the more difficult.

It is perhaps needless to say that this economic and professional situation has also deeply undermined my sense of myself as a woman and a feminist. Since I was a child, I always knew that I would have lifetime employment. It was not to be an ordinary job, either, but an important one. This construct of myself as a career woman was not something I chose; it was something I simply knew. In a world where the neighbor's car sports a bumper sticker proclaiming, "My kid beat up your honor student," I continue to feel I have not merely an important, but a vital and urgent, role to play. I feel infinitely frustrated by my inability to pursue what I feel to be my vocation—my calling—in life.

By dint of my current unemployment, however, I have been relegated to extremely overeducated hausfrau, responsible for all the household chores while my dutiful spouse maintains our economic status by going to the office every day. Were I a man in the same situation, would I have been duty and honor bound to continue my "temping" in order to bring money into the household? It pains me to admit—probably yes. To occupy my impatient brain and idle fingers, I have begun a needlepoint project. The creation of beauty is something I have always found therapeutic; I love to cook too, and have never been ashamed of that or thought it inappropriate for a serious-minded woman. But there are times, when my needle is flying, I realize with horror that I have become a Jane Austen (anti-?)heroine: isolated, intellectually frustrated, barred by her social (or, in my case, educational) standing from any useful occupation. I frequently feel that the pursuit and attainment of my doctorate has left me exquisitely unprepared for anything but that for which I have trained and now seem unable to reach; for I am certainly now overqualified, as well as ill qualified, for what my past training binds me to believe is lesser work.

The greatest trouble I have, therefore, is also the most painful. It concerns my own personal feelings of confidence and self-worth; it is the emotional conundrum with which the educational process

left me entirely unequipped to deal. For five years, I dedicated myself wholeheartedly to the goal of earning a Doctor of Philosophy.
The psychological condition of my doing so was an absolute belief
that this was the highest and worthiest goal toward which I could
aspire. How else is one to complete the gauntlet of classes, language
tests, papers, conferences and symposia, comprehensive exams both
oral and written, and the completion and defense before a committee
of a book-length research project? How else can one justify remaining a student of the humanities well into one's late twenties when
all one's friends and peers are embarking upon careers or preparing
themselves to be lawyers, doctors, and business managers? When
immersed in the process, one breathes the rarefied air, the pure,
heady ether of academia, and believes, as one might of a religion,
that this particular education is destiny. I felt that, by participating
in this process, I was part of an intellectual elite, and that being
entitled to append "Ph.D." after my name would constitute a pass-
port guaranteeing me a place in this realm forever. Indeed, I was
led to believe more concretely than by the atmosphere alone that a
job would await me when I was done. One of my professors assured
me outright that when I was through, I would have a comfortable
career to support me for the rest of my life. I cannot blame him for
my predicament; I think he honestly believed what he said, and it
has been a very long time since he himself was a seeker in the
academic job market.

To be fair, times have changed too. In 1989, when I embarked
upon the final phase of my education, I had read several articles in
magazines and newspapers about a study recently conducted by the
former president of Princeton, William Bowen, concluding that just
about the time I would be through with my degree—just about now,
in fact—there would be an alarming shortage of professors in the
humanities.[1] He foresaw a wave of retiring professors, an influx of
baby-boomer offspring reaching their college years, and a shortage
of students who had entered Ph.D. programs in the humanities during the seventies and eighties. He could not, of course, have foreseen
the recession, the budgetary cutbacks, and the unemployment that
came into being during the years when I was happily ensconced in

my studies. I was likewise unaware of the effects they would have upon me, personally, when 1994 rolled around and I would be looking for a job, Ph.D. in hand.

The shock of reality, therefore, has struck me doubly hard. From community college teaching jobs, sabbatical replacements, and museum internships, to Ivy League fellowships and tenure-track positions, rejection after rejection arrives in the mail in response to my carefully crafted letters, my perfect transcripts, my "impressive" (as I have been told nearly as often as I have been rejected) curriculum vitae, my glowing recommendations. Once, I felt that I deserved a teaching job—because I was a good teacher, a good researcher, a good writer—even, I flattered myself, a good person. My confidence in my own abilities, my belief in the value of the five years I spent on the doctorate as well as the doctorate itself, my faith that good work is rewarded, have slowly been eroded over the past two years; so much so that I have had to reconstruct my entire sense of self in order to be able to handle my present situation. My idea that because I was good at teaching and loved it, I should therefore be a teacher, has taken as much battering as my self-esteem, and I have reevaluated myself and my predicament to the point that I have realized there really is no other alternative than to abandon the goal I once held to be my inalienable right, the proper reward to a job well done, and to begin to think of myself and my life path in terms of a different career. This realignment has been difficult and painful. The triumph of hope over experience still leads me to put some small amount of faith in this spring as the one that will find me that elusive teaching job, but I still fail to understand, as a friend once remarked, "What more do they want?" This nagging question still accompanies every letter of rejection: "Where am I lacking? What else could I have done?" My husband tries to reassure me that it is simply a matter of supply and demand. Certainly the statistics published by the professional organization to which I belong and which purports to represent me support this contention: art history positions receive a ratio of about forty-two job applicants per position. Who gets these positions? I have not been able to determine. Do they have a great deal more experience? Are they overqualified for the positions for which I am certainly qualified? Are they trained in the popular or politically correct specialties I was not savvy enough to choose? Such questions, as legitimate as I believe they are, serve also to undermine my faith in the choices I have made in the past. When I embarked on the course that would lead me to my Ph.D., I never would have guessed then that I would now have to rationalize my intelligence and abilities in terms of perhaps mistakenly possessing a doctorate.

One may well ask, what do I hope to accomplish by thus unburdening myself? I am not sure. Is it to make others feel sorry for me? They needn't; I feel quite sorry enough for myself as it is. What do I hope to gain? Nothing but a job; and this philippic will certainly not accomplish that. Perhaps I merely wish to have my plaint heard; perhaps its publication will validate my experiences, put on my failure some stamp of approval that is otherwise lacking. Perhaps I would simply like to know that I am not the only one undergoing such an intensely frustrating experience. Or, perhaps, I serve myself up as an object lesson to others who are undergoing the same situation or are about to: do not bind yourself too closely with self-identification as a Ph.D.

My own position has, finally, become intolerable. I can no longer beat my head against a wall; I am too battered and bloody. I have made the decision that if I have not secured an academic position by the fall—and my requirements are generous, for it can be an adjunct position, a sabbatical replacement, or a non-teaching job with a museum, gallery, or foundation—I will denounce my doctorate, professionally speaking, and start anew. What will I do? Where will I end up? I do not know; I may try publishing, advertising, the world of computers, interior design, or who knows what else. And I can always fall back on my typing and organizational skills. I make a great secretary.

Notes

[1.] These articles all referred to a study sponsored by the Andrew W. Mellon Foundation: William G. Bowen and Julie Ann Sosa, *Prospects for Faculty in the Arts and Science: A Study of Factors Affecting Demand and Supply, 1987 to 2012* (Princeton, New Jersey: Princeton University Press, 1989). The result was articles, e.g., in *The Chronicle of Higher Education*, with such titles as "Big Faculty Shortages Seen in Humanities and Social Sciences" (Vol. 36, September 20, 1989) and "Universities Must Lead the Effort to Avert Impending National Shortages of Ph.D.'s" (Vol. 36, January 17, 1990).

(Academic) Sense and Sensibilities: Confronting Ambivalence About the 1990s Job Market

Diana Dull

When I saw this call for papers, I was immediately intrigued by the creative—and perhaps cathartic—possibilities. That I am even willing to talk about my experiences with the academic job market in this forum is ironic. The topic came to dominate my life this past year, so much so that my family learned not to utter the words "job search" at holiday gatherings, lest they kill the mood. They understood that a series of difficult, private decisions in my life had been publicly scrutinized, leaving me feeling exposed and defensive. Friends, colleagues, and mentors had formed strong opinions about how I should "play" the tenure-track game (an ill-fitting term for an activity that feels like anything but play). Sometimes this resulted in my being offered much appreciated, helpful advice. At other times, I received unsolicited, judgmental lectures. Petty departmental gossip also found its way to my ears. And one formerly civil colleague even sent me hate mail via the Internet; apparently my indecisiveness and "attitude" about the job market had offended his sensibilities, and he felt compelled to share this fact with me. But I digress, for this essay is about *my* sensibilities at being a new Ph.D. facing the 1990s academic market. To tell that story, a few background notes are in order.

During 1994–95, I was an ABD in sociology, one who allowed herself to be convinced that taking an early shot applying for a tenure-track position was a good idea. Keeping up with application deadlines was the first challenge, as I was simultaneously teaching a new class and trying to finish a half-written dissertation (ask me how cleverly I lied about my progress to all concerned). About two months into the application period, the phone began to ring. Six departments liked my file well enough to book interviews. I felt giddy and flattered as each call came in, though such responses gave way to anxiety fairly quickly. In eight chaotic, exhausting weeks, I visited more states and time zones than I had in all of my thirty-six years. In the end, two schools had made offers, and I had made myself crazy. I had not fully anticipated what I now felt: that my common sense about the realities of the market conflicted dramatically with my sensibilities—about who I am, what I value, what I feel I am worth, and what I am seeking in this academic life.

Such lofty concerns did not arise immediately. Pragmatic issues warranted my attention first. For example, I learned early on that I was naive about the pricey wardrobe issue. This penny-stretching graduate student faced a rude financial awakening when it came time to pack interview clothes. My California-native attire did not suffice for the blizzard-condition states I was to visit. Thankfully, friends disabused me before I traveled of the fantasy that I owned a "real winter coat." I had no sooner maxed out credit cards purchasing acceptable winter boots, suits, gloves, and coat, when I received interview calls from two other universities, one in a desert setting, another in a tropical setting. By the time I headed off to the mall a second time in search of "cool, tasteful linens that breathe" (a search committee chair's exact words of advice), I was looking at short-term loans from family members.

My job market experiences also began to provide me with some of the best cocktail party stories I've had to share in years. People seemed to enjoy my tales of strange faculty members I met on my travels. There was the professor who leaned in so close I could feel his coffee breath on my face as he whispered, "So, what I really want to know about you is this—are you secretly one of them closet feminists? 'Cause I see you're writin' about gender here, and we don't really need a feminist in this position." Then there was the elderly emeritus who made a ten-minute speech about all manner of unrelated things at the end of my job talk, finally bellowing his question: "Answer me this—*what is truth?*" (Actually, I thought I fielded that one pretty well, under the circumstances.) And for sheer dramatic imagery, I enjoyed telling the story of my interview in a beautiful, tropical locale. The search committee had graciously offered to combine informal interviewing time with a half-day scenic tour. I imagined we would still be discussing my research as we drove past the ocean views and palm trees. I didn't imagine the horrified look on my interviewer's face as he saw—too late—that a couple of feral pigs were crossing the highway. After fighting to maintain control of the van (we were briefly airborne), my host found himself at a loss for words for the first time that day. I remember feeling both sickened and perversely grateful to those piglets, whose ill-fated evening stroll bought me at least a half hour on the job market where I could stop smiling insipidly.

I found myself telling such tales of boars and boorishness in order to find some humor in a difficult situation. My interview experiences have left me with a sense of deep ambivalence, uncertain as to what I am even hoping for in this market. Common sense tells me that I need to grab any job that I am lucky enough to be offered. The reasons seem obvious, numerous, and compelling. I understand that the market is exceedingly tight and competitive, making any job offer in these times a coup, if not a gift from the gods. I also understand the logic that one has to get in the game to play the game. As one of my advisors keeps stressing: "A first job is a first job; take it, then publish your way out. But you've got to take the job to get the better job." Common sense also reminds me that I have clocked eight long years in graduate school, incurred the usual amount of mind-numbing debt, and now have even more bills to pay. Coupled with the fact that I'm turning thirty-seven—beyond the age where I should be musing about what I want to be when I grow up—this would seem to suggest that the time to act is now. Thus, when those two offers came my way last year, common sense told me not to hesitate in signing on one of those dotted lines.

And yet, I did hesitate, for reasons that I am still grappling with today. For what made perfect common sense to me—to take any job I was offered—was in direct conflict with the sensibilities I feel about my life at this time. Some of these sensibilities are admittedly emotional and, hence, may seem irrational to the reader. But we all bring our desires, experiences, and baggage to life's difficult choices, and I was no exception. For example, I am a single woman who is deeply saddened and concerned by the fact that I have not yet begun a family. I have had much time to question how, and to what degree, the pursuit of my career has hindered my opportunities in this regard. It may not be fashionable or professionally savvy to admit that my desire to have a family vies with my desire to have a career, but it is true. So even as I go through the steps it takes to secure a tenure-track position, I feel troubled—When will there ever be time enough to pursue these other neglected parts of my life? When I'm a first-year, junior faculty member trying to get settled in a new job? When I'm coming up against tenure? I was not the first, nor will I be the last, academic woman to voice such concerns. But being in good company did not allay my fears. I found myself looking at my life after my doctoral graduation with mixed feelings. I was proud of my accomplishment, but frightened by the sense that life had been passing me by all those years in graduate school. Right at the time I was supposed to face the market with bright eyes and purpose, I felt a strong urge to run the other way (a feeling I am still fighting).

Other emotions played themselves out with a fierce intensity as I weighed job offers. I am a daughter who learned a formative lesson from her father's early death, at age fifty: life is short, and you've got to live it fully each day, embracing what makes you happy. The daily, ongoing struggles my father had experienced with his career seemed to matter very little when all was said and done. What mattered was the love of his family, and that we were by his side at the end. When I tell people this story anecdotally, they nod their heads and appreciate the sentiments. When I bring up this story to make a point about how my family relationships affect my feelings about moving across the country to take a job, most people lose patience with me. Colleagues did not, or would not, understand the salience of my relationship with my family of origin. They would say things like "Hey, you're single! You have no one tying you down, no children, no husband who can't move because of his job! So what's the problem?" When I stressed that I did have complex ties to people I loved, they would respond with comments like "They'll only be a phone call away!" or "Diana, it is time to cut the cord!"

It seems we are surrounded by dominant cultural messages that say only our families of choice should factor into our adult life decisions. To factor in the feelings and needs of one's family of origin, on the other hand, is to be deemed "childish." Having lost one parent too soon, I find myself very resistant to seeing my other parent only once or twice a year (my two job offers were in locales three thousand miles from my family). I treasure similarly close bonds with my siblings, and my young nieces and nephews. Bimonthly visits with my family members are an integral part of my life and happiness. The idea of being a long-distance daughter, sister, and "Auntie" feels unacceptable to me. Few people view these sentiments as logical reasons for my hesitation within the academic job market. In fact, I've been told that I have "a problem" and "had better change my attitude." For these reasons, I have learned to keep these feelings to myself. It has left me resentful and angry—not just at people's comments, but at the painful conclusion I have come to face: I will have to leave the state and all those I love to be employed (the California job market has proven even more hopeless than the national market). To make such a choice goes against my most deeply held values. Before my academic life, I had never experienced a career where I was so helpless to get around the geographical dictates of the profession. I wish I had been less naive about the realities I am now facing in this regard.

My emotional sensibilities about leaving loved ones were not the only concerns I faced last year. The job market experience also forced me to examine what I felt I was "worth"—and what I should hold out for—in this process. Because I made the choice to go on the market ABD, I faced salary offers that were significantly lower than those I would have been offered with the Ph.D. in hand. While no one goes into this business for the money, these offers were lower than my worst fears. Some faculty mentors advised me that "a few thousand one way or the other" did not mean that much in the long run. In terms of a literal ability to pay a few more bills each month, they were probably right. But there was a symbolic issue at stake for me here. The dollar offers were so low, and I had worked so long and hard, that I found the numbers insulting. After eight years of sacrifice to obtain this advanced degree, I was being offered a salary that matched the administrative salary I had earned a decade earlier (when I had only a two-year degree). Coupled with these low salary offers were nonexistent moving budgets and limited research support possibilities. Such offers left me stewing. I didn't blame the individual departments, as each was facing a budget crisis. But the cold reality of how little we honor teaching in this country was now hitting me where I lived. My laments about the nation's mixed priorities aside, I still struggled with a strategy question: should I hold out one more year on the assumption that having a Ph.D. in hand would lead to better offers? It seemed a reasonable assumption, even to those who told me to take what I could get.

Finally, I had—and have—a certain sensibility about the kind of collegial environment I hope to experience. I am not so naive as to think I will find a department where colleagues hold hands in a state of blissful harmony, everyone respectful and supportive of one another's work. I have witnessed firsthand the political factions, petty quarrels, and behind-the-back commentary that occurs in any academic department. From these troubles, there are surely only degrees of escape. But I thought I would at least be spared departmental dirty laundry on the job market scene; didn't faculty trot out their best behavior in these situations? As I was to learn, the answer to that question is "not necessarily." The faculty of one of the departments that expressed interest in me also expressed less than kind sentiments about one another. Each took a turn—over drinks, office interviews, and tours of the city—to let me know about a particular colleague's "professional troubles," "strange style," and "cold, difficult personality." I noted that the sole woman in the department received more than her fair share of this commentary. When we had some time together, she spoke frankly about her unhappiness, her isolation, and her ongoing desire to leave the department. This left me wondering if I would be taking her place as the new object of the men's criticisms. In another, similar interview, the lone woman in the department took me out for a private dinner and, with tears in her eyes, said, "I hope you can come here, because then there would be two of us women, and a possibility for a fair fight" (this in reference to her two "colleagues" who held private "departmental meetings" whenever she was out of town). Faculty I met in several departments also told me "behind the scenes tales" of what I would be facing should I come on board. I flew home from such trips feeling less than inspired. I recall thinking, Why should I leave behind everyone I love to come spend my days with these people?

An offer did come from this last interview, leaving me to face a personal moment of truth. The fact that I had already turned down an offer from the first department that had interviewed me weighed heavily on my mind. While the first department seemed to have a kind group of colleagues (except for the man who feared feminists), their offer was poor and non-negotiable (i.e., extremely low salary, no moving expenses, minimal research or travel support, etc.). As a single woman, I was also concerned about the isolated community and lack of amenities in this location. At the time I declined this job, I rested hope on the three other interviews I had yet to complete. By the time I faced my second offer, I had received three job rejections. Could I truly afford to say no twice?

I had five days to make the decision. The list of pros and cons I was drawing up grew longer and longer, but I don't know that it helped much in the long run. As I described earlier, advice—some helpful, much stern and judgmental—poured in from every direction. My family struggled to be supportive, no matter what I decided. Friends and colleagues offered their range of views; those willing to truly listen to my deliberations acknowledged that the decision was complex. Others just kept shouting at me for days. It became hard to hear my own voice in all the din. I knew I could not base my decision solely on the emotional pull I felt not to move from my loved ones. But it was not clear what would constitute "the right criteria" for making this decision. Salary? Job security? Departmental reputation? Collegial environment? Teaching load? Research support? And I still faced the unknown variable: would I have more, and better, choices if I just waited a half year and returned to the market with my doctorate in hand? With five minutes to go before my deadline, I made the call and declined the job. Since I was too uncomfortable to state the messy mix of actual reasons for my declining, I claimed I had taken another offer. The phone receiver was barely back in its cradle before I burst into tears, and cried till I was all cried out.

As I write this essay, it is almost a year to the date since I made that difficult decision. While I have learned to live with the choice I made, I remain ambivalent about whether I did the right thing. Did my sensibilities get in the way of the commonsense approach to this market? And if so, was this such a bad thing? Hindsight is not always twenty-twenty. My view of my situation now, as then, is blurry. I know I was relieved and thrilled to actually complete my dissertation once the job market pressure was off (no small feat; I had strong doubts that I was going to meet that goal in a timely fashion). My family and closest friends wept happy tears when they realized I would be around for at least another year, and I shared in these emotions. Fate also smiled on me when my home department offered me a one-year lecturer appointment; this has temporarily deferred some of the ramifications of my decision.

On the other hand, I know that I am mere months away from my last known paycheck. To date, I haven't had the same number of "nibbles" on the job market scene as I had last year, thus challenging my theory about securing greater choices with the Ph.D. in hand. I have had one interview with a department that I think I would have enjoyed as a first position. While it was a great distance from my home, it did offer a pretty environment, research support, and a very fine salary and benefits package. But I was not offered the position. As of today, I am long-listed at two schools, one of which is actually offering a lower salary than the lowest offer I received last year. Should I be forced to take this job—I cannot financially afford to turn it down at this point—what will I have gained in this process?

The answers are as difficult as the questions. I fully appreciate the fact that I have made whatever bed I now find myself lying in, and that my potential impending joblessness (or move to Timbuktu) does not warrant any sympathy. But I never wanted anyone's sympathy in this process. What I did want was for people to respect my decisions, even if they did not agree with them. I also wanted the chance to talk about the conflicts this process can raise, without judgment. To that end, I have truly appreciated this forum.

I have no conclusive final thoughts to offer here; my story is clearly still in progress. But I would like to close with these observations. The constraints of the academic job market represent a reality that we all face collectively. But the choice to pursue, accept, or decline a job is ultimately a private, personal decision. I am sure that, for many, the only problem with this market is that it is flooded with new Ph.D.'s that look just like them. (One department just wrote me with the news that they had received five-hundred-plus applications for one position, but had lost their funding. The double message in this letter was not lost on me.) My common sense tells me that I could learn a lesson from those Ph.D.'s who would be happy to land wherever the job winds take them. And it tells me that continuing to cater to my sensibilities may be a fool's gamble. As my father would have said, such sensibilities will not pay the rent or put food on the table. But I can't help reflecting on the fact that this was a sermon my father made throughout the healthy years of his life. Months before he died, he wondered about the paths not taken, the compromises he regretted, and the hopes he had let go of much too soon. I remember this too, and feel caught between the two lessons my father tried to impart.

The Sad and Candid Story of an Immigrant Woman in Canada and Her Unsuccessful Job Hunt

Veronica Vazquez Garcia

Should I go back to Mexico? Should I stay in Canada? These are the questions that I was asking myself when I saw the call for papers by new Ph.D.'s looking for work in the unappreciative labor market of the 1990s. I had printed the e-mail message and put it on a stack of papers next to my computer. I had not touched it for nearly two months, since I was suffering from a post-defense trauma and I could not pull myself together even to write a letter. Suddenly, three months after my defense, I could think again of the possibility of spending days at home, facing the computer screen. I had recovered my energy. That day, I celebrated my Ph.D. for the first time, and above all, my love of exploring ideas.

Why did I have such a hard time after my defense, in which, after all, I was recommended for a university medal? Why could I not feel happy about myself? There are several answers to this question. The doctoral program is a difficult, time-consuming process. It takes many years of unpaid labor and diplomacy. All decisions (getting a full-time job, relocating, having a baby) must be postponed until "later." For those who cannot afford to postpone them, doing a Ph.D. can be a real health hazard.

I get upset when I hear people saying that those who pursue graduate studies are avoiding the "real world." In graduate school I learned more than the sociology of elevators. Departmental politics taught me many things about power and competition. Dealing with my supervisor, forming a committee who would follow me throughout the process, getting respect and funding for a non-mainstream area of research (gender and development in the third world) required an amazing amount of real-world experience. Fortunately, I did not only learn about power and competition; I also learned about the importance of networking and organizing.

Being an international student from Mexico did not make things easier. I had to unlearn some things, and learn others: how to write a paper for a graduate course; when, where, and how it is appropriate to talk to a professor . . . Believe it or not, these things, which some people take for granted, change from place to place, and I had to learn them in order to survive in the Canadian academic environment. On top of this, of course, was the fact that I was writing and doing presentations in a language other than my mother tongue, that I was far from family and friends, and that I was on a low-budget scholarship which I knew would come to an end before I could even reach the stage of writing the dissertation. As an international student, I was not allowed to work in Canada, other than as a teaching or research assistant at the university where I was doing my studies, and only for a limited number of hours per week.

I survived the first two years of the program (courses and three comprehensive exams) and became an ABD. When I had no more money to pay international student fees, I applied for a leave of absence from school, took a job in Mexico City, and applied for landed immigrant status in Canada. A year later I came back to Canada as a new immigrant and thought to myself: "This will make things easier for me." I made a big effort to finish my dissertation and planned my new life in Canada. For the first time, I could apply for all kinds of jobs while writing my dissertation. I was so excited.

Yet I did not expect to get the greatest job as an ABD. I was totally aware of the fact that as an ABD and even as a new Ph.D., I could only expect to get temporary teaching positions. I knew it would be more difficult for me, not only because of my gender, but also because as a new immigrant I had no "contacts" in Canada. I could not go to my old university and teach a summer course, something which many of my Canadian-born friends did. So I completed the Ph.D. program with no "Canadian" teaching experience because I did not get any of the teaching positions I applied for as an ABD. I did have teaching experience in Mexico, but that did not really count for my Canadian employers.

So my first shock as an ABD was that I could not even get a temporary, part-time, poorly paid teaching position. I applied for specific courses at two universities in Ottawa and could not even get a job teaching at my own university, where I had finished my M.A. with honors and was completing my Ph.D. with high standards. What is even more amazing is that I applied for courses directly related to my area of expertise, i.e. gender and development, social anthropology, the development of sociological and anthropological thought, and introduction to anthropology. Employers always had good reasons to hire someone else. I was told that they had found exactly what they were looking for, i.e., someone with a graduate degree in social anthropology. But let's not fool ourselves. We know that someone who has spent years doing literary reviews, comprehensive exams, and seminar presentations, can teach *any* course if he or she is given enough time to prepare it. I came to believe that the people who got the courses had more contacts than I had, or at least had been more visible than I was during the hiring process. I also knew that my lack of Canadian teaching experience put me at a disadvantage, to the point that no one was giving me the opportunity to acquire it once and for all!

I did not even reach the interview stage for any of the permanent, tenure-track positions for which I sent applications as an ABD. Unfortunately, I know little about the process whereby search committees make short lists of candidates. They usually sent me a standard letter referring to the "tough choices" that had to be made due to the "impressive backgrounds" of applicants, including myself of course. But I know there is more to it than that. I have been involved in hiring processes at my own university and I know that sometimes it is hard even to agree on the area of specialization that the department is looking for. More tragically, I have seen excellent candidates dismissed, and dubious ones invited for interviews.

Only once was I able to get a hint as to why I was not being invited for interviews. I met someone who had been involved in the hiring process at one university where I had sent my application. I asked him for feedback, and he made very useful suggestions. I wish I could meet someone like him more often, in order to avoid making the same mistakes over and over again. But then he said something that made me think a lot. He said that just by looking at my résumé and cover letter, it was hard to tell that English was not my first language, because my writing was very good. I took this as a compliment, and perhaps he intended it to be just that. But then I realized that in his comment there were some discriminatory assumptions regarding my professional abilities. First, he had assumed that English was not my first language, something which is not self-evident in my résumé. Second, he had assumed that my English would be bad because it is my second language, and he was surprised to see otherwise. I could picture the search committee thinking the same thing, looking at my résumé, with my funny-sounding name, and deciding not to hire me because my English would not be good enough. They never gave me the opportunity to prove otherwise.

After so many bad experiences I decided to take a more "aggressive" approach, as "experts" recommend to job hunters. I called friends and acquaintances and asked for their help. I realized that none of the people I knew from the Ph.D. program had permanent jobs in academia, and that very few actually had full-time jobs. Most of them were part-time instructors, or were on short contracts with the government and other organizations (unions, for example). They either had very good contacts in the government, or a long history of activism in these organizations. They were not publishing and most of them had forgotten how to write a research paper; many had not even finished the Ph.D. program.

One day, my husband suggested I talk to the mother of a friend of his who works at a community college. I did. I was very nervous because I had never met her before and I did not know what I would say. She was extremely nice to me. She passed my résumé on to the chairperson of the Department of Social Sciences and I was given one course, which I am presently teaching. I love the material I teach, the group size (thirty-four students), the college's approach to education and the people teaching there. The only thing that I do not like is the salary. The job pays $30 Canadian per hour and only classroom hours count. So I teach four hours a week, and I make $480 Canadian a month. It is less than I would make living on welfare, even considering the welfare cuts made recently by the new right-wing government of Ontario. With an unemployed husband and this salary, we had no choice but to move back in with my in-laws, since we could not afford rent. Pretty depressing when you are in your early thirties and have spent the last twelve years of your life "upgrading your skills," isn't it?

Although I am glad that I am teaching this course, I find it sad that the only possible way to get it was through contacts: my résumé went from the mother of my husband's friend, who happened to be the coordinator of the Department of Social Sciences, to the chairperson's desk. I kept thinking that if I had mailed my résumé directly to the department, it would probably now be inside a file cabinet, and I would not be teaching this course. What was even more amazing was that this nice woman, who treated me like her daughter, did not know anything about my professional abilities; the people who know about them—i.e., the people at the university where I did my two graduate degrees and worked as a teaching and research assistant for years—have done nothing for me.

I was so desperate that I attempted a career change. I went to the local offices of Canadian non-government organizations working on international development and asked for information. Even though I heard the same story everywhere ("This is not a good time to start a career in international development"), I thought that my area of expertise, my fluency in English, French, and Spanish, and my fieldwork experience in Mexico would get me a job. I applied only for jobs in which I had fulfilled most of the requirements: an M.A. in the social sciences; a knowledge of Latin America; fluency in English, French, and Spanish; willingness to travel; good writing and social skills. I lost heart when I did not even make it to the short list for a job in which I had fulfilled *all* the requirements. The argument was lack of "practical" and administrative experience, as if spending a year doing fieldwork and being a student representative at the departmental board of my university had not taught me anything. And again, let's be honest. The people who are telling me today that I have no practical or administrative experience had *none* when they got their jobs twenty or fifteen years ago. They learned on the job. The generation of radicals from the 1960s are now the gatekeepers of the 1990s.

My thesis defense came and I stopped looking for work for about a month. After my defense I decided to give up the idea of a career change for a while and focus again on academic positions. A few bad experiences had taught me that outside academia a Ph.D. is seen as a handicap instead of an asset, because I was "overqualified" and had no "working" (meaning administrative) experience. Since there were few academic openings in Canada, I decided to try the American market. I subscribed to the *American Sociological Association Bulletin* and began applying for jobs in the United States. This geographical change provoked the hostility of friends and relatives, who believed that I was giving up a "nice" country such as Canada to go to the United States. I understood their reaction, since Canadian nationalism has always been based on the country's more benevolent welfare state and world reputation as a peacekeeper. What people do not want to see is that the gentler, kinder Canada is disappearing rapidly under provincial Conservative governments and even a federal Liberal government, which is presently undoing its own social legacy. I dislike the myths that make us feel good about a particular nation. This is even true for Mexico, the country where I was born and spent most of my life. All I want is a place that can support my personal and professional development. In fact, I think that Canadians in general will soon have to target other labor markets, and some are doing so already. For example, a friend told me that recent university openings in New Zealand have been inundated by Canadian applicants. It is very simple. If you cannot find work in your home country, you have to look elsewhere.

I started to apply for tenure-track, assistant professor positions in the United States last November (my defense was in October). So far, I have applied for approximately forty positions, and I have received letters of acknowledgment from most of them. By now, most search committees are looking at my file, and I cannot tell whether or not I will be as disappointed, as I have been with Canadian universities and non-government organizations. In order to maximize my chances, I decided to position myself as a person with broad interests who was capable of teaching courses that are taught in most universities, such as introductory surveys and social theory courses. Most of us have taught courses that have little to do with our area of expertise, and we did it well. However, research interests are more difficult to negotiate. Most U.S. openings are in criminology and quantitative methods, and I cannot really present myself as an expert in these areas. So I usually respond to ads that include gender and/or race and ethnicity in the job description. I write a short summary of the major contributions of my dissertation and ask my references to describe my research achievements in their letters of recommendation. I know that many employers may see my research interests as "narrow" because my area of expertise is not the United States. I also believe that my Mexican nationality will limit my chances of getting a job in the United States. I just hope that some employers will see the potential benefits of hiring someone with a different cultural background and geographical area of expertise.

Even though this time I really hope that I will make it to the short list at least once or twice, I am full of fear. What will happen if I do not make it? Will I have to turn to plan B, which is to go for a postdoctoral fellowship, prolong my poverty and instability, and "upgrade my skills" even more? (Until when?) I know that my funny-sounding name will play a role in any decision, and that even if I make it to an interview, there is going to be someone who has trouble understanding my "accent." Students at the college where I am presently teaching just reminded me of that. In the meantime, I will have to keep on presenting papers and submitting them for publication. How can anyone bear the costs of all this with an income of $480 Canadian a month? Putting aside the issue of money, how can anyone keep up her spirits until something better happens?

This is why I am asking myself these questions: should I go back to Mexico? Should I stay in Canada? Two weeks ago, I received a tentative job offer from a Mexican research center doing exactly the kind of work that I am doing. In Mexico, new Ph.D.'s are currently in demand. Academic institutions are increasingly raising their standards and offering permanent positions only to people with Ph.D.'s. Salaries are not and will never be good (I would make approximately $1,000 U.S. a month), and one of the reasons I want to stay in Canada is the potentially better life that I could have here. But now I ask myself: how long am I going to think of a better future in Canada and decline offers elsewhere? The demand for Ph.D.'s in Mexico may be over soon, since people with M.A.'s are now doing their Ph.D.'s. So I am waiting to hear more from the Mexican research center, and am seriously considering going south.

I know there are a lot of people in my situation. This does not make me happy, but at least it gives me a sense of perspective. In the last two or three weeks there were at least two stories in the most important Canadian newspaper, the *Globe and Mail,* about unemployed Ph.D.'s in Canada. One was about an engineer who had been living on welfare for a number of years. The other described a specialist on African history. Both were males and the first was of Arab descent. I am sure there are many women too, perhaps even more than men. I belong to that generation of women who, according to the 1995 United Nations Human Development Report, were able to get an education, but have not been incorporated into the labor force. Perhaps we will never be. In fact, many of the part-time instructors who are currently losing their jobs in a number of universities and colleges are women.

I wonder how historians will characterize end-of-the-century North America. What term will they use to describe the unemployment and underemployment of perfectly skilled and creative people? Depression? Crisis? Transition to a technologically driven society that requires little human power? Social revolution? Personally, I hope they use this last phrase. And that this time, we really mean it.

Postscript: April 1996

This morning I got an e-mail message from the editors of this anthology saying that this essay had been accepted. I was happy to receive some good news among the many "We regret to inform you" letters that I have been receiving lately. I was told by the editors that I could add new material, especially if I have had some job offers from the U.S. search and my situation had changed in the last couple of months. . . .

My situation has indeed changed, but not in the direction suggested by the editors. I only had one job interview—to teach in Eastern Europe with the Civic Education Project—but I was not offered a job. I made it to the semifinals (I was among the ten best applicants) in three American universities. In two cases the hiring committee asked for more information and I spent a week of my salary sending materials by courier. I do not regret it. But I did not hear from them again.

I have learned an important lesson from this job hunt. Now I know that my chances of getting a tenure-track position in American academia today are extremely low. The three institutions that showed an interest in me were looking for people in my area of specialization, but I just did not have enough publications and teaching experience. I have the impression that the few people who are currently getting tenure-track, assistant professor positions are in their late thirties or even early forties. They have spent many years teaching part-time and getting published. Most of them have a book already published or in print. I simply cannot compete with them. I am thirty-two years old and I just recently finished my Ph.D.

Another new development in the last couple of months is that I started to look again for positions in the Canadian academic market. A friend had told me that openings in Canadian universities usually take place between January and April. A week ago we both expressed our dismay at the amazingly low number of openings in the country. I applied for no more than ten, and I recently received letters from two of them stating that the positions had been canceled due to "budget problems." I applied for summer teaching positions in two other Canadian universities, and I received a very unusual letter from one of them. The author had taken the time to go through my publications and showed a genuine interest in my work. He regretted being unable to offer me something (the position had been advertised but they were not hiring anybody) and even apologized for the bad academic market. I must say that I appreciated his letter a lot.

So things are clearer to me now. I know what it takes to get a permanent position in North American academia. I will have to spend the next two or three years applying for temporary and poorly paid teaching positions. I will have to target universities outside Ottawa, where I have been unable to get teaching positions in the past. In the fall I will have to apply for funding for a postdoctoral fellowship. This means that for the next few years of my life, I will be living on a permanent low budget and will be constantly relocating. More important, I will continue to postpone any real decisions in life.

Or I will go back to Mexico for good. Indeed, I have also spent the last couple of months working on a research proposal for the research center in Mexico, and I am close to the final draft. If approved, I will be offered a permanent position to do research in my area of specialization and teach graduate seminars. I will accept it. Mexico is a country in crisis, but so is Canada. Not only for me, but for many people like me.

S ix

Different Paths

Introduction

Victoria C. Olsen

We graduate from college and begin graduate school. We complete our course work speedily, pass our exams on the first try, and begin our dissertations. We research and write each chapter in sequential order. We finish within the mandated six years. We go on the job market as ABDs and we have tenure-track jobs waiting for us when we receive our degrees. We revise our dissertations into books, publish, teach, advise, and get tenure five years later. We progress through the ranks to full professor, and send our children to our home universities.

If this "classic" academic career was ever the norm, it hasn't been for decades. A few of the senior faculty in my graduate program fit this pattern, but they were all hired in the sixties. Many forces, from the personal to the institutional, make this pattern unlikely today, yet it remains a hidden assumption behind much of our thinking about academic careers. And there is little coherent information about different paths within the academy, even as they become more and more populated. The lack of information then only adds to the inevitable anxiety associated with leaving the beaten path.

This section aims to remedy some of that lack by describing several (not, of course, all) possible routes through the maze of academia. Marilyn Bonnell details the life of a visiting professor, roving from job to job on one-to-two-year contracts. Allen G. Hunt shares his decision to retrain himself by going back to graduate school in geology. Eleanor B. Amico tells the story of her reentry into academia after raising her children, and recounts the difficulties she has encountered when judged against peers who have taken a less circuitous career path. Christina Boufis relates her solution to the problem of "waiting out" the market: she has found an interesting job teaching in a women's county jail, but she wonders how portable her experience will be when and if she attempts to reapply for academic jobs. Unlike the contributors in the "Alternative Careers" section, these contributors all identify themselves as academics, though the academy doesn't always acknowledge them as such. Their attitudes are as various as their career choices. From Hunt's dispassionate analysis of his professional past to Bonnell's enviable contentment in a life of constant relocations, they demonstrate the truism that every situation is personally unique.

My own situation parallels and complements those described in this section (see my essay in the "Alternative Careers" section). Like all these contributors (and, in truth, everyone else) my career decisions have been shaped by equal parts of chance, choice, and necessity, and it is a rare academic (like Bonnell) who happily accepts the consequences. Like Amico, I wonder how to present my child-rearing responsibilities; they do not fill out my c.v. and I may find myself unable to "account" for these invisible years later on. Like all of the academics on different paths—from adjuncts to office temps—I struggle with the problem of the ticking clock. How do I account for all this time without a recognizable academic title or role? Like many others, I fear that the passing years only make me less and less marketable in an already overcrowded market.

Which is a shame, because as Hunt and Amico point out, teachers and scholars with varied life experiences have a lot to share with students. Hunt and Amico both argue persuasively that their time off the main track makes them better teachers, with more sympathy and insight into their students' diverse circumstances. The academy has often given lip service to this ideal of having "real world" experience as well as academic credentials (especially in the sciences and increasingly in creative and business writing programs), but there is little attention to the costs and difficulties of these paths. Specifically, they require coping with job insecurity, finding alternate sources of income, and juggling multiple roles to a greater extent than a tenure-bound academic.

Yet it is important to remind ourselves too that the straight path in academia is largely mythic everywhere now. We are entering the age of academic free agency (though without the inflated salaries that implies): even the tenured and the tenure-track bounce around from department to department, whether from choice or necessity. The market glut of new and promising Ph.D.'s also makes it harder and harder to get tenure in some departments. These assistant professors, while perhaps lucky early on, sometimes have it hardest, as the rug is pulled out from under them after they have made even heavier personal and professional investments in academia than the rest of us. The recent example of tenured faculty being fired at Bennington College shows that no one is safe in this market, and all academics will have to adjust to the new corporate model of university "efficiency."

But as Allen Hunt complains, most of us have not been trained to think of efficiency as our goal. Nor did we usually expect to find our academic prospects as mysterious and intangible as they have become. As odd as it may sound now, many of us went into academia because it seemed secure and certain. Like medicine and law, the professional track was clear: you put one foot on each rung of the ladder and you get to the top. I know that when I was trying to devise a career in writing and research it was the very straightness of the academic path that appealed to me. It is only now that I have been forced to reconstruct an idiosyncratic route toward my original goal, and to acknowledge that that can in some ways be liberating as well.

So my best advice to graduate students and Ph.D.'s is this: Form alliances and friendships with those on the margins. Find mentors who have had different career paths and ask them explicitly for advice on how to handle your own situation. Read anthropologist Mary Catherine Bateson's *Composing a Life* and believe her argument that change, disruptions, and improvisations shape the most rewarding lives and stimulate creativity. Most importantly, keep repeating to yourself, "There are many ways to get where I am going . . .".

The Gypsy Scholar: Making a Living as a Full-Time Adjunct

Marilyn Bonnell

"Stayin' alive, Stayin' alive!" Little did I imagine that the job market would bring new meaning to the lyrics of, of all things, a Bee Gees song! The good news is that I am staying alive. The bad news is that to do so I have been forced to modify my concept of my profession (which in the end, turns out to be good news too). Like most new Ph.D.'s, I envisioned the security of a tenure-track position and a place to call home. The reality is that I have had to join the Navy (in a manner of speaking) and see the world, as the old recruitment posters proclaimed. The parallel in academia is being a visiting professor, the person who steps in when faculty members go on sabbatical or educational leave; when they retire, resign, or take administrative positions and a full-scale search has not been yet launched; or when an institution wants to offer certain courses but does not want to commit to a tenure-track position to do so. That's when I step in.

What I've discovered is the job of the gypsy scholar. Let me add this distinction: this is not a job that involves racing around, teaching two courses at one college, jumping on a beltway, and teaching another course at another college and an evening course at yet another institution. What I am talking about is a job that is full-time for generally one-to-three years, with a nine-month contract, your own office, secretarial support, health insurance, and a retirement plan.

Being a full-time adjunct is not for everyone but, I suspect, it is a job that few consider seriously enough. Newly hatched Ph.D.'s do not see it, after all, as the job for which we spent years preparing. In fact, to many of us, it smacks of substitute teaching (and conjures up how we tortured that fifth-grade substitute by giving her false names). But in the current job market, there is no use holding out for the job of your dreams—or even the job to which you feel entitled.

Everyone bemoans the fate of the poor adjunct, but you do not necessarily have to be a victim of the system. For instance, I am generally "abused" to the tune of $30–40,000—currently of over $40,000—for a nine-month contract (with full benefits). And some universities will even pay for my move! What's the catch? Well, they want you to teach. Here, then, is the rub if you are a research-oriented academic. It is very hard to publish to the tune of three, or even four, courses a semester when you are prepping new courses. Unfamiliar courses mean new syllabi, but a quick look through the files in your new department will provide you with plenty of models and a great opportunity to see what other people are teaching. In addition, a temporary adjunct position generally comes with fewer strings than a tenure-track job. Think of it—no committees, no advising, no staff meetings, no million-and-one distractions from teaching! For me it's heaven, although as a gesture of goodwill I do volunteer for committees in which I am interested and attend meetings of general interest in my department. And the thing that most impresses my peers is my commitment to my students, which comes naturally to me. My tenure-track colleagues, running to and from committee meetings, think I am a teaching super-star. Unburdened by many of the extraneous responsibilities they have, I can lavish my attention on preparation for my classes. If you enjoy teaching, these jobs are for you.

Being a gypsy scholar does require some mobility. But what better time to be a gypsy than when you are first out of graduate school? You probably do not own a dog, let alone a home; do not have a spouse, let alone children. Think of the advantages. These one-to-three-year stints will allow you to sample a variety of settings rather than prematurely settling down for life, only to discover that you hate the city—or the country—that you have settled in. They also allow you to sample institutions of various sizes and types of populations. (For instance, I have taught at universities ranging from 1,400 to 40,000 students and now know what type of student and university suits me best.) If you haven't thought about travel, adventure, excitement (and my experience with English Ph.D.'s is that they would rather read it than live it), I encourage you to do so. If you have a yearning to settle down where you did your graduate work, get over it. The smaller the geographical area you consider, the smaller your chances of finding employment. So leave that comfy nest. Stretch your wings.

Of course, for some strange reason, some people do not like to move every few years. I have come to look upon moving as a challenge (and a great opportunity to give to charity old books, out-of-date clothing, and that cookie jar in the shape of a cow that moos when you lift the head). And listen, when in the future will you have so little furniture to move? So get a move on! It takes me an hour tops to pack and unpack all my belongings into a small U-Haul—what grad student has a fridge or washer and drier? Before moving, I usually go to the location of the college and scout around, buy newspapers, and leave my name at various real-estate offices; oftentimes a member of the hiring committee will put me up for a few days or will give me the name of a B&B. Sometimes the university itself can set you up in the house of someone on sabbatical. If you belong to a church, get the nationwide directory and call the branch in your new town. Members of their youth group will descend en masse when your van pulls up and have you unloaded in no time, for the price of pizza and soft drinks. Arrangements for utilities can be set up in advance by phone (another thing to check on when you get to town—find the local telephone office and wrangle a phone book out of them).

In order to facilitate your acclimation, swim at the university's pool, go to church, find a health club, get a therapist, locate a good chiropractor, join a food co-op or a reading group, get an e-mail account—join, join, join. Introduce yourself. Say hi to your fellow colleagues in the hall. Ask to observe the classes of professors who have reputations as effective teachers. Don't be shy. Go to lots of university functions. Give a little "Friendly Friday" at your place when the semester starts (you'll never again have the time)! And bring the department secretary flowers—believe me, she can make you or break you.

And keep thinking of the advantages of the position. You get full benefits (and take advantage of the portable retirement programs). You usually don't vote (or vote on anything momentous)—so you don't make enemies. Everyone likes you because you pose no threat to anyone's territory (just wait till you get a tenure-track job!). If you enjoy teaching, remember that that is what you will get to focus on. And after you have done several of these job assignments, and done them well, you will be the first choice when another faculty member goes on sabbatical or the university has an unplanned resignation for which there is not enough time to do a full search. And whereas being a part-time adjunct seems to confer no status (or even to confer a negative status), a visiting professorship has panache. And getting your next position will be even easier (actually, my one-year offers have always turned into two years), not only because each position increases your network, but also because your colleagues will have seen enough of your work to write you very good teaching evaluations (invite them in to do this, even if the department has not set up a system of teacher observations for visiting faculty). To say nothing of being a known quantity when an opening in your specialty finally arises.

Now that you have opened your mind to the possibility of being a visiting professor, how do you get a position? Naturally you want to search *The Chronicle of Higher Education*. Some departments have anticipated their openings and can advertise in the late fall or early winter, but do not lose hope. Many of these jobs become available very late—in the summer, in fact—due to unforeseen circumstances. Application for a visiting position requires a modification of your standard letter of application. First of all, not that they don't think your dissertation on Shakespeare is the bee's knees, but really, so what? What any department head really dreams of is someone who can write a syllabus, who can deal with students, who can teach—in other words, someone who requires very little (read: no) guidance, supervision, or effort on the part of the department head. So take the page you have written concerning your dissertation and telescope it to a small paragraph and, if possible, show how it will tie in with your teaching (many job advertisements give an idea of the courses you will be teaching). A humongous paragraph on your research may signal a researcher, who will be disappointed/disgruntled in a position that requires intensive student contact. Don't give the impression you might be a petulant pedant! Next, talk up your teaching. Recount a wonderful teaching experience or an effective unit or assignment you have devised. Enclose a particularly creative syllabus, but be careful not to present anything that may not be acceptable to the department. (For instance, some English departments have specifications for the curriculum and methodology of their first-year composition courses.) And enclose testimonials from your colleagues/department head, especially if the school to which you are applying does not require a dossier. And include copies of your particularly stellar computer-generated student evaluation summary sheets too.

If you get an interview, make sure your mind-set is dedicated and professional. Do not tell the hiring committee that you want to rest for a year or two before getting a real job. Do not even think of applying for the job if you want spare time to finish writing your dissertation or novel—heaven forbid you verbalize such fantasies during the interview (I have witnessed this happen). Remember, what the search committee is looking for is an effective teacher who will not bring shame down around their ears by turning out to be incompetent, unsuitable, or disgruntled. These positions are not antecedents to the profession of teaching; they are the profession.

A word about anxiety management. When I got my first temporary assignment, I was, naturally, beset with worries concerning the possibility (or rather, impossibility) of finding my next job—until a friend sat me down and asked me what my worst case scenario was. What was it? I would end up a bag lady, of course! Did that mean, she queried, that if I did not have a job in academia I wouldn't work anywhere? Now, I had pumped gas at my father's Sunoco station as a kid, and since that time had held a variety of inauspicious jobs. If it paid (and it was legal or almost legal), I would do it. I immediately stopped worrying. After all, they were hiring at Taco Bell. And I'd make a great greeter at Wal-Mart! But facing the worst case scenario really helped me put my dilemma in perspective. I would be overqualified, but I'd work no matter what! And if I lived frugally and used my salary (that, after the stipend from grad school, seemed like a fortune) to pay off my loans, I'd be fine. And, in fact, I have managed to put away about $34,000 in mutual funds for retirement and buy a new car (which, after graduate school, I really needed). Besides, a tenure-track position is not without anxieties of its own.

Many graduate programs seem to prepare their graduates for the best case scenario—stepping into a full-time tenure-track position. Temporary positions are beneath contempt, a sign of failure. But if I am failing, I am failing to the tune of an excellent salary and benefits. I pick locations that I like. I am exposed to a variety of teaching models. And I am much happier than most of my cohorts in the field, who feel trapped at institutions they hate in locations they loathe. So consider the job of gypsy scholar!

Life-Path Sexism

Eleanor B. Amico

My career as an academic has never followed a straight path, and I'm still not sure what is around the corner. I have been a full-time mother, a graduate student, a women's studies administrator, a college teacher in religious studies, and an editor. I have been on the job market for the last six years, and I am still looking. I am forty-eight years old. What follows is an attempt to understand my situation. . . .

1980. My daughter is now in kindergarten. Time to think about what will be next. I spend the few hours a day she is in school brushing up on my biblical Hebrew, filling out the charts in job-hunt books, and making lists of possible career moves.

I have an M.A. in religion, Old Testament studies. I got that primarily because I simply could not help myself. I love university life. I love teaching. I love writing. I desperately needed to return to school at that time, and I had decided that someday what I wanted to be was a college professor. I started that degree in 1971, had my first child in 1973, and graduated in 1974.

My first and primary priority, however, was always the dream I, as a child of the fifties and sixties, had grown up with: to be a homemaker and mother. I had bought the "feminine mystique," hook, line, and sinker. But when the new feminist movement came on the horizon, I also bought it. The result was conflict. I knew I was intelligent, I knew I was fascinated by topics outside the realm of my family life, I knew I wanted to teach college someday.

My solution was to stay at home while my children were little, and then, when they entered school, begin a career. It was in many ways a good solution, although, now, looking back, I think I would have liked to stay home a few more years. My children were negotiating the struggles of school; my marriage, as it turned out, was on very shaky footing; and I ended up entering an inordinately stressful graduate program. Not a good combination.

I chose the University of Wisconsin because of my interest in the Old Testament/Hebrew Bible, and while they did not offer a doctorate in religion, they had an excellent program in Hebrew and Semitic studies, and Madison was within commuting distance. I could go to school without uprooting my family.

I still felt young; I was in my mid-thirties. I began in 1981 what would be a grueling process, beginning with a year of undergraduate courses to bring my Hebrew up to par for Madison's graduate program, and resulting in a second M.A. in 1984 and a Ph.D. finally in 1989.

Meanwhile, of course, life goes on. My husband's job necessitated a move, fortunately after most of my course work was finished, so for that first year after the move, I only had to make the longer commute and an overnight stay once a week, and then I was ready to work on my dissertation. However, at that point, my marriage finally fell apart, and I ended up single parenting my two then teenagers through some very rocky years. The move was in 1985. The separation was in 1986, the divorce in 1988, the major parenting crises were between 1988 and 1990. If you compare these dates with the ones in the previous paragraph, you can see I was juggling, bigtime.

But I was lucky enough to land a job in the small university city to which we had moved. My graduate minor was women's studies, and when I found out that the current coordinator of the

Women's Studies Program was leaving the position, I made myself known. I ended up coordinating a barely visible, severely under-funded program on a quarter-time basis. In addition, I also heard that one of the religious studies professors had accepted a position as associate dean. His field was Old Testament. So I contacted him too and ended up with several years of ad hoc teaching in religious studies. Contracted for barely enough time to receive benefits, I was in that category the University of Wisconsin system calls "academic staff." While many of my colleagues were moaning about the strug-gle to get tenure, I was not even on the tenure track!

I was initially told I had not been hired as faculty because I did not have my Ph.D. I got a fellowship and finished my dissertation and degree in 1989. Of course, since then I have found that other people without Ph.D. in hand had been hired as faculty, not only on other campuses but on my own, and then given support to finish their degrees. Next I was told that women's studies could not hire anyone as faculty, since it was not a department and therefore had no faculty who could make tenure decisions. And, of course, all along, there were the budget discussions. Women's studies just was not a priority, not deserving of the kind of funding that would pro-vide the support it needed. Then there was the reasoning that there were so few students in the program: at the time I started, there was no women's studies major and only one student minoring in it. One problem, of course, was that no one was funded to teach the intro-ductory classes. It's a little hard to develop a minor under those conditions! Eventually the dean was convinced to increase my time so that I could teach one of the introductory classes, and finally the other class and the seminar. And the number of students began to soar.

Women's studies then became a presence on the campus; fac-ulty interested in the field began to contact me and became a core of supporters; students began to choose minors in women's studies to complement a variety of majors; word about women's studies classes began to spread so that every class was filled to overflowing; students not even in classes began to contact me for resources. And the interdisciplinary Women's Studies Council, which guided the program, became a much more focused and visible group.

Meanwhile, however, funds in the religious studies department's budget had been cut, and I lost my ad hoc teaching opportunities there. I was still supporting children, and I needed a full-time income. My solution was to obtain an additional job, which I worked for two years, till the fragmentation of time and energy became so frustrating that I quit my other job and determined to live on part-time pay, while searching for a tenure-track position.

Between 1986, when I began at the university, and 1989, when I completed my Ph.D., people were advising me to enter the job market and be prepared to move. But it was not that easy. I had two teenagers at home, both of whom had gone through significant trauma already, and who desperately did not want to move before they finished high school. Again, I put my children first. And I am not sorry about that. But this decision put me in a different class from the "normal" Ph.D. candidate. I chose to remain in my marginal positions and provide what stability I could for my children.

I was also urged to publish, and I understood the importance of this. But I was still working on my dissertation! And one thing I had never had in graduate school was serious mentoring on the publication process and its importance. I really had no one, it felt to me, to help me shape articles in such a way as to be acceptable for scholarly journals. Of course another large part of the problem was that my time and energy were fragmented and limited by the necessity of juggling two separate jobs, running my home as a single parent, and trying to finish my degree.

But finally the day came when our constant cry for a full-time, tenure-track coordinator was heard. A search was to be held. However, because women's studies was not a department with faculty and could not grant tenure, the dean decided to house the program in an existing department on campus, arbitrarily chosen for reasons never clear to anyone else. He began negotiations with this department, the members of which were most unhappy with the prospect of including a faculty member who would contribute nothing to the department's work—whose portfolio would be totally in women's studies. As it turned out, the department, probably as compensation, insisted on and received total control over the search. Looking back at what ensued, it is clear that their top priority was to obtain someone highly published in that department's field.

Thus, although I was the top candidate in the judgment of the Women's Studies Council, when candidates were ranked for the interviewing process, I was nineteenth! My work in building the program, my teaching record, my experience all counted for nothing. I was not even interviewed because I had not published a book. I was fired.

Technically, through an interesting type of contract I had been required to sign for the past eight years of my employment there, I had actually been fired every year. My contracts stipulated that I was hired for nine months, and that my employment would be terminated at the end of that time. Each year I had to reapply for my job, although usually this was somewhat of a technicality. Thus, I had no recourse when it became clear that I would be terminated.

Publish or perish. It used to be the bane of professors at large research universities. Tenure depended on publication of books with the right kinds of publishers, and articles in the right kinds of journals. Now the rules are changing. Now it is not just the large universities that require this kind of publication, but also small, comprehensive schools supposedly devoted to teaching, where faculty are expected, in addition to doing research and publishing, to teach four courses a semester and perform significant community and university service. And, in my case, not being faculty, I did not even have the kind of support faculty can get for research and publication. It was all done on my own time, and I was ineligible for study grants in the summer because, of course, I was not an employee at those times.

And publication is no longer just a requirement for tenure: it has become a requirement for hiring in the first place. It is not that I have no interest in research. My curriculum vitae is filled with papers read, conferences participated in, research done, and work in progress. But none of those has translated, yet, into the proper books and journal articles. And so, by these criteria at least, I was considered unqualified.

I was looking for a tenure-track position with fervor by this time. My last child had finished high school in 1993, and I was ready to move to wherever I could find a position. For three years I have searched (one of them while unemployed), both in religious studies and in women's studies. Now I know that the job market in academe is extremely difficult these days, and my two fields also happen to be particularly crowded. Therefore, it being a buyer's market, for everyone who lands a position, at least ninety-nine do not—so clearly I am not being singled out for failure. I can do the math.

However, as I proceeded through these three years of intense searching, landing two interviews a year but no job, even at the institution I had served for eight years, I began to see a pattern. I have begun to think about something I am calling "life-path sexism." It is, it seems to me, a combination of sexism, ageism, and elitism that is none of these and all of them. I am beginning to suspect that schools, probably unconsciously, are looking for one of two possible candidates. One is someone who, like me, is recently out of graduate school, full of energy and enthusiasm, with lots of potential—oh, and incidentally, unlike me, probably twenty-something. The other is someone near my age (I am now in my late forties), with an academic vita commensurate with a whole career of scholarly work.

I, on the other hand, am a person with a new degree and the academic experiences of a much younger woman, but the life experiences of a middle-aged woman. I have received enough years of evaluations to know that I am an excellent teacher. I have received enough feedback on my administrative skills in coordinating the Women's Studies Program to know that I am also good at that. My conference papers are always very well received. My publications are good, but so far they are limited to book reviews and encyclopedia articles.

Well, one might suggest, I should work on that. And I have continued to do so. But all of this has been done in the context of finishing up the responsibilities I have taken on in my life before academe (child raising) and of trying to put bread on the table on a regular basis. Unemployed, I cared for my ailing mother in exchange for support, and wrote a book. Will this book get published? Will it help me get a job anyway? Who knows?

Now I am working as a commissioned book editor for a publisher of reference books. I receive about half the pay I would expect as a beginning professor, and no benefits. But it is a job, and it allows me to live on my own again for the two years of the contract. And it gives me a year off from the interminable and demoralizing job hunt.

Now I wonder whether it was all worth it. I love the whole educational process. I spent many very difficult years preparing myself for an academic career. But I didn't do it in the right order, apparently. I am being asked to fit into a traditionally male model of professionalism that, in fact, even fits fewer and fewer men in this age of career shifts.

I try to look at it as a challenge and an opportunity to be at my point in life and still facing the unknown. However, it very often does not feel so positive. I am aware that in less than twenty years I will be eligible to retire, and so far I have nothing to retire from. I am aware that eventually I am going to need retirement money, and I do not have much. I have been economically marginal since my divorce, always with the belief that soon I would have a professional position and begin earning enough to save for my retirement, and develop at least some pension. But now I do not even have health insurance. A forty-eight-year-old woman on the market does not face these concerns in the same way as a twenty-eight-year-old.

I believe there may well be a problem of life-path sexism in our colleges and universities, and that it is affecting my life, and preventing me from entering the profession I have chosen and prepared for and want to be a part of. Furthermore, it is preventing potential students and colleagues from receiving the benefit of my knowledge and experience, both of which have been enhanced by the path my life has taken.

The Job Search As Career: 1983–1997

Allen G. Hunt

Introduction

In 1983 I received the degree of Ph.D. in theoretical condensed matter physics from the University of California, Riverside, although then we simply called the field solid state theory, and usually said "a Ph.D." We used to make lighthearted jokes about Ph.D. really meaning "piled higher and deeper." In 1995 I returned to school at Duke University in the Department of Geology to work on a second Ph.D.; and although I have been here only one year, it has sufficed to have me reassigned to the master's degree program. I should receive this degree in December, and will be actively seeking a job by August at the latest.

My views and the apparent views of potential employers regarding my qualifications have diverged during this thirteen-year period. In the beginning of my career we agreed that my qualifications were promising but unproven; now we don't agree on this.

And over this time the academic job search has become an odd one. Instead of providing value for money, the searcher is supposed to provide money-value, making the meaning of "value" equivalent to the worth of a commodity, or better a bond, which should go on producing dividends for its lifetime. As a corollary, older job seekers (as well as students) are regarded as shorter-term bonds, with a higher associated credit risk. Thus retraining is not usually regarded as an asset. In applications for academic positions one is judged chiefly on one's grantsmanship, a word which probably did not exist ten years ago. The process of applying for grants, with its emphasis on describing exactly all the ramifications of the project, leads to incrementalism in scientific research—or merely filling in the holes. This strategy for research fits in nicely with the emphasis on generating dollars for ideas; an idea can best be sold as a grant proposal if it is shown that the associated research can be carried to a conclusion on schedule and if all ramifications of the research can be enumerated.

In turn, criteria formerly applied to professors are now applied to students. Nowadays, "prospects" are offered graduate student "positions" based on their ability to provide value (published research leading to financial support of the professor and institution) for money, not on nebulous criteria of academic promise, and the traditional academic apprenticeship of graduate study has been redefined as an internship.

A number of phrases from competitive sports and business are also entering the vocabulary of young professors. These include "track record," "proven track record," "team player," "go-getter," "competitive edge," "research endeavor," "downsizing," "entrepreneurship," "vision," "leadership," "communicate your ideas," "sell your ideas," "marketplace of ideas," "networking," "meet the needs of," "return on our investment," "accountability," "communication skills," "interpersonal skills," "time budgeting," as well as such standbys as "grantsmanship" and "prospects," already mentioned. This list is just the tip of the iceberg, which underscores how much the academic market in the sciences resembles a more corporate model now.

History

I estimate that I have spent nearly one year of full-time work searching for steady employment since early 1983. As I have had steady employment during two one-year periods since then, a Fulbright fellowship for two years, and part-time work for the rest, it seems to me that there may be great inefficiency in the search for a job. Of course this inefficiency is presumed to reduce any subsequent inefficiency *on* the job by matching precisely the candidates' qualifications with universities' needs. During graduate school, I spent much time earning money, mostly by teaching part-time at local colleges and universities. This was not an absolute necessity, although it seemed to be a good "investment" at the time. The very word, "investment," of course, is merely my current description; at the time I would have said "experience."

After receiving my doctorate in 1983, I continued teaching part-time and then full-time while applying for industry and academic jobs. I spent two years in Germany on a Fulbright and published collaborative research articles with my former advisor. My most successful year of job-hunting (1988–89) yielded an offer for a temporary teaching job, which required a cross-country move, and an offer to supervise the physics education at an Air Force base. I turned both offers down. I wouldn't relocate for a temporary position and I didn't want to be an administrator. By then I had applied for over fifty positions over a five-year search, and had enlisted the help of a professional résumé writer.

In 1990 I became fully independent in research. This transition was, however, somewhat painful, as it led to a conflict between me and my dissertation advisor which took several years to put aside. In the next five years I published over thirty-five articles as sole author in some of the most important physics journals (but not *Physical Review*). I found part-time work at California State University, Fullerton, where I taught on average about eight hours a week for the next two years. I also resumed teaching at Loma Linda University where I had taught in 1984, which was now being divided into two schools. At the same time I was translating German industrial guidelines from German into English for the Association of German Engineers. With this whirlwind of activity, I was sure that I could begin to attract attention in my applications.

In spring 1990 I applied to the South Dakota School of Mines and Technology. The department chairman was enthusiastic about my application and tried to reach me by telephone. I was never home when he called, and I had not believed in the value of an answering machine, so we never connected. I applied there again in 1991, and was interviewed, but did not receive an offer. I had at that time some eighteen publications, but the faculty preferred a physicist from the former Soviet Union who had over forty publications as well as approximately fifteen years of experience as a professor. The experience was interesting for other reasons, however. I was uniformly favored by the students, and detested by the administration. I relate this story because it bears on uncertainties in interviewing techniques. In books that I had read, I had learned that blue pinstriped suits were considered inappropriate for academic jobs, as were jeans and T-shirts. So I compromised. I bought a new pair of slacks, a new shirt, a burgundy sports coat, and new socks, and polished up my dress shoes. I ironed my shirt before I went to bed, and I ironed it again the next morning.

Between 10:30 and 11:00 I was scheduled to meet the vice-president (for academic affairs, I believe). He was fifteen minutes late for the meeting on account of a phone call. Then he invited me into his office and asked me what my dissertation research concerned. I said it was about the Coulomb gap in disordered insulators. He asked me what the Coulomb gap was, and I explained that localized electrons in disordered semiconductors repelled one another; the (Coulomb) energy gap arose from subsequent transport of an electron into the proximity of other electrons, which was resisted through the electronic repulsion. This explanation took about one minute. Then the vice president started to tell me about his modeling of the magnetic moment of the electron, and said it was really just an escape, not intended to produce any meaningful results. I unfortunately do not remember what I said next exactly, but it was certainly intended to be neutral. He continued to talk about his model for about five more minutes. Then he received another phone call and ushered me out of his office.

My next "interview" was with the president, who discussed his business ventures as president, including some large land transfers, for the next thirty minutes. I listened politely, although with little enthusiasm. I had expected something regarding the objectives of the university, the means by which they might be accomplished, the role of the physics program, the interaction of the administration with the faculty, the expectations of the administration, and so forth. When I did not receive the job, I called the department chairman to find out what the decision was based on. He told me that the faculty had ranked me second, while the administration had ranked me last. According to the administration I had not even taken the position seriously enough to buy appropriate clothes. The faculty had worried more about the absence of a letter from my dissertation advisor (which had occurred because of the conflict mentioned above).

In the following year my applications did not generate an interview in physics. In January of that year, I was in the physical sciences library of the University of California at Riverside. I saw someone I knew vaguely, although I did not know exactly what his position was. In a spirit of euphoria, I pulled out five issues of the most recent physics journals (unbound) and showed him an article of mine in each. He asked me if I would give him a copy of a résumé and a publication list. I did so. Shortly thereafter he asked me if I wanted a post-doctoral appointment in soil sciences. I dithered awhile, but when it became clear that I was not generating any employment in physics, I said yes. I started with him in September, 1992. This position was for one-to-two years. As it turned out, the grant was not renewed, and I worked only one year full-time. There was enough money for me to work a second year at 20 percent. In the second year, I concentrated on my own research, while my advisor concentrated on job hunting. At the end of this year, summer 1994, my post-doctoral advisor left for Duke University. I applied for yet another tenure-track position, at California State University, Fullerton, as well as for many others, but was not successful. I returned to teaching part-time, coincidentally at the university where I had begun teaching fifteen years before (when I had just received my master's degree). This was peculiarly significant to me.

In October of 1994 my contact at Duke convinced me to apply for a student position at Duke in the department of civil and environmental engineering, where he was now associate professor. He thought that I could get a Ph.D. in a very short time doing groundwater physics (because calculations of transport coefficients using percolation theory apply to these disordered systems also), and be supported by his department. I applied, retook the GRE (scored 1,510), and was accepted into the program, but not funded, because I was too old (the department wanted to spend its resources on younger prospects). So my contact got in touch with a professor of geology, who was himself a former physicist, and they tried to interest me in a plan to get me a second Ph.D. in geology. I bit.

I arrived at Duke in the summer of 1995, expecting a quick Ph.D. in geology. The time frame had never been discussed specifically, however, so we had conflicts from the start. My wife lives in California, and I was not prepared to commit to an indefinite time span. Now we have decided to salvage a "professional" master's degree from our investments in each other and the program. I did, however, try one final approach. I attempted to get admitted to graduate school in geology at the California Institute of Technology, within driving distance of my home, but was turned down. I was told that Caltech was not in the business of retraining people to make them employable, and that I did not have a sufficiently long and productive career in front of me to make the retraining worthwhile anyway. The fact that I had published nearly forty articles in the last five years did not sway them. In fact, a look at one of my articles was sufficient to convince them that I certainly did not need Caltech. I was told many times that "this is a free country," an aspect of political ideology the applicability of which to my career was not obvious to me.

Now I am forty-one years old, pursuing a master's degree in

geology, and I do not know what I will do with it when I get it. From what I can see about the job market, there is very little chance that this additional education will increase my opportunities for academic employment, and its impact on industrial positions is also uncertain. The only chance that appears to exist may arise from the annual Exxon interviews of graduate students. Every year, a representative of Exxon comes to Duke in October to check out the geology student talent pool and interview anyone interested in joining Exxon. At the moment that seems to be the most likely opportunity, because my work in groundwater hydrology should be of interest in reference to the problem of petroleum extraction, and my (new) experience in seismology and general geology is relevant to petroleum exploration.

Lessons and Uncertainties

There are several perspectives from which to consider this history. If you regard my financial security as the goal of the job search, then this search obviously has not been successful. If the objective was to find the job for which I was best suited, then the answer is uncertain. It has always been my feeling that the purpose of an educational system is to educate students—a form of service to future generations, of building for the future. This no longer seems to be the main emphasis of physical science divisions at the university, where one most often hears of ''competitive edge'' as a reason for quality education. Perhaps these various institutions were right not to offer me a job, and the limits of my search constrained my opportunities. This interpretation seems to me to be very unrealistic, personally and institutionally, unless the main purpose of the university has now become to survive. My career decisions have certainly contributed to a great deal of personal growth, so that I am now in a much better position to do students an educational service than I ever have been. People also grow into jobs: I would have undoubtedly made advances under other circumstances as well, and

I would have been paid. Also, there would be a better chance of continuing to work in an environment in which I could be of service. So a neutral evaluator of my career would probably say that the experience has not, as yet, been worth the years of effort.

If one agrees that this search has, up to now, had a negative outcome, what could be the lessons learned from it? These are numerous:

1. Plan for a career while still a student. Many authors have outlined this process, and I will not add to it.
2. Be aware of changes in the market. In my case these included profound changes in emphasis, from research and teaching to earning a school money, as well as more mundane changes, such as obtaining word processing abilities and an answering machine.
3. Be aware of the subtleties of academic connections. In my case, the most important journal was *Physical Review*, and the most important venue was the March meeting of the American Physical Society. The most important people, however, I have not incorporated among my circle of respected and respecting colleagues to this day. I am not certain I know who they are.
4. Emphasize successful grant applications over publications; make sure that your publications help you get your grant applications funded.
5. Do not alienate your dissertation advisor, or other potential recommenders. This advice is so basic, one might wonder why I give it. I do this from my own experience. Swallow your pride when necessary. I, of course, cannot tell you when this is necessary, as I could not recognize the events in my own life until they were past.
6. Do not teach part-time for a long period. This creates the impression that you are incapable of generating income, and thus have not met the only standard that does not need to be evaluated neutrally or in depth (as do the quality of the published article, the quality of the jour-

nal, the quality of the refereeing, the quality of the venue, the "level of the competition," etc.). You become known as a "part-timer," another word for the modern intellectual lower class. The business designation, "temp," has not caught on (which may seem strange), although part-time employees are always temporary employees. The reason for this, I assume, is because a "temp" employee has a function, only his or her lifespan is uncertain. Part-timers are part-time in a second respect. They are known to have a short lifetime as part-timers before they are replaced by the next generation, i.e. they are on the way down. And this classification emphasizes that they were, from the very beginning, different. They are not ordinary employees who suddenly became temporary. They simply never made it. I have been advised to avoid the classification "part-time lecturer" in my vita, although using "part-time" lecturer when it was accurate would have allowed the distinction of being able to write "lecturer" when I had a full-time temporary position.

7. Recognize the corporate mentality that is permeating the academic job search. This means that there is an extraordinary emphasis on your ability to be a "team player," a concept whose increasing emphasis simply sticks in my throat. I do not see education as a political compromise, or as a business, or as a hierarchy; the future, i.e. the students, must always be the raison d'être of a university. But typical search committee members, and especially deans and administrators, imagine a rather different purpose for the university.

8. Recognize the importance of prestige, or stature. Prestige and stature are conferred upon you mainly through association with important people or institutions. People with stature may be instantly recognized. They occupy chairs, or have won prizes or scholarships, or have given lectures that are named after people. Even if neither

name means anything to you, these people have some
stature, and may diffuse some of it to you. Of course,
in physics, Nobel is one name that everyone recognizes.
Thus, it has now become important to receive a recommendation from someone with a Nobel Prize. Equally
useful is to receive a recommendation from someone
who was an early supervisor or colleague of a Nobel
Prize winner, and who can say about you that you are
at a similar stage in your career as the Nobel Prize winner was at that age.

9. Wear the appropriate clothing to an interview. I did not
know what clothing was appropriate. I followed the advice of eschewing the "Wall Street" corporate look. But
in some academic environments, this may be more appropriate than you think, particularly when the school is
in the Midwest, has a strong engineering background,
and is trying to emphasize its business skills. Of course,
this last piece of information would not have been easy
to obtain without actually visiting the school.

All of these lessons require adaptation to a market and to a
potential employer. Of course it is ridiculous to expect that you can
really adapt yourself (unless you have no strong personal convic-
tions) to each employer, university, and department to which you
are going to apply for a job, just as it is ridiculous to imagine that
you can provide for the needs of all the organizations to which you
apply for grants. You want them to believe that maybe you can, so
that they will think that if they grant the money, or if they hire you,
they can exploit your feelings of indebtedness as well as your de-
pendency. After all, they have invested in you (not really hired you,
and not because you showed that you can comprehend, discover,
and teach), and you must continue to give a return on that investment. This control is implemented through the tenure evaluation
process, in which financial contributions to the university are rated
most highly. In fact some universities have used as a criterion for
hiring in the physical sciences that a potential faculty member be a

source of sufficient income to the university to balance his/her perceived financial burden, specifically a quotient of the operating costs of the university and the number of dependent faculty members.

The changes in the academic environment and in the qualities sought in job candidates are illustrated by my fortunes in the job search, which initially rose and then declined, although my qualifications continued to improve dramatically. Of course there is an additional influence: the increasing period of time since I obtained my Ph.D. undoubtedly generated distrust. I imagine that my representation of the academic job market and search will tend to turn off exactly those people I personally would like to see successful in their search for employment, those whose purpose is to serve the needs of students. But this is not my objective. Actually, I hoped in this essay to outline the present realities of academic life and employment, so that others could better prepare themselves for this challenge. Maybe, unlike me, they can understand how to "play the game," without compromising the interests of a real education and its less tangible benefits for future generations.

Ordinary Women:
Teaching at the County Jail

Christina Boufis

One out of every two hundred people residing in the state of California lives or works in a correctional facility, and I am one of those people. Trained as a Victorian scholar, with a minor in women's studies, I teach GED preparation to women at the San Francisco County Jail. In some ways it seems strange that I should be doing this; both the educational level (high school not college) and the location (jail not university) are far different from any job I imagined myself getting after I completed my Ph.D. But given the reality of the job market—there are only a handful of positions for new Ph.D.'s, and employment opportunities in the California penal system are at a record high—it seemed only logical. Furthermore, with women as the fastest growing segment of the inmate population—and I teach only women— I can put my academic feminist principles into practice: to teach, to listen, to learn, to help.

I began teaching in the jail as a substitute, taking over from a man who needed a break, and who was more than eager to turn his class over to me. Before I could start, however, I had to go through a security clearance process and study the pages of rules (for the inmates and myself) given to me by the assistant coordinator of inmate programs, a woman I'll call Cassandra. Explaining the punishment system, a combination of treatment and accountability for crime, she informed me that this jail was different from many others; inmates were expected, nay required, to participate in programs, and education was one of them. Though the Sheriff's Department per se had no money to spend on education, programs such as the one in which I would be teaching were funded by various community colleges. Both men's and women's adult basic education, GED, and ESL classes were staffed by low-paid part-time adjuncts. Knowing full well that I would be working far more than I would be compensated for—as indeed is the case with all adjuncts—I nevertheless felt that I'd rather be exploited teaching at the jail than teaching anywhere else. And even on the most difficult of days, when I feel that I am pushing a rock uphill and my twenty-five students are doing their best to push it back down, I still feel that way.

My introduction to the students came when I observed the last class taught by the previous teacher. When Cassandra and I entered the classroom, I was shocked to see everyone wearing bright orange sweatpants and sweatshirts; the students looked like fluorescent ice pops. And the class appeared to be in a constant state of chaos. There were twenty-four students, some working on math problems, others passing papers, a few reading magazines, one student who looked like she was crying, and one sprawled out over several desks in what appeared to be a prone sleeping position. Cassandra immediately interrogated one student as to why she wasn't working, and the woman responded that she didn't have to answer her if she didn't want to. "That's not an appropriate way to talk to me," Cassandra replied. The student became even more heated and started telling all her classmates that she didn't have to talk to Cassandra or anyone else if she didn't want to. Cassandra radioed to request a movement deputy to come and escort the woman out of the room.

After this disturbance, the class quieted down and returned to the lesson they were doing on the human reproductive system. "How many of you women have had children?" their teacher asked.

Twenty out of the twenty-four raised their hands. They next read a short passage and answered a few comprehension questions, which were fairly straightforward. But two women keep motioning for help. "Mr. Man, Mr. Man," they called—which was a shortened version of their teacher's last name, but also an indisputable fact— "we're tripping on this word here." Mr. Man went over to help them figure out the word they were having trouble with. The term was "amniotic sac." I was hooked.

After class, Cassandra explained the punishment system to me again—changing the behavior of the inmates through treatment and accountability—something I agreed with in theory, but hoped I would not be called upon to enforce. I was a teacher, not a jailer, after all, and I believed in a non-hierarchical classroom where all authority (including my own) was decentered and shared. Besides, they were students to me, not inmates. "Now, they know the rules, so don't be afraid to write them up, " she told me on the first day. "If one girl slaps another one across the face, you write her up. If they curse, you also give them a notice of rule violation. Then they'll lose their privileges," which meant no phone, no visits, and most importantly, no commissary, where they were allowed to buy candy once a week. As many of them were former substance abusers, such sugar restrictions were considered severe punishment. I didn't feel comfortable writing anyone up for anything.

Cassandra then went on to explain a little about how the women lived in circular units called pods. There were no bars or locks on the doors; apparently, no one could do anything they shouldn't in this nonlinear setup. I would have women from two pods in my class, both those who were required to participate in a drug treatment program, and those who weren't. I assumed that more than half of the students wouldn't necessarily want to go to class, but everyone had to sign a contract in this jail, so they were forced to participate. I would have no murderers in my class, Cassandra assured me in what I thought was an attempt at humor. "We keep them on the seventh floor," she added. I thought of all the years I'd been teaching—one year in a New York City high school before I returned to graduate school, six years at a local college "apprenticing" as it were, while I was a graduate student—and though nothing specifically had prepared me to teach at the jail, nothing in my training, I felt, was inconsistent with it either. Besides the teacher part, the reformer in me, steeped in Dickens and Victorian literature, took over: I was there to help; the system was to blame. But as if reading my thoughts, Cassandra warned me, "Now, they're all here because they did something. Don't forget it. They've committed some crime."

My first day of teaching, I am late and disoriented. I enter the jail to find all the corridors strangely unlit and spookily quiet. I find out that there is an Eddie Murphy movie being filmed in the jail, which accounts for the fact that the parking lot (and all street parking for blocks) was filled. Nothing seems real yet in this liminal space; the new facility, built only two years ago, feels like it is part school (with a sometimes overwhelming smell of industrial-strength macaroni and cheese wafting down the hall), part jail, and now part movie set. I am equally uncertain about how to address my students: their former teacher called them "ladies" all the time; to me the term smacks too much of Victorian class divisions. I settle for "class" and recognize the irony.

The students are there when I arrive, and one, Nina S., is sitting in the classroom pretending to smoke a tampon. I choose to ignore this, and hand out math exercises (though I've never taught math) that I think are easier than the ones they were doing when I observed them. But they're not. Many students claim they don't know their multiplication tables. Many others say they don't want to work, and that they don't have to (clearly a rule violation), and others keep asking where their former teacher went. Others want to know if I've seen Eddie Murphy, and when I tell them I haven't, they look away, slightly disgusted and even more uninterested. I am losing control. I'm worried I will have to radio for a deputy. I think how foolish I was to think about feminism or Victorianism or about putting any ideas into practice. These women are not my sisters, I think. They don't care that we are all women in this classroom, all here together. I think I have made a big mistake. I panic, then I decide to hand out a Lucille Clifton poem I brought called ''The Thirty Eighth Year of My Life.'' We read the poem and the class is relatively quiet. They're paying attention; they even respond to my questions, and some of the students are amazed by the mere fact that the speaker has survived to be thirty-eight. We write a response to the poem about what it means to be a woman at this time, in this country, at this point in their lives. And though the speaker in the poem is bemoaning her ordinariness, her plainness, most of the women write poems praising the ordinary; this is what they want to be. Drugs have made them different, but they want to be as ordinary as the woman they read about: just an ordinary woman in jail, arrested for carjacking and assault, caught with drugs, at nineteen, and with two kids, one woman writes. I have succeeded somewhat in reaching them, but still I feel disappointed; I can't forget Nina S. with her tampon, and I think that this is not the great feminist moment of recognition I had hoped for when I handed out the poem. I wonder at my idealism, my naïveté, my hope. I leave exhausted and read a couple of the poems that a few students handed me on the way out. There are several on masturbation, and I feel as foolish as I did when I asked them if they expected their lives to turn out a certain way, the very question that the speaker in the poem asks herself. ''Did I expect to be a homosexual in jail?'' Nina says to me contemptuously, ''No, I didn't expect to be no homosexual in jail, but I was a homosexual before I was in jail.'' The woman sitting next to her laughs.

When I return two days later, the students tell me they liked the poem I brought them the other day. Some have even brought poems and letters they want me to read. One woman shows me a letter from her daughter, who writes that she wants to help her mother get through her time in jail, that she's not angry with her, but that she's proud her mother is getting help. The daughter, who sounds remarkably mature for her age, is only fourteen, and is expecting a child of her own, her mother adds. Another woman shows me a letter to her two-year-old son that she hopes he will keep until he is able to read; she isn't sure where he is, or if she will be able to get him back from foster care when she gets out of jail, but she wants him to know she cares. I abandon the math exercises I have prepared and turn instead to some poems by Langston Hughes. I tell them how good they are at interpreting poetry. It's true; they have a razorlike sharpness about sensing emotion in these poems. But Nina S. won't look at me. She won't accept any of the Xeroxes I hand out.

We next read oral histories dictated by homeless people who live in a nearby shelter. My students immediately pick up on the lingo of recovery, and what's more, they completely identify with the autobiographical speaker. They call her a sister. It dawns on me that this is also the acronym for one of the drug treatment programs many of the women participate in—Sisters In Sober Treatment Empowered in Recovery—and that this is probably one of the primary ways they define sisterhood. It certainly never occurred to me to include recovery in any definition of feminism, and suddenly I'm enlightened. I hand out multiplication tables at the end of class, and everyone takes one.

The class tells me that their former teacher always showed movies on Friday (an untruth, I later find out) so I promise to bring them a film the following week if we get through enough work. We each keep our end of the bargain, but I'm nervous about my choice of movie. I planned to show *Sarafina*, but I also have *Waiting to Exhale* as a backup, though I could not in all good conscience show the latter one; I thought the characters so far removed from my students' lives. When I tell Cassandra about the movie, she disapproves; she thinks showing movies wastes a good day. I tell her I disagree, and I list my choices, including how skeptical I am of *Waiting to Exhale*. She tells me that she really liked it, and that her mother was just like one of the characters in the movie. A faux pas. I am already self-conscious about my position; I'm a white woman talking to the assistant coordinator of programs, who is an African-American woman, telling her what kind of movie I think my predominantely African-American students should watch. I kind of dislike myself at this moment: I'm uncomfortable; I question my motives for showing each movie, and for taking race into account. I don't know how not to, and I don't know how to, it seems. I wasn't trained for this, I think, and try to see if I can remember something helpful from one of my women's studies classes. Nothing specific comes to mind.

But luckily, a different program director approves of *Sarafina*. I agree to show half of it and discuss it. I don't; I show the whole thing in one day. The students are grateful that I kept my word about bringing them a movie. We sit with the lights out (the surveillance cameras are still on, of course) and they fill out the question work sheet I prepared for them. But they are visibly disturbed by all the violence, especially when one young boy gets shot. And they are moved by the scene when Sarafina gets out of prison and goes directly to her mother. "I came to you first," the character says as she embraces her mother. My students all nod in agreement. "Where else but to your mama?" Sarafina's mother replies. "That's right," one of my students chimes in, "where else?"

When I leave for the day I notice the deputies in the control room watching the women in the pods; I can see them all moving in their circular dorms: black and white shapes on the screen. From the 101 freeway in San Francisco, you can see these semicircular pods with opaque glass and tiny slivers of windows that form the new jail. I had never really noticed this building before, but now I can't get this vaguely menacing structure out of my mind. Zooming along on the highway, I feel only the magnitude of the building and its mixed message: we can sort of see in, and, I assume, they can vaguely see out; but not really. One of my students says she spends her days trying to peer through the cracks. I ask her what she is going to do when she gets out; she tells me emphatically that she is going to walk right down the middle of the freeway.

When the semester ends, I am asked to teach through the summer in a program that is funded by a different community college and which, incidentally, pays far less. I decline, deciding I need the time to return to my academic work and think about my "career." I also decline an NEH summer seminar for similar reasons: no longer certain about the Victorian scholar path I once was on, I feel I would be attending the seminar under false pretenses. It isn't that I have decided to leave academia altogether—though the tight job market and the different path I'm taking at the moment may decide that for me—it's just that the route I had planned suddenly seems too narrow. Teaching at the jail, I feel more connected to some of the material I studied in graduate school, and more like I am living the knowledge I have gained. At this point, I'm not sure if I would feel similarly as an assistant professor teaching Victorian literature, and I'm not even certain anymore that I want to find out. I am certain of only one thing: that I want to teach again at the jail, and I tell the program coordinators that I will return in the fall.

Before the next semester begins, I am offered two other adjunct teaching positions in two different departments at two colleges. Unable to find even part-time teaching when I first moved to San Francisco two years ago, it is ironic that now I have to choose between several classes, all of which conflict with the daily teaching schedule required at the jail. I hesitate only briefly. I have thought a lot about these women over the summer, and want to have my own class for the entire semester. I give little thought to how this may look on my c.v., or how I may be ruining my chances for a full-time position by turning down a part-time position in an English department where I desperately wanted to work. Something tugs at me at the jail; something feels unfinished there.

When I return in late August, I see many familiar faces, and lots of new ones. I think about the incredibly high rate of recidivism, particularly for women, and recall how many of my students have told me they are afraid to be released from jail for fear they will get "in trouble again"—start selling drugs or their bodies or end up with the wrong people at the wrong place and time. I tell them a million times that education is the key and the only way out, and in my heart of hearts I believe that. I suppose that is why I am still teaching, and still teaching at the jail. "If prison guards were required to hold doctorates," Louis Menand has recently written, referring to California's 40 percent increase in expenditures on corrections (compared with the state's 29 percent reduction in higher education in the same five-year period), "the academic placement rate could be reversed overnight."[1] If that were the case, I wonder if the recidivist rate could be magically reversed as well, and if my students would indeed have the chance to lead ordinary lives like the ordinary women they yearn so desperately to be.

Notes

[1] Louis Menand, "How to Make a Ph.D. Matter," *New York Times Magazine* (September 9, 1996), pp. 78–82.

Seven

Alternative Careers

Introduction

Christina Boufis
Institute for Research on Women and Gender,
Stanford University

areer? What career, you may very well ask when, for a number of reasons, you find yourself at the crossroads of academia and some unknown, unmarked territory. The doubt about what may lie ahead, and the regret about the academic road that wasn't, is more than enough to leave many new Ph.D.'s both bitter and unsure about their ability—and marketability—in any profession. And who wouldn't be? Having spent the better part of one's youth in graduate school, having thought that completing the degree, impossible as it seemed at times, would guarantee a teaching position and place in the profession, who would not shrink from the cruel possibility that the long-awaited career you had trained so long to enter was over before it even started?

But this is not entirely true. For the good news from the essayists in this section is that after getting through the initial pain and disappointment of not using one's Ph.D. in the traditional sense— and by not dwelling on it here, I don't mean to minimize the intensity of this pain—there are other alternatives, and they are not as gloomy or devoid of intellectual satisfaction as one might imagine. Nor does switching fields necessarily mean that one must leave ac-

265

ademia altogether. In fact, as Eliene Augenbraun and Adam Bresnick make clear, the outcome of "unsuccessful" job searches can lead to a rethinking of one's relationship to the academy, a process that in many ways can be both liberating and empowering.

Perhaps the first step in thinking about other options is to set about exploring with as open a mind as possible. This may sound trite, but I know from personal experience that the tendency is to do the opposite: to be extra hard on oneself, to go around singing the "what am I going to do with my life" melody every hour of every day, thinking all the while that you're about ten years too late. It's especially helpful if your friends are going through the same thing that you are at this point. I was very lucky in this respect; the writing group I belonged to during my dissertation writing days became an incredible source of support when many of us began to contemplate other careers. If you don't have such a group, you can form one or a similar one, as Augenbraun did when she worked to establish support systems for post-doctoral scientists. Or you can try to lobby for departmental or school-wide seminars on alternative career options for new Ph.D.'s in your field, which might include inviting alumni who are not in tenure-track teaching jobs in the field of their degree. If you can't get institutional support through seminars and professional organizations, at least try to find friends to shore up your self-esteem. This is particularly critical on those days when you've spent the morning looking for employment and convincing yourself that you have no marketable skills.

This secret belief—that you possess no skills at all or none that would be good to anyone at all—seems to strike especially hard when you try to turn your c.v. into a résumé. But all those who have written a dissertation usually have exceptional research and writing skills; they can also conceptualize, organize, and synthesize lots of complex information—skills that are valuable in any field. The problem may be in translating these "academic" skills into the business language a résumé requires.

Career placement centers, both your own or a nearby university's, are useful here. Despite the horror of having to sit with people much younger than you, these offices often have contact files, samples of résumés, and even pamphlets about who is hiring recent Ph.D.'s (as was the case with my local university). There are also many private employment agencies—where you don't have to sit with recent undergrads and where everyone is in a career transition—that can provide similar services, usually for a fee. It is best to approach these places with the somewhat detached attitude of a researcher, if you can. Remember that you are investigating options, not making major life decisions, at this point. It also helps to think in terms of jobs rather than careers: having invested so much in preparing oneself for a career that didn't lead to a promised job, the essayists in this section demonstrate that the opposite holds true as well—that taking a non-academic job may instead lead to a very fulfilling career.

What's important to keep in mind throughout this process is that while such rethinking often brings up a lot of doubts and insecurities, it also affords you the opportunity to use those skills or parts of yourself that may have been underutilized in graduate school, such as artistic ability, in Augenbraun's case, or computational linguistics, in Brian Ulicny's. Trained to do one thing for so long, we are actually amazed to find that we can do other things, and do them well. It may take additional training to develop or sharpen specific skills that employers want, but as Ulicny explains, the time spent may indeed be what gets you a job.

Indefatigable persistence (and the need to find a way to keep eating) does pay off. Eventually, one does get an interview which leads to a job, which then may lead to another job, which then may lead to fashioning a new career. There is no predicting the play of circumstances that can lead to finding satisfying work. Nor is there only one way. I found my current teaching position through a seemingly circuitous route that began when I volunteered to teach literacy at the local library. Augenbraun writes of the "happy accidents"—including the fortuitous rearranging of offices at work—that helped turn her degree in cell biology into a career in political science and media. While it helps to be in the right place at the right time, it is also important to do things you haven't done before, from volunteering, to taking a job you might not have previously considered, to talking to people in non-academic fields, and lastly, to allowing yourself to imagine other possibilities and other careers. Victoria Olsen found an alternative career where she least expected it, in motherhood, which allows her to reexamine her own and society's ideas about professional identities.

Finally, not having a full-time tenure-track teaching position does not necessarily mean that the door to academia is forever closed. Your degree and years of learning are not things bestowed on you that vanish when you leave the academy, though it may feel that way. You can, as Augenbraun and Bresnick did, find new ways of reconnecting to the profession, ways which feel even more complete and satisfying because you created them yourself.

If You Can't Join Them, Beat Them

Eliene Augenbraun

Transitioning into Transition

I felt like a star. Top of the world. A medical degree, a Ph.D. in cell biology, a post-doctoral fellowship, and my own post-doc grant. A great post-doc project. Wow! Life was great!

But my "high" didn't last. My graduate school advisor, whom I admired, committed suicide. My "great" post-doc project turned out not to be so great. I realized that after nearly fourteen years of lab work I was tired of it. Burned out. And that my interests were shifting away from the lab toward media and organizational problems. I took a year off the hard career track to decide what to do.

Thin Envelopes and Thick Skin

First, I tried to fit myself into many jobs for which I thought I had talent and training. I turned my c.v. into a résumé, wrote cover letters, and sent out dozens of job applications. Two- and four-year colleges, science museums, science news services, pharmaceutical and health insurance companies, management consulting firms, multimedia developers, environmental groups, technology transfer departments in law firms, financial firms, and many others received the most carefully crafted and personalized cover letters I could then imagine, my résumé, and appropriate writing samples or statements of purpose.

I got nothing back but a fourteen-inch pile of rejection letters and one interview, which went miserably. Uh-oh.

Drawing on Everything

It was back to the drawing board. Literally. For many years I had freelanced as a medical/scientific illustrator. I still was doing it part-time to make ends meet. I leveraged my illustration/design experience (not my Ph.D.) into an internship at a science museum. Before long, I was making my post-doc salary working twenty-five to forty hours a week as an artist. (What does that say about the pay of biology post-docs?) I took advantage of my extra time to volunteer, write more job applications, and read in fields I considered entering. I spent an hour or two a day on the Internet. But mostly, I just decompressed from having worked so hard during the last sixteen years of my post-secondary education and training.

In a couple of months I started generating interviews, and a couple months later one led to a science policy fellowship. The American Association for the Advancement of Science (AAAS) runs a program to bring scientists of all ages and from all disciplines to Washington, D.C. Diplomacy fellows, like me, work at the U.S. Agency for International Development (USAID) or the State Department. There are also congressional and executive branch fellows.

I work on international science policy issues: science communications, emerging and reemerging infectious diseases, crisis prevention, and human resource policies. I write policy analyses and briefing memoranda for senior management at the agency and interact with other U.S. government agencies and counterparts in other governments. I travel to places you read about in the newspapers, meet with amazing people, and learn firsthand about the issues on which I advise policy makers back home. The fellowship lasts for two years, and then? During these years of government downsizing and furloughs, it is very hard to imagine that I will be able to progress professionally in this field. But at least I am learning enough to do many different things. In the middle of my second year, I realize how much I am a part of the growing community of scientists in transition.

Besides my day job at USAID I still do work for which I receive no salary. For a while, whenever I got a(nother) thin envelope, I worked even harder on young scientist career issues, my unpaid work of choice. I am (still) working to change policies that make work life and career transitions difficult for scientists. In 1993, my colleagues and I formed the Johns Hopkins School of Medicine Postdoctoral Association. Working with the administration and faculty, we developed policies to improve the lives of post-doctoral researchers: minimum salary and benefits guidelines, parking privileges, and access to the sports facilities. In 1995, I organized a conference call for a dozen young scientist activists throughout the country. We formed the Association of Science Professionals, the first national, multidisciplinary, young scientist policy organization in America. We advise policy makers, professional societies, and science funders. We give talks at professional society meetings and federal institutions (the AAAS annual meeting, the National Academy of Sciences, the National Institutes of Health, and the National Science Foundation, to name but a few). Because of these activities I have been invited to do all sorts of fun things—like appear as a guest on National Public Radio's *Talk of the Nation Science Friday*, a call-in show for science issues (more on that later).

Bite (Byte?) and Switch

In looking back at all the challenges and twists and turns of my career, I realize that though things did not turn out the way I expected they would, I am pleased—no, amazed!—by my career. I am taking bites out of life that I never would have—or could have—on the academic track. Why am I amazed? We all know that crossing disciplines is a good thing, if you can do it. By a series of happy accidents I am now shifting my marketable expertise from cell biology (in which I am now three years behind) to political science and media.

Curious about what happy accidents let me switch fields? First of all, a bunch of people moved offices at work. I ended up sitting next to the agency's senior-most political science policy advisor. Then, the research team (of which I am a member) started drafting an agency-wide research strategy. One of the new topics we were asked to explore was what we would need to know to prevent deadly political conflict. Nobody on the research team knew anything about it; my assignment was to learn about it. I spoke to my new office neighbor (and about three dozen people in and out of the agency). In the meantime I was becoming an expert on American broadcast media because of a business venture I was setting up. To make a long story short: my neighbor liked my work, was intrigued by the project, and was leading a team of political science researchers to El Salvador to investigate a closely related topic. He asked me to join the El Salvador team as the communications expert.

I went, praying that I could muddle through it. I'd never done social science research before. Well, the team was very understanding and helped me out a lot. And it turned out that I have a lot of directly relevant experiences, but I would never have guessed it. Like interviewing information sources—it turns out that this is not much different from taking a history from patients, which I did for two years as a medical student. Or analyzing the data—I did that,

272

too, while working on post-doc policy issues. It turned out I was pretty good at it. How do you like that? Scientific training really can cross disciplines! And I've been asked to extend the study for USAID, write papers, give talks—the whole academic shtick. Cool!

Jack May Be in the Box but I Thunk Out of the Box

I am pretty sure I can put food on the table. But that is not my greatest goal or my greatest comfort. I am excited by the impact I have on people's lives at USAID and through my political and journalistic activities. I want to remain part of the scholarly community. And I am terrified only once a week or so, which is better than before.

I gave up on finding one ready-made job that "has it all" boxed up and ready to go. Now whatever I do must be entrepreneurial, something "thunk out of the box." I spent the last few years opening my mind to all the possibilities that would work. Academia is not the only option, that is for sure. To paraphrase Louis Pasteur, opportunity favors the prepared mind.

Remember I mentioned that I was on NPR's *Science Friday*? This was another happy accident. For many years I knew that I wanted to work with a partner, whether as a scientist or something else. Since leaving the lab, I realized that I wanted to do something that combined business, art, science, and communicating with the public. After the radio show I chatted with the host and executive producer of *Science Friday*. He is not someone I would ever have met during an ordinary academic life. Nor would he have ever considered working with me if my résumé had crossed his desk. But as we started getting to know each other, it became apparent that each of us had experiences, interests, and talents the other needed in a partner. We both wanted to increase science news coverage in the mass media. This is how our media production company, Scien-Central, was born.

Go with the Flow

So here I am—traveling around the world, working on incredibly interesting issues, starting a business. For the moment, I'm on a high again. I do not expect it to last forever. Only the next time I hit a low, I hope I'll remember that what goes down can go up. That a career is not like a one-way railroad track where you enter at one end and continue straight ahead along the only path you can take. It is more like a little river flowing down a wooded mountain—obstacles might change your direction but in the end you cannot stop the flow of a determined dream—uh—stream.

How I Got to Collegiate

Adam Bresnick

I. Business School

When I decided to go to graduate school, I did so because I had developed a passion for literature and criticism as an undergraduate at Brown University, and I wished to make a life of this passion. I decided to study comparative literature at Berkeley mainly because the program demanded extraordinary things of its students. Rather than confine them to a specialization early on, in the manner of so many current programs, Berkeley's department asks that students study several literary traditions from the medieval period onward, that they learn at least two modern foreign languages and one ancient language, that they undergo a rigorous battery of written and oral exams for the masters and the doctorate, that they teach introductory literature courses, and, of course, that they compose a dissertation worthy of publication. Graduate students in comparative literature at Berkeley take nearly twice as many courses as their counterparts in the national language departments; as a result of this, their intellectual formation and range of reference tend toward the catholic. While many university literature and language departments have begun an inexorable move away from a curriculum that insists on the primacy of literature as an object of scrutiny, the Berkeley program maintains the tradition it inherited from the great generation of European exile philologists who inaugurated the discipline of comparative literature in the United States after the Second World War, and while graduate students learn the regular gamut of contemporary interpretive methodologies, from structuralist semiotics to queer theory, literature remains the mainstay of the program.

What did I want as a student of comparative literature? In the deepest sense of the term, I sought to deprovincialize myself, for as a third-generation American Jew who grew up in the suburbs of Washington, D.C., during the seventies, I wanted to find out how I might get back to Europe, how I might reconnect myself to a continent from which my great-grandparents had definitively severed themselves in the first decade of this century. But I did not want merely to find my roots in Europe; rather, I wanted to find Europe's roots in me and to understand my stake in Western culture. So my project was not merely to study one author or one decade or one problem; rather, I set out to learn the Western tradition in the grandest sense of the term, from Homer to Montaigne to Joyce, from the Bible to Shakespeare to Musil, from Plato to Kant to Freud. And amazingly, Berkeley was just the place to begin such an undertaking, for there were so many compelling professors and so many offerings in the mid-eighties that I was able to have my cake and eat it too in the company of a hungry and convivial peer group.

Graduate school was for me a time of fabulous intellectual expansion; as I look back on it now, I can hardly believe the luxury of that existence. True, I made very little money as a TA, and true, there were intellectual pressures and self-doubts with which I had to deal as I prepared for exams, but by and large the life was one of remarkable personal freedom and great intellectual discovery. My work was disinterested in the best sense of the term; while I did my best to fulfill departmental requirements as quickly as possible—the average time in the Berkeley comparative literature Ph.D. program is nearly ten years—for the most part I studied and wrote with hardly a thought about the practicality of my intellectual pursuits. While such broad and rigorous training is conducive to the development of a scholarly sensibility, it is not particularly well suited to the current intellectual environment and job market, for as I was soon to find out, the name of the contemporary academic game is specialization and identity politics.

What I wanted above all was the psychic expansion that attends great learning, and I wanted to convey this in my written work and to my students in class. What I didn't understand, of course, was that graduate school in the humanities is essentially a form of business school, and that the job market rewards learning less often than it does savvy self-promotion and canny invocations of the latest trends in academic criticism. What makes the business of academe so crazy is the fact that its product is speculative in the truest Hegelian sense of the term, for its value cannot be adjudicated in anything vaguely reminiscent of an objective manner. While those of us who believe in psychic expansion, both for the pleasure and the knowledge it affords, are happy enough to say that the things of the mind are the most useful things of all, the market knows only exchange, and the currency of that exchange for the past several years has borne the watermark of identity politics. Academic writing that does not invoke the holy trinity of race, gender, and sexuality cannot be traded easily in today's market, and work such as mine that focuses on canonical authors and the problem of the aesthetic is often thought to be retrograde, even if that work seeks to tease out the contradictions and aporias of the aesthetic ideology rather than simply to endorse it as a social panacea.

As a straight white Jewish male with a love of literature and aesthetics, the identity politics card was never really a consideration for me, and my resolute desire to study what interested me rather than what might make me marketable turned out to be more problematic than I thought it would be. For in a fractured job market, it was not so much that I fell through the cracks as that I fell directly on them. Paradoxically, the shrinking market demands more specialization rather than less, and the aspiring professor who cannot be easily pigeonholed might as well fly the academic coop. In today's politicized academic world, literature must serve as the warhorse of the consciousness-raising vanguard; disinterest be damned. I believe that it does not take great sophistication to understand the politicization of the academy in the name of identity as a rather desperate attempt by disenfranchised contemporary intellectuals to salvage a political efficacy in the face of a culture that regards them ever more as eccentric parasites to be cordoned off from the real business of post–Cold War America, which is expanding the crushing hegemony of capitalism as the only world system.

II. A Litany of Jobs That Might Have Been

How could one not hate the academic job market? I know I did. In 1992, having completed my Ph.D., I set out to find a job as an assistant professor in what was fast becoming a truly depressed market for positions in the humanities. My first year out, everyone assured me I had done well, as I managed to obtain four interviews, two for positions at prestigious state universities, and two with private institutions of good repute. All four were in places I could at least imagine living, and the communities at each school were said to be congenial enough. Given the virtual nonexistence of positions in comparative literature, all four interviews were for positions in French departments, the language in which I specialized, so I selected my nattiest clothes, silently rehearsed my job spiel in French as I daydreamed about the impending interviews, and set out for the MLA conference with high hopes of being offered a position as an assistant professor.

My first meeting was with the French department of an erstwhile school for upscale women now known as a college catering largely to artsy-fartsy types from the northeast. Entering the small hotel room, I was greeted by three women who graciously conversed with me in French and English, asking me about my background and interests. While they were friendly enough, it became clear to me halfway through the interview that they were far less interested in my opinions about literature and criticism than in my abilities as a language instructor, and while my French is solid enough (indeed, my coiffeur, an ultra-chic Frenchman from Grenoble, once acidly assured my wife that I speak with an accent more Parisian than that of the Parisians), I am not a native speaker, nor am I particularly interested in teaching French language. As this became clear to them, it became clear to me that I would not be getting this job.

For my second interview, I was ushered into a room filled with professors I knew well, as I had studied with many of them and had read their books. The interview went swimmingly, as they knew and respected my work and were happy to debate the crucial points in my arguments. The hitch came when they told me that there would probably be no position after all, as the most famous member of the department was in fact not going to leave for a rival institution, as rumor had it, but was merely using the rival university's offer as a bargaining chip in order to negotiate a more propitious salary at his home school. While I was happy to hear that this man, whose work I so admired, would now be even more handsomely remunerated than he was formerly, I was miffed to see my second dream go up in smoke.

The following year, I had three more interviews, one of which was for a job as an assistant professor of comparative literature at an outstanding state university in one of the nation's great cities. This, I thought, was the job for me, and truth be told, the interview could not have gone better than it did. The search committee was composed of several truly distinguished scholars of uncommon intellectual acumen, and the discussion we had was *fairly crackling* with energy and good humor. When I left the room, I was floating on air, and as I zoomed toward the elevator, I was approached by the departmental chair, who assured me I had done extremely well in the interview. A month later, I received a letter of condolence which began by congratulating me on my work, only then to deliver the bad news in two sentences: ''Please do not interpret the fact that you were not selected as one of our finalists as relating in any way to your own fine work. Our decision had to be based not only on our own particular needs, but on complicated university issues related to the state budget crisis.'' I didn't know whether to laugh or cry: I was glad the committee liked my work, but if my work was not the ticket, what was? When I informed my advisors at Berkeley of the contents of this letter, they suggested that the chair had done a risky thing, for he had euphemistically admitted that his department had no choice but to hire a member of a designated ethnicity or gender or lose funding for the position (this was before the recent attacks on affirmative action). Put a bit more baldly, they argued, such a statement would potentially have been grounds for legal action. As a white male on the left, I am sympathetic to the claim that literature departments need to be diversified, but when it happens at my expense in a virtually nonexistent job market, it is difficult for me to celebrate the fact that our best universities have embarked on the project of becoming more reflective of the general population's racial composition. I had seen another job come and go in a flash.

One year later, in an even flatter market, I apply for a job in one of the nation's most renowned French departments and am granted an interview. Even better, this department has decided to forgo the MLA entirely and simply invite a handful of candidates to the campus to give papers and be interviewed. This seems a wonderful thing, as I will be spared the misery of the annual MLA conference—which, in a perfectly appropriate act of sadism, the association sees fit to schedule every year between Christmas and New Year's, just in time to expunge any vestige of holiday cheer in the name of higher learning—and will be able to meet the department on its own turf.

Through the grapevine, I hear that there are troubles, as the department is spectacularly riven by internal conflict. A junior faculty member has recently applied for tenure and been rejected; it seems he falsified information about his publications and was caught. Though he hasn't a leg to stand on, the fact that he is married to the department chair complicates matters gravely, as they had hoped to railroad the tenure application through the university bureaucracy. Meanwhile, the university has imported a scholar from a well-known university to take over the chairmanship the following year, and the spurned duo takes him to be their mortal enemy. I am told to beware, as I am perceived as the candidate of the chair-to-be, and the situation is delicate, if not downright dangerous.

When the call offering the interview comes to me, I am thrilled, as I will be one of four candidates out of a pool of more than two hundred. I agree to come in five days to give a paper, only to be confronted with a major hitch. The committee requests that I give a paper on Zola in French; meanwhile, I have a job talk prepared on Balzac in English. What to do? I tell the secretary I shall need time to translate my work on Zola, and we reschedule for three and a half weeks later. I agree to this even though my wife is expecting our second child in the interim, thinking that as she had our first child ten days early, number two will follow suit and there will be no conflict. By placing a few calls to people I know at the university, I arrange to have one requirement waived: the department now allows that the paper can be in English as long as I offer a five-minute introductory speech in French detailing my interests and background, all by way of proving my linguistic competence.

My wife gives birth to our second child ten days late, just five days before the date of my interview, and there are some minor complications that cause her to have to spend extra time in the hospital. Our house is fairly chaotic when I leave for the interview, as I have a wife who is still in pain from the delivery and its complications, a first child who is somewhat bewildered by the arrival of his brother, and a pullulating baby who doesn't allow us much sleep. The chair-to-be, my ally in the war about to be fought, drives me to his house, where I meet his wife and enjoy warm conversation.

When I arrive at the university to give the paper, I am both exorbitantly wired and inordinately tired. The chair greets me coolly but politely; her husband, by contrast, is abrasively rude. During my talk, he sits on a sofa against the wall with his back turned to me, only occasionally craning around to gaze at me with black ballpoint eyes through his greasy hair. He is a ghastly individual. When my talk is done, I receive some questions from the audience, which I field gracefully. Indeed, I am particularly happy that I am able to face down the chair's husband, whose utterly provincial questions only indicate that he sees everything in terms of the machinations of the sixteenth century, his area of specialization. Having fended off his attacks, I turn to the chair, who begins to ask me questions about Zola. As it turns out, she has read every one of his books, and rather than ask me questions pertaining to my paper, which is part of a project on aesthetics and affect in nineteenth-century fiction, she grills me on all the Zola novels I haven't read, all by way of proving my ignorance to the crowd. I am caught between a rock and a hard place, as I have no choice but to admit that I've not read the entire Zolian corpus even though I never claimed to have done so in the first place. So it is that the chair makes her point to the crowd, showing me up as one without thorough knowledge of one of the most prolific writers of the nineteenth century.

The next day, when I explain to a well-known faculty member that I had been forced to read a paper that I had not chosen for my job talk, he remarks that the chair always cheats to get her way. While she lost the game for her husband's tenure decision, she wins the game against me. Another job down the drain.

III. How Things Shook Out

In the fall of 1988, having passed my Ph.D. orals, I went into exile from Berkeley in order to live with my wife in the Bronx, where she was about to begin attending medical school at the Albert Einstein College of Medicine. It is well-nigh impossible to convey the culture shock I experienced, for whereas in Berkeley I belonged in the community, in the Bronx I was an interloper, an intellectual stranger in a working-class Italian neighborhood in which comparative literature was a nonstarter. While I spent most of my time writing my dissertation in Bronxian obscurity, I was able to cobble some work together in order to help pay the bills and in order to maintain my sanity for thesis writing, which demands a certain self-absorption, the deleterious effects of which were only amplified by a sojourn in the Bronx, where no one spoke my language. In 1989–90, I taught the famous literature-humanities core curriculum at Columbia, which was an exhilarating experience, as it allowed me to crystallize much of what I had learned during my four years of course work at Berkeley. In addition to that, I taught English to sixth graders in a Manhattan program called ''Prep for Prep,'' which takes unusually gifted inner-city kids and prepares them for admission to the city's elite private schools. The teaching I did at Prep for Prep was in fact not unlike the teaching I did at Columbia, with the difference of course that the rhetoric I employed for the college course was more specialized and complex than the rhetoric I used with my sixth graders. Still, I was struck above all by the continuity of the pedagogical enterprise, for what I sought to instill in all my students was the ability to read for form. I wanted them to understand, as I have intoned hundreds of times by now, that the specific glory of literature resides less in what is said than in how it is said, for it is in the how that we locate the fascination of the literary. The kids in the Prep program were eminently well equipped to read for literary tropes, and they evidenced an astonishing aptitude for discerning irony, for such subtlety of mind is no doubt in part inborn, waiting to be coaxed out by a challenging teacher. I quickly realized that the challenges and rewards of teaching extraordinarily gifted sixth graders were in some ways greater than those associated with college teaching, for an eleven-year-old child is open to thinking in a way that many undergraduates no longer are. I was able to convey to these kids by performative example that one's work can and should be a form of play, and the classroom buzzed with electricity.

In 1991 Columbia was unable to offer me the position as preceptor for lit-hum, and I needed to find some other form of employment, so I sent my résumé around to various Manhattan independent schools to offer my services as a substitute teacher. In due time, the English Department chair of the Collegiate School, perhaps Manhattan's most intellectually demanding boys' school, called me for an interview, and I went to see him in the fall of 1991. He was a truly committed teacher who had done graduate work in

English at Cornell before deciding to opt out of the university world for a career as a secondary school teacher and administrator, and we hit it off immediately. Shortly thereafter, I began to sub at Collegiate, and found the level of the classes to be not unlike that of the freshmen courses I had taught at Berkeley and Columbia.

In the spring of 1993, shortly after my wife and I had moved from the Bronx to Manhattan in order to regain something like a normal social life, the chair informed me that there would be a position open at Collegiate for the fall of 1993 and asked me if I would be interested in applying for it. My initial response was to refuse the offer, for I had set out to teach in the university world, and it seemed a comedown to accept a real job in a high school. But the more I thought about it, the more reasonable it sounded. The school would pay me more than a college would, and I would be able to design a number of elective courses to my liking. I would be able to work in a friendly, stimulating environment with far less grandiose people than one finds in the university world. And, of course, I would be able to continue living in Manhattan as opposed to shipping out to the boonies in the quasi-missionary fashion of so many young academics who are educated at the nation's best universities and then forced to take positions in schools few have ever heard of.

It's now my fourth year teaching at Collegiate, and it has been a salutary experience in most ways. My peers in the English Department are a remarkably talented, generous lot who are committed to the life of the mind in a way many in the university world no longer are. It is easy for me to say that I like and respect my departmental colleagues, which, as far as I can tell, is something that few junior professors struggling up the tenure ladder can say. The administration of the school is progressive and humane, and when I have something to discuss, I go directly to the headmaster, who hears me out in a judicious, open manner. Most gratifying, the school has embraced me with open arms, and has encouraged me to set a very high level in my teaching, so that I have been able to teach courses quite like the ones I would teach and have taught at the college level. This fall, for instance, I taught a twelfth-grade seminar called "The Art of Horror; The Horror of Art" in which we read works by Mary Shelley, Balzac, Hoffmann, James, and Wilde that treat the lives of artists and artworks. I also taught an eleventh-grade survey on aesthetic philosophy largely modeled on a course I took as a sophomore at Brown for which we read works by Plato, Aristotle, Burke, Nietzsche, and Freud, among others. This winter I will teach a survey of twentieth-century Central European literature and a seminar on Ralph Ellison's *Invisible Man*. The great irony, of course, is that Collegiate allows me to teach comparative literature courses and to draw on my broad training as I see fit, while the teaching opportunities in the vast majority of college jobs I have applied for tended to be much more rigidly circumscribed. And the students are absolutely first-rate. They read with verve and focus, they discuss the works with acuity and passion, and while at times the energy in my seminars can spill over into an untoward rowdiness, for the most part my students work at a very high level and would be the envy of most college teachers. Indeed, two years ago, I taught as an adjunct professor at Fordham, and I was struck by the fact that my students at Collegiate wrote far more compelling essays than did the sophomores and juniors at Fordham. The pedagogical relation at Collegiate is both more intense and more sustained than it is at the college level, as I meet students in their tenth-grade year and then often teach them for six or seven of the next nine trimesters. In short, I have the opportunity to mark these students in their most formative time and the privilege of creating courses that ask them to push themselves as far as they can go.

There are, of course, some things that mitigate the rosiness of the picture I offer. First, I grade a ridiculous number of student essays, and while the lion's share of these papers have something to recommend them, it still is a fairly punishing regimen, and I worry sometimes that such a steady diet of student writing will rot my mind, as a colleague who teaches calculus even though he earned a Ph.D. in comparative literature at Princeton claims they invariably will do. Second, I have to spend a great deal of time in the school, as I teach three or four periods a day and must consult with students about their papers and problems with material. Third, I worry about the prospects for long-term growth, for while the teaching as it stands is superb, it's hard to imagine continuing at this pace for the next thirty years. The ambitious people in the secondary school world tend to gravitate toward administration, and I have decided definitively that this is not the road I wish to travel. I went into the field in order to read, write, and teach, and this is what I want to continue to do. As it stands, however, the benefits that accrue to me are obvious. I have the opportunity to teach super-smart kids in a congenial atmosphere with colleagues whom I genuinely admire. I have job security without the anxiety of tenure looming above me, and I do not have to worry much about cozying up to anyone in the school if I do not wish to do so. I have as much independence, both in my day-to-day routine and in my pedagogy, as I could reasonably expect to have, and I have the respect of the institution. And when the day is over, I exit the school and find myself happy to be able to prowl the streets of Manhattan, for this is no doubt the most interesting city in the country. To keep my fingers in the academic pie, I attend a research seminar at Columbia and occasionally work as an adjunct assistant professor at Fordham, and I continue to publish academic criticism and essays. Perhaps it is no surprise, then, that this year I ordered the MLA Job Information List, and for the first time in four years have been unable to bring myself even to apply for a college post. As far as I can tell, when it comes to jobs in the academy, there's very little out there that I want more than what I already have.

Ex-Philosopher

Brian Ulicny

I n 1993, MIT gave me the somewhat redundant title of Doctor of Philosophy in Philosophy after seven years of graduate school. Two years later, I found myself doing fulfilling work in the corporate world, even applying what I had worked on in my dissertation. That is, I am now a happy former academic. Here's my story.

Rule Following

In 1986, I was a senior at Notre Dame, about to get a bachelor's degree in both philosophy and electrical engineering. I had a couple of job offers and a couple of fellowship offers and no especially clear ideas about the practicalities of a career. Does any college senior? I knew that I didn't want one of the standard careers that most of my classmates were going into: law, investment banking, accounting, engineering at a large corporation. I knew that I wanted to do something creative and innovative. I had become very interested in cognitive science in college. I was especially fascinated by John Searle's 1980 article "Minds, Brains and Programs" (published in *Behavioral and Brain Sciences* 3, pp. 417–424), which argued that computers could never understand language. I couldn't accept Searle's conclusion, but I realized that I didn't have the intellectual background adequate to grapple with the issues at that point. I thought that studying at MIT with Jerry Fodor, one of Searle's critics and a major figure in the philosophy of mind, would give me the training I needed to participate in the debate over intentionality, meaning, and understanding that was, and still is, at the heart of cognitive science. I was also an admirer of Noam Chomsky's work, and since the department at MIT was a joint department of linguistics and philosophy, I thought that I would be able to have some contact with him there, as well. Because of all this, the fellowship at MIT seemed like the most interesting option, and, at that point, I didn't value practicalities over intellectual curiosity. So, off I went to MIT to study with Fodor.

The department at MIT hadn't bothered to tell me that Fodor would have left MIT by the time I got there, having gone on to a joint appointment at CUNY and Rutgers. I was disappointed, but I began the usual course of study in philosophy at MIT anyway. In addition to the required courses in philosophy and logic, I spent several semesters taking additional courses in linguistics and in natural language processing through the artificial intelligence laboratory. For my qualifying exam, I had picked an advisor, Jim Higginbotham, now at Oxford, who had a joint appointment, on both sides of the department. Higginbotham was trained as a philosopher, but he had done important work in linguistic semantics as well. Eventually, when it came time to write my dissertation, I wrote on the foundations of lexical semantics, the study of word meaning. Higginbotham remained as my thesis supervisor; Robert Stalnaker and Noam Chomsky were the other readers.

A Plea for Excuses

In 1992, the semester before I graduated, I went on the job market for the first time. There's not too much to relate about this episode. Like several others from MIT, after all the essay writing and letter begging and résumé tuning, I got no interviews. Of course, one had to make the arrangements to go to the American Philosophical Association meeting (in Washington that year) before one knew whether or not one would have interviews, so I went to Washington anyway. It was certainly depressing to walk around D.C. in the cold during the day, trying to keep busy and applying for last-minute jobs that I wouldn't have wanted anyway. They didn't call, either. I had no stomach for hearing the distinguished lecturers and symposia. At night, there was the horror of the "smokers": those relics of days gone by where candidates might get signed to tenure-track jobs over ballroom cocktails and a smoke. Now no one in his or her right mind with a job to offer attends the smoker. Anyone doing so would be instantly swamped by candidates begging him or her to consider their dossiers one more time.

After three depressing days, I went back to Cambridge to spend the end of the Christmas holiday with my girlfriend (now wife . . . see, this all ends happily) and her parents. I wasn't looking forward to this. I had gone from being a philosophy graduate student to being a philosophy graduate student with no immediate prospects. Had I done everything I could to get an interview? I assured them I had. Had I checked my résumés for typographic errors? Yes. Had I documented my achievements fully? Yes. Had I considered what would happen if I didn't get a job? No. I tried to convince them that the market was currently overcrowded and my chances would be better next year when I had actually graduated.

Graduating under these circumstances was frightening. When you are in graduate school, you can deflect expectations indefinitely with the excuse "I'm still finishing my dissertation." You can blame your lack of life plans on your thesis supervisor's unreasonable expectations for your work. You can rely on the fact that there will be an important new book or article that you must address in your own work every few months. Thus you can remain in the realm of becoming. Once you've graduated, especially in philosophy, none of those excuses hold up.

I was extremely lucky in that I had been able to scrape together several teaching gigs and was making a comfortable amount of money. For the previous two or three years, I had been teaching at two or three colleges a semester as an instructor or teaching assistant. Logistically, this was quite involved, since I didn't have a car. I relied on Boston's commuter railroad and subway, my bike, various college shuttles, a one-day-a-week car rental (my girlfriend loved this for going to the supermarket), and my feet to get back and forth from Waltham and Lowell to Cambridge in time for various classes. Most semesters I had some intro philosophy or logic sections at Bentley College, a business-oriented college in Waltham, Massachusetts. For three years, I also taught in the Core Program at Harvard. It was a dream job to teach at Harvard, no matter how low on the totem pole I was.

That year, the APA meeting was in Atlanta. Once again, I made the arrangements to go in advance. And once again, I had no interviews when I got there. One of the MIT faculty managed to line me up an interview while I was there, however. Nothing came of it. I continued teaching five or six sections a semester at Harvard and Bentley and other area schools. That meant a lot of grading and little time to work on getting anything published. By now, my girlfriend and I wanted to get married, and the lack of a permanent job was a constant worry and a tension. Each semester I had to scramble to line up sections for the following semester. Luckily, once I was in the Harvard system, it was relatively easy to get other sections. I wound up teaching all sorts of material there: from quantum theory to political philosophy to history of science to museology. In the meantime, I won two teaching awards at Harvard and good teaching reviews from the other schools.

My last year on the market, I finally got an interview at the APA. That year, the conference was in Boston, so I didn't even have to buy a plane ticket. The interview was for a specialist in the philosophy of artificial intelligence at Kent State in Ohio. The interview went well, and I was invited to come out for a campus visit and to give a talk. The department chairman there had one condition, however: before I accepted the trip offer, I had to promise that I would take the job if it were offered. Our placement officer had warned me that their hiring practices were a little bizarre.

My girlfriend and I had basically had it with the philosophy job market at that point. I declined the chance to accept a job at a place I had never seen with colleagues I had never met. We had no desire to get married and move to Kent, Ohio, under those circumstances. I was done with the whole business: applying for jobs where they didn't even have the courtesy to tell you that you hadn't been accepted. Or demanded that you agree to take a job without knowing anything about the conditions under which you would be working and living.

Why hadn't I done better on the academic market? I had graduated from a prestigious program. Although I hadn't seen my letters of recommendation, neutral observers had assured me that they were excellent. My teaching record was very good. On the other hand, I didn't have any publications to my name. My dissertation was focused on concerns that didn't travel very well outside of MIT. Further, two of my advisors were linguists. (Higginbotham, by that point, had gone on to Oxford to head up their linguistics program.) This reinforced the impression that my work was a little too marginal to philosophy. Moreover, my advisor wasn't available to round up interviews for me. But I don't want to make excuses for myself.

In the end, I'm happy that I didn't get an academic job. Teaching, I discovered, was not a vocation for me. It was surprisingly easy for me to walk away from it. I miss the joys of being able to disappear into a university library for the afternoon. I miss the students whom I got to know well. I miss the trappings and rhythm of campus life. But I don't miss the teaching.

My Way Out

After my first unsuccessful year on the job market, I began to think about alternative careers. I had initially gone to MIT because of an interest in artificial intelligence. I had a computational background. I had linguistic training. I began to think about refocusing on working in the artificial intelligence field rather than doing philosophy. I immediately set about learning some additional computer languages and looking at technical journals.

A big source of encouragement came that summer. I prepared a résumé emphasizing my interests in computational linguistics and went off to the Association for Computational Linguistics meeting at Ohio State. I tried aggressively to get my résumé into as many hands as I could. The positive responses surprised me. While I hadn't done anything but school projects in computational linguistics, companies like Microsoft and NEC were interested in talking with me. My skills weren't quite at the level they wanted. No offers were made. It was clear that it wouldn't take too much to get there, however. After the APA, I basked in any attention at all like a puppy.

The next summer, I managed to get involved with a project at the Artificial Intelligence Laboratory at MIT that was both related to the subject of my dissertation and that allowed me to spend the summer programming. It was an unbelievably lucky coincidence. I had saved up enough money from all the teaching I was doing to be able to work at this all summer without pay. The skills and experience I got would end up making all the difference.

The next winter, after my last APA, computational linguistics and natural language processing jobs were being advertised all over the Internet, which I patrolled daily looking for opportunities. I was sending out my c.v. almost daily in response to new jobs, and I was getting responses. I was even flown to Germany to give a job talk at a computational linguistics research institute there.

Finally, one of the leads turned into a job. I signed with a start-up I discovered based on a very elliptical advertisement posted on the Web. The company was just opening its doors and was set to do very innovative things in information retrieval on the Web. They needed a computational linguistics developer on the team. Moreover, they were interested in the ways I thought we could apply commercially some of the things I had worked on at MIT. I moved to Southern California the summer before my girlfriend and I got married, and everything worked out unbelievably well. The team works incredibly well together and includes very talented people with backgrounds in computer science, library science, physics, and machine learning. The technology we developed was a great critical success, and our start-up was acquired by a larger corporation last summer, a year after it began. That, of course, is one of the best things that can happen to someone who joins a start-up at the beginning.

Lessons

So what can be learned from my story? Wittgenstein argued that no rules can be induced from any finite set of data, no matter how large. Surely, then, nothing can be gleaned from the very particular set of circumstances in my story. But, perhaps that's not entirely true.

One lesson to be learned is that if the academic market looks bad, begin to investigate alternatives early. I certainly had to be prodded to do this. (My girlfriend served as chief prodder. Another lesson would be to get involved with someone who is not swept away by the romance of academia.) Each year, I had a thousand reasons why I would surely get a job the following year. But each year, I taught too much and published too little, and nothing changed. Since nearly all of the people you know are aiming at academic careers, it is hard not to consider looking at alternatives as giving up or failing. But it isn't. There is just no denying that there are more doctorates awarded than jobs available, and it will simply decrease the quality of the jobs that are available if everyone refuses to consider other careers. Why should a university hire two new assistant professors if there are desperate job seekers willing to take on the teaching load of both? Or of three? And gladly do committee work. While publishing like fiends.

Better, go into graduate school with an exit strategy in mind. When I was entering graduate school, there were all sorts of rosy forecasts my parents would clip from *The Chronicle of Higher Education* predicting a dearth of academics by the time I would be ready to graduate. You have the benefit of knowing this isn't true now. Keep reminding yourself that there aren't enough jobs to go around. Maintain your viability in another career all through graduate school.

Best, don't get your doctorate until you don't really need one. The students in my program who got excellent jobs at Ivy League schools—and there were, excruciatingly, several of these—came into the program vastly better prepared than I was. Mostly, these happy few had put in a few years at Oxford or already had some more or less doctorate-equivalent credential in a European system. They didn't come to MIT to come up to speed. They were already functioning at an extremely high level when they arrived. Many had an impressive list of publications already to their credit. As such, they impressed everyone from the day they hit the doorstep. They wrote beautiful dissertations quickly. And they got good jobs. Make no mistake about it: they worked extremely hard. It was never a matter of luck or favoritism of any kind. My suggestion would be, if you don't fit this model, leave your current program and start a new one as a wunderkind.

Expectations

Victoria C. Olsen

When I was young, I was obsessed with names. My own name seemed to promise a regal destiny, and I wrote and rewrote lists of heroines' names for the daughter I would have someday, when I was a professional. I tested my theories about the future on my little sister Margrit, giving her questionnaires about names and identities. In between neutral questions like "Which nickname do you prefer, Meg, Megan, Peg, Peggy, or Daisy?" I would stick in a hard one: "Do you want to grow up and have a career or do you want to be just a housewife?" Recognizing a loaded question, she picked the career—as I would, as our mother had, and as all the other mothers we knew had. My sisters and my friends all knew we would have jobs and raise our kids as we were raised, by teams of baby-sitters, housekeepers, teachers, and parents. My family never had much cash, but we had lots of credit and we lived high. It was a privileged upbringing that will be hard for my generation to match: live-in au pairs, alternative

NOTE: A version of this essay first appeared in *Barnard Magazine* (Fall 1996): 56.

private elementary schools, summer trips to Europe . . . And it was made possible by the necessity (in economic terms) and the privilege (in historical terms) of my mother's work.

My mother has a successful career now, and Margrit is working on hers, but my own career has disappeared. My name did forecast my future, but "unemployed Victorianist" is not the identity that I had hoped for. My early love of research served me well through college and graduate school: it earned me a Ph.D. in English literature at Stanford University, but it didn't get me a job. The promised expansion of academic jobs in the mid-1990s never materialized, and like thousands of other new Ph.D.s, I find myself unable to do the job I was trained for—in my case, teaching and writing about nineteenth-century British culture. Instead, I find I have the job that would never have made any list I concocted while growing up: stay-at-home mother. It is a job for which I have no experience, no training, and no role models. It is a job that isn't a job at all in American culture, and certainly not a career. I don't have one friend who is raising a child without working outside the home. Feminists all, my friends and I assert the invaluable and neglected importance of women's work in the home, while never, for a moment, seriously considering it as a lifestyle. My faith in the work of child rearing has been battered by society's indifference to it, feminism's ambivalence about it, and my own experience of its daily drudgeries.

Now, on a good day, my daughter is my best baby friend, and we spend companionable time hanging out together; a bad day pits me against her and my own boredom. Today I have already changed one spill-over diaper, washed all the bed linens, and cleaned out the toaster oven. It is raining and my eighteen-month-old daughter and I are stuck indoors, where our entertainment comes from watching out the windows for dogs. It is a bad day. I write this as she wanders around me, pulling books off the shelves, needing a bottle, a toy, attention. The floor is a mess but I've learned not to pick up after her until the end of the day, or I will spend all day doing it. I can't believe this is my life.

The work of childcare is unbelievably dreary and monotonous. Between feedings and changing diapers, the physical care of infants is almost constant, and it is replaced by the nonstop supervision required by toddlers. Like Pip in Charles Dickens's *Great Expectations*, my daughter is being brought up "by hand": for Pip that meant he was raised by a sister who beat him; for my daughter it meant that as an infant she had to be held at all times. She was born the month I submitted my dissertation and her infancy coincided with my first round of rejections from academic jobs. After a year and a half, she is thriving, while my career is still stalled, and I have no expectations at all for the kind of tenure-track assistant professorship in my field that I trained for. During the deep depressions that have plagued me through these months, I have throught a lot about this problematic idea of expectations. Struggling with dashed hopes, I have tried to have none, and found that alternately demoralizing and liberating. On the one hand, to be free of expectations seems so admirably independent and self-contained. On the other hand, to have no expectations means to be without a future at all.

My profession is now engaged in a similar conundrum: does graduate study in the humanities imply the promise of an academic job or not? The question itself has dramatic consequences. If graduate study is vocational training, then the collapse of the academic job market is an epic crisis that departments, disciplinary organizations, and academic institutions need urgently to confront. If graduate study simply trains the mind, then all those unemployed and underemployed scholars are just the inevitable casualties of the (over?)privileged pursuit of knowledge. Departments nonetheless exploit their graduate students' love of learning in order to provide underpaid teaching assistants to high-paying undergraduates. If the purpose of doctoral programs in English, like my own, is to train young professors, then this job market means that it should train many fewer of them and raise the barely subsistence levels of teaching wages and fellowship grants. (My peers and I competed for part-time jobs and fellowships that paid at most $10,000 per year.) Graduate study was always a privileged vocation, at best and at worst: wages and job opportunities were perceived as irrelevant to the life of the mind and for a long time scholars necessarily came from backgrounds that could support such ill-paid but prestigious work. Yet socioeconomic forces are making that ivory tower more illusory than ever. Graduate students squeak through the long apprenticeship of a Ph.D. degree only to face the huge student loan payments and lifestyle expectations of other professionals without the income to support them. As usual, the academy is having a hard time keeping pace with the changes outside its walls.

But how can I complain when I am forced to exchange the privileged life of an academic for the privileged life of a full-time mother? Both positions are old-fashioned, middle-class ideals: my daughter and I are supported by my husband's salary; she and I have the opportunity to spend a lot of time together during her formative years; I spent seven happy years in full-time graduate study. While neither my role as a mother nor my role as an academic has turned out as I expected, I am learning to live with this plot twist. And I have a revised understanding of my own childhood and my mother's work: I am suddenly aware of how her own expectations for a family and a career were disrupted as well. My parents' divorce coincided with New York City's near-bankruptcy in the 1970s, and my mother's civil service job was always in peril. In fact, I am living out her middle-class fantasy of family life, while she embodied my idea of the career woman. Our expectations have failed us both, but she has become my role model for living with these failed expectations. She and I, like many women, like many academics (and like Pip too, the Victorianist in me adds), have found our expectations to be painfully deluded, but we may still have happy endings yet.

Eight

Where Do We Go from Here?
Critiques of the Academy

Introduction

Anne M. Menke
Department of Modern Languages and Literatures,
Swarthmore College

Colleges and universities are big businesses. This declaration is a common thread that runs through the three essays that comprise the final section of this book, "Where Do We Go From Here? Critiques of the Academy." The cherished myth, which held that the ivy-covered walls of academe guarded the liberal arts from the crass world of money and power, receives short shrift here. Once considered by many as noble, even ethical, endeavors, literature, art, and learning, which achieved a certain autonomy from government and religious authorities in the nineteenth century, have ended up under the rule of the almighty dollar. There is apparently little to celebrate and much to fear in this new order of things. The tone of these articles suggests that far from being a haven for intellectual exchange, places of higher learning are now oppressive worksites closer in spirit to other normalizing institutions analyzed by Michel Foucault, such as prisons and asylums.

All three contributors insist on exposing the similarities between places of business and of learning; nonetheless, their responses to the advent of "edubusiness" vary in these personal narratives. In

301

"The Economy of Letters" Lesliee Antonette pragmatically suggests that we assume our new roles as entrepreneurs and openly adopt a business attitude. Dismissing the supposed ethical differences between academics and the corporate world as groundless, she proclaims that "[t]he sooner we learn to value our ideas and ourselves as valuable commodities, the better off we will be in an increasingly difficult job market."

John Dixon also calls upon the vocabulary of economics, but in order to suggest a quite different approach to the dilemma of employment for Ph.D.'s, one that firmly grounds itself in the tradition of class struggle against the alienating effects of world capitalism. In "Hidden Injuries of the Job Market," Dixon urges us to "break with the ideologies of professionalism and meritocratic individualism" in favor of a collective identity which is more in keeping with the solidarity many academics profess in their writing about other exploited workers.

While Antonette and Dixon chip away at academe's self-image as guardian of truth and moral values by focusing on the economic plight of graduate students, Laura Stempel Mumford addresses another manner in which the hallowed halls of higher learning exercise dominance over intellectual workers. "Independent of What?: Rethinking Academic Marginality" speaks to the devalued status of so-called "independent scholars." In Pierre Bourdieu's terms, thinkers and writers who do not have institutional affiliations suffer from inadequate "symbolic capital," and this regardless of their scholarly publications. Mumford thus challenges another (American) academic myth, which holds that universities are "the center of intellectual life and work." Intellectuals without academic posts are then by definition marginal, and by implication second-rate.

Missing from these critiques of the difficulty of obtaining academic jobs in the late 1990s is an analysis of the effect edubusiness has on the practice of teaching. For just as the continued infiltration of the profit logic of capitalism has dramatically altered how professors view themselves and treat one another, it has also radically transformed their relationship with students. We professors may view ourselves as scholars eager to challenge young minds with the vast knowledge we have gleaned from years of arduous study. Our students are more apt to view us through the lens of the consumer society they make no pretense of having escaped. We are there to provide a service to them. For their steep tuition fees, they expect in return a product: good grades (let's be honest, an A) and the credentials to enter the job market or pursue further job training in graduate school.

Not only do students not distinguish education from other products available for consumption, they insist on learning being promoted, packaged, and delivered in the same sleek, superficial way as movies, TV, music, and videos. What's more, students increasingly demand the right to rate the performance of their professors, applying what I think of as the *American Bandstand* yardstick: "I'd give it an 87, it's easy to dance to." In other words, if it pleases me, if it makes me feel good, if I feel okay (the new deity being strong self-esteem), then you're an okay professor and your class is worth taking. Unfortunately, students armed with this newly found source of power as consumers who are always right have found ready allies in business-conscious administrations. Why professors seem to be the last ones to awaken to the realities of edubusiness and what the best way is for us to respond to these changes are urgent questions for intellectuals inside and outside of academics. And it will surely be no easy task to forge a collective identity and establish solidarity given the fierce competition for jobs and the polarizations effected by the differences in status among the Ph.D.'s described in this book.

The Economy of Letters

Lesliee Antonette

I entered the academic job market in 1995. I graduated from a state university in June 1996 with a Ph.D. in composition and American literature. My dissertation is a reconsideration of the theories and practices surrounding multiculturalism in the academy. Do I sound marketable to you? This is a common question among graduate students entering the job market. We talk about ourselves in terms of commodities up for auction and we discuss the market in terms of supply, demand, and surplus. We are relatively unselfconscious in our promotion of ourselves. We are anxious to perform well in order to sell ourselves to the best institution. That is what we have been trained to do.

However, somewhere between brand-new Ph.D. and tenure a lapse of memory occurs. To those in positions to hire us the market metaphor becomes something crass. The time-honored practice of hustling for the best position is forgotten and distance from economic need allows many faculty members to divorce themselves and their institutions from any relation they may have to the business end of the university. There is a historical distinction made between the world of big business and the world of academia which is based upon the perception that the former functions independently of ethical standards and the latter is founded in them. This is where our problems begin.

At the Modern Language Association's 1995 convention in Chicago, I met a fine old gentleman whose retirement was being celebrated by the many graduates he had produced and some of his colleagues. We sat in the lobby of the Hyatt and smoked cigarettes and talked about "the market." During our conversation one of his colleagues approached and the old gentleman was kind enough to introduce me. He introduced me as "new meat." As the colleague shook my hand (delicately), a look crossed his face which reminded me of the look a baby gets on her face when she is engaged in passing a particularly painful gas bubble. He tried to smile, but he seemed perplexed at the introduction. I was not sure if he was embarrassed by the introduction itself or by my nonplussed response to it. It seemed to me that the whole notion of "the market" left a bad taste in this gentleman's mouth and having to touch the "new meat" made him incredibly uncomfortable.

I was, in fact, not offended by the old gentleman's introduction. I *was* "new meat," and I was there trying my damnedest to sell my ass to the highest bidder. I have been a student for ten years, I have accumulated massive student loan debts, and I want a job. I don't feel that I am in the minority here at all, and I think it silly to disdain an accurate portrayal of my position. I admired the honesty with which the old professor engaged me. We had a thoughtful and interesting discussion about the quality of the institution and the problems of the job market.

These are terrible years on the job market. Many public universities across the country have been experiencing their own version of downsizing: early retirement programs, doubled teaching loads, and larger classrooms, not to mention the slowdown in replacing those retired fellows. Those of us who are not yet in an academic position find ourselves after years of education in a position of unemployment, or underemployment if we are lucky. Downsizing is good for the university, we are told. The bottom line for the university is the same as for big business. The preservation of the institution—and after all, if there is no university there is no possibility of employment for us—overrides the needs of those who inhabit it. We accept this logic from big business, so why is it so difficult to accept it from the academy?

In fact, our academic training prepares us to compete with one another and cooperate with the institution and its representatives. We are taught to perform in class in a way that will be pleasing to the professor. We need to pass the class. Hustling for grades is a precursor to hustling for jobs. The institution is set up to provide an atmosphere in which we can openly compete with one another for teaching assistantships, A's, research grants, panel presentations, and publications. We are trained to sell ourselves and at the same time the ethics of the institution demand that we not talk about it. The whole process of being groomed to maintain the status of the institution is occluded by a rhetoric of higher ideals. This allows for all of the smaller corruptions that plague our existence as graduate students and prepare us for the larger inequities suffered by ladder faculty clamoring for tenure.

Graduate school is full of petty humiliations, yet how many times have I heard someone say, "Don't take it personally"? This insistence on objectivity effaces our presence as individuals and produces us as cogs in an educational wheel. Teaching assistant ranking practices, grades received on papers written, and fellowship selection—all of these practices work to reinforce a depersonalization of the educational system. Only "good" students are rewarded—it is nothing personal. But it *is* personal. When one individual in a class is supported by a grant and one is supported by department funds through a teaching position and one is living on loan money, there is an uneven playing field. Add to that the subjective nature of grades and evaluations and you have a situation that is highly personal.

It is a personal struggle every single day to perform—and not only for the student at the bottom of the hierarchy. The student at the top now has to deliver. She has been marked as a "good" student and now she must perform in ways that please the administration that chose her. She has no choice but to become a "company man.'' The fellowships, the teaching support, the publications, the panel presentations all prepare the student for the job market. The ethics of the institution confirm that the institution functions to preserve itself.

I enjoyed meeting the retiring professor. I was not offended by this sweet and interesting man when he referred to me as fresh meat. I chose to be in Chicago, I chose to sell my ass, and I choose to become interpellated by an institution that cares not one whit about me as an individual. This is the job market at its best and at its worst. This is the nature of any job market in a capitalist culture. I do take it personally, however: I am a person with ideas and interests and I bought into all those higher ideals. Further, I continue to compete because I believe I will be different. I will not become a ''tenured radical,'' like all of those tenured radicals before me.

I understand that the institution is the bottom line and that ethical behavior within it is defined as that which supports the institution. It is for this reason that I suggest that graduate students learn to think of themselves as entrepreneurs. The sooner we learn to value our ideas and ourselves as valuable commodities the better off we will be in an increasingly difficult job market. We will then be able to understand not only the fiscal value of a degree, but the intellectual and ideological value of the work we do in the academy. That is what we will be paid for, and that means that every time we produce a piece of work it will not only address the larger interests of society, it will reproduce the institution. Once we understand that the ethical quality of our work is its ability to maintain the privileged position of the academy as a cultural institution charged with the production of knowledge, we may one day figure out how to make the institution itself, and its market, less dehumanizing.

Postscript

Nearly a year has passed since I wrote ''The Economy of Letters.'' As I read it now, as an assistant professor in a tenure-line position, I cannot help but notice the edge of desperation in my tone. At that time I had vague prospects of employment, but much of my fervor may have been inspired by fear. However, now, on the other side of the dichotomy I set up in the essay, I could become that "tenured radical" who, separated from financial need by time and employment, forgets her own past. At this point I see no danger of that occurring. I remain a commodity. I sell my soul for a good teaching evaluation in my tenure file. I kill myself working on committees that the institutional system of governance will not allow to make effective decisions. I subscribe to the Modern Language Association's Job List because "I know there must be something better out there," and now I have a new line on my c.v. In short, I am still painfully aware that my life in the academy is life on the market.

Hidden Injuries of the Job Market

John Dixon

onsidering the scant media coverage given to labor disputes, it is remarkable that the January 1996 "grade
strike" called by graduate teaching assistants at Yale received so much attention.[1] What fascinated reporters and
commentators about the events at Yale was that this strike involved
elite professionals-in-training at one of this country's most prestigious universities. Here were skilled middle-class professionals identifying themselves as exploited workers, forming a union, and
demanding that they receive official recognition. Behind the media
interest in the strike was anxiety that an era of downward middle-
class mobility might be weakening this class's faith in enterprise
and self-reliance. Some commentators were exasperated that elite
students were rejecting the values of personal responsibility and professionalism at the core of middle-class life. Others were perhaps
secretly drawn to the idea of collective action as a means to address
their own sense of insecurity.

In this essay I want to suggest why I have come to feel, along
with those Yale graduate students, the need to break with the ideologies of professionalism and meritocratic individualism informing

graduate education. I have recently received a Ph.D. in English literature and have been on the job market for two years. In completing
my degree and searching for work, I have witnessed the way people
live out and suffer from these ideologies. My story tells how my
experience of competitive individualism during the job search grad-
ually forced me to question my own values. Looking back on my
early years at graduate school, it surprises me how readily I embraced the individualism that I now find so suffocating.

I arrived at graduate school with the attitude that the experiences
awaiting me were tests of character. It is easy to see now how this
outlook made me less than skeptical about institutional arrangements. As a first-year teaching fellow I welcomed the chance to
teach sections, to prepare exams and paper topics, and to handle all
the grading and conferencing in a course for which the professor
only had to read the lectures he had long since written. I was not
indignant that I hardly had time for my own studies, because I saw
my teaching responsibilities as an essential learning experience designed by wise authorities to prepare me for the profession. A year
later, when the department announced that we would be expected to
complete the Ph.D. program in four years, not five, I accepted this
as a personal challenge. All of us saw the new oral exam focusing
on dissertation research as opposed to traditional literary periods as
a salutary concentration on professional specialization. No graduate
students complained about the obvious fact that the whole change
was instituted by the administration to turn teaching fellows more
quickly into lower-paid lecturers. We all accepted at face value the
claim that these changes would be good for us and improve
our education.

Other mundane facts of our life in the department were likewise
taken as part of the natural order of things. The "graduate lounge"
was a dingy, out-of-the-way room with a single square-foot bulletin
board. Not surprisingly, the room was not frequented, and the board
served only for an occasional announcement of lectures, not for any
lively expression of opinion about graduate student affairs. At the
time it did not occur to me to question why we had no central
meeting place for exchanging experiences and ideas. Later I learned

that since the early eighties, bulletin boards around the campus had been mysteriously dwindling in size and moving to remote and inconvenient places. Once focal points for student organizing, they had become little-used spots to advertise spring break travel packages or used furniture sales. The one vehicle graduate students did have for keeping in touch with one another was a newsletter updating us on the scholarly successes of our fellows. Obviously it did more to stir competitiveness and anxiety than to generate solidarity.

It was not until the later years of graduate school, when we all began worrying seriously about the job search, that I started experiencing this competitiveness as an oppressive burden. A particularly alienating moment was a conversation I had with a fellow graduate student after a departmental party. As we stood chatting, he suddenly rebuked himself for having just wasted his time talking to an assistant professor without clout or reputation while others were "networking" with prestigious senior professors. This same student was doing a Marxist reading of the representation of workers in nineteenth-century fiction. How could this friend of mine not see this contradiction between his professed intellectual allegiance and his personal moral conduct? My first impulse was to charge him with hypocrisy, but then I thought that perhaps he was just giving frank expression to a way of thinking we all quietly succumb to under the force of circumstances. While as literary critics we increasingly vow solidarity with the marginalized and oppressed, as job seekers in a tight market we fixate on career advancement, brooding over how to "package" and "market" ourselves in a time of plunging demand. No small measure of our capitulation to circumstances is the way terms like "job market" and "networking" no longer jar our sensibilities. We regularly describe our personal attributes as commodities without thinking what such metaphors imply about our relationships with one another.

The problem with my friend, of course, was not his pursuit of a career per se, but his particular manner of pursuing it. When we start seeing others solely as means to our own ends, when we begin dividing the world up into winners and losers, when we catch ourselves labeling bright, affable young junior professors with superior credentials to our own as "losers" because they lack departmental prestige, then surely our professional seriousness has degenerated into pathological careerism. We can aspire to a career, I hope, but eschew careerism. The values of service and dedication implicit in the idea of a "career" as opposed to a "job" are worth defending. Recent downsizing trends in the academy should be attacked precisely for shutting so many of us out from a life of social commitment. Yet professionalism also involves an individualistic sense of self. Professional life brings with it a belief that each individual is responsible for his or her own destiny and that one's position in society and one's career success reflect inner merit.

Over the years it began to strike me how few graduate students had escaped the destructive power of this mindset inherited from our Calvinist forebears. At first I assumed that I was alone in dreading that I was a second-rate impostor as an academic, a reprobate without hope of salvation. But the more I talked with my peers—all talented, idealistic young men and women with contributions to make to society—the more I realized how widespread this impostor complex was. Behind our confident facades, we were all living under the shadow of nagging self-hatred. In addition to the personal harm this caused, it tainted our relations with others. We despised in others what we hated in ourselves. Fear of failure produced contempt for "failures." I began seriously to doubt whether I could feel genuine solidarity with the oppressed if I viewed the world in terms of winners and losers and dreaded falling into the latter category. On a theoretical level one could perhaps be convinced that class conflict and structural poverty and unemployment exist, and one could give lip service to the values of community and cooperation, but on the level of lived experience one was likely to look at the poor and unemployed as the undeserving and to find satisfaction in individual competition more than in social commitment.

The view of the world in terms of winners and losers implies the metaphor of life as a "race." From early on, we all have drummed into us that every citizen of this country should receive an equal starting position in the "race" of life, and that almost all of us do. Past injustices, we learn, have largely been rectified by progressive reforms. This is now a society of unprecedented equal opportunity and merit rewarded free from the rigid class hierarchies of European societies, a view reinforced from many directions. Our representative political institutions convince us that sovereignty resides not with any "ruling class," but with the people. Our "free enterprise" economy affords enough rags-to-riches stories to give credence to the idea of our society's exceptional fluidity. There is the apparent inconsistency that, as recent studies have shown, economic inequality in the United States exceeds that of any other Western industrialized nation.[2] But meritocratic individualism only makes claims about equality of starting position, not equality of outcomes. No institution plays a more crucial role in lending plausibility to the notion of equal opportunity than our extensive system of public and private education with its promise of universal access to the means of self-improvement. Of course none of these claims is completely false; they would hardly carry such weight if they had no foundation in reality. But systematic inspection of them demonstrates how selective and oversimplified they are. They are partial truths concealing unpleasant facts about class and exploitation.

An important reason why I, and many people I know, decided to pursue an academic career is that we believed in the liberal mission of education. When we arrived at graduate school, we wanted to participate in achieving a more equal society in which everyone would have a chance to realize his or her talents. Inspired by an ideal of civic-minded professionalism, we chose a life of teaching and scholarship over the self-seeking individualism of more lucrative careers. We hoped to be valued and paid modestly according to the services we would provide, imagining that we would thus shelter ourselves from the storms of the market, achieve a comfortable and well-deserved middle-class life, and even find in our scholarly work something approximating unalienated labor. We ourselves had worked hard to achieve distinction in school. No wonder if academics as a group tend to believe implicitly that one's occupation is a badge of talent, initiative, and commitment. No wonder if graduate students are prone to experience success and failure as a measure of inner moral worth, even in spite of what we claim to think.

Graduate school and the job search work to reinforce this individualistic mind-set. In the strike at Yale the administration insisted that "There's no union to recognize because there are no employees to recognize."[3] For them graduate students are the privileged beneficiaries of professional apprenticeship, not cheap labor. My university makes a point of drilling this self-understanding into us. At an annual, mandatory orientation program for teaching fellows, the dean and the provost speak about the honor and privilege the university has bestowed on us, the generous tuition waivers we have been granted, and the substantial stipends we have received to help us through our period of professional apprenticeship.

This ritual protests too much. A professional sense of self is more subtly, and therefore more powerfully, instilled by interaction within the department. Every stage of the graduate program serves as a rite of passage in which we are hailed, or as Althusserians would say, "interpellated," as colleagues on our way to a career. After my dissertation defense, as I stood smiling and shaking hands with the professors, I felt a proud sense of professional identity. Yet on some level, aware of the dismal job market, I knew that this very sense of pride would be likely to haunt me soon in the form of self-blame.

The way the faculty prepare us for the job market fosters this self-blame. A placement meeting held each autumn to counsel job seekers conveys the implicit message that while it is a difficult job market, you can find a position if you play the "game" right. Our professors have devised numerous ways of encouraging us and showing us how to play the game. At the placement meeting they distribute examples of the c.v.'s of persons who have succeeded or failed to land positions in our own department. Beyond revealing something about the department's tastes, this exercise chiefly has the effect of making most of us secretly wish that our c.v.'s could be half as long, and our letters half as clever, as those that "failed." Some professors also imagine we will be inspired by colorful anecdotes of their own luck and success. It does not occur to them that perhaps their experiences as Ivy League graduates in the late sixties might not be entirely relevant to what we are going through today. Others seem to think that if you have secured an adjunct position at a prestigious place, you should be able to turn it into a full-time one by making a favorable impression on your new department. For years afterward, when they spot you in a hallway, they ask how that job turned out, implying that a person with the right stuff would have parlayed it into a career. But the most common way to encourage us is to tell stories of successful graduates they once had under their tutelage. While such anecdotal evidence of success abounds, the department, I discovered, keeps no records of where its Ph.D.'s end up. It is impossible to acquire any sense of how Ph.D.'s from your department are likely to fare on average. But at the placement meetings, in conversations with professors, and in gossip among graduate students, the success stories endlessly circulate.

Arguably, anything less than this single-minded attention to the means for professional advancement would be unprofessional. Of course professors should encourage us and advise us on writing application letters, publishing articles, and interviewing. Yet implicit in this treatment of us is the notion that if we do not "make it," we have only ourselves to blame. In my experience professors find it convenient to stick exclusively to this role of professional mentor because they can then avoid addressing uncomfortable issues of graduate exploitation and overproduction. Graduate students appreciate advice and encouragement. At the same time, however, we would welcome it if professors occasionally dropped the mentor role with its focus on individual improvement and showed some sympathetic recognition of the systemic nature of the problems we face.

The competitive individualism encouraged by graduate school corrodes any sense of graduate student solidarity, making us an unlikely group to turn to unionization as a solution to our problems. I was surprised when I heard about the collective action at Yale and the spirit of solidarity among graduate students there; it seemed so distant from the situation in my department. Here the bad job market just intensifies an atmosphere of quiet desperation and invidious comparison. Our behavior in trivial matters testifies to our atomization. Last year I began to notice that in the weeks before the MLA annual convention we were all reluctant to reveal the number of interviews we had. Those who had no interviews were ashamed to admit it. Those with several, on the other hand, feared that saying so would make others resentful. Moreover, the latter group worried that if they let it be known they had many interviews, they might later be stigmatized as failures for receiving no job offers despite so many chances. Another instance of our alienation from one another is the way otherwise polite and sensitive people will let slip expressions of happiness at the news that a fellow student has dropped out, their better selves unable to restrain the relief they feel at the thought of one less competitor.

With little sense of solidarity among graduate students as a whole, we usually turn for support to spouses, small circles of friends, and therapists. Our sense of isolation is increased by the fact that our own families have difficulty comprehending our situation. When I tried to explain the bad job market to my parents, they took me to mean that Ivy League jobs were hard to come by and that I might have to settle temporarily for one at a small private college or state school. Then I mentioned the latest MLA statistics indicating that only 45 percent of the graduating Ph.D.'s in English found tenure-track positions in 1993–94.[4] Unexpectedly, they took these figures to be very encouraging. I could not convince them that their bright son would not easily find a job in these circumstances. How could I blame them for thinking this way when many graduate students think that way about themselves? On several recent occasions I have mentioned the same figures to fellow job seekers. To my amazement, the response was one of surprised enthusiasm that the percentage was that high. They voiced no indignation that so many persons like themselves were committing eight years or so of their lives to careers that would never materialize. I suppose my associates secretly felt that they were among "the elect."

The bleak job market, however, will increasingly push us toward a sense of collective identity. The idea that we are serving apprenticeships is hard to maintain when no jobs are waiting for us at the end. Despite the grim situation, I will continue to look for a job in the academy. But my attitude toward the pursuit of a career has changed. The experience of graduate school and the job search has taught me to identify with workers and to think of society in terms of class as opposed to meritocracy. I am now much more wary of labeling myself or others as undeserving. The more I learn to appreciate the talents of my colleagues, regardless of their outward "success," the more indignant I become at a system that lets so much merit and commitment go to waste. At many universities, graduate students and professors are uniting to prevent this squandering of human potential.[5] They are fighting together for benefits and living wages for teaching assistants and adjunct instructors, for reasonable workloads and class sizes, and for more permanent tenured positions, so that a greater number of us can have the opportunity for fulfilling careers. I admire their work and hope to have a chance to join them in the struggle. While we all claim to value democratic participation and social commitment, I doubt whether many of us truly appreciate these virtues, because we are so conditioned to feel a sense of satisfaction through competitive self-advancement. Some experience living in accordance with them may make it harder for us to accept anything less, either in the academy or in society at large.

Notes

[1.] For details of the Yale "grade strike" and of the six-year effort of the Graduate Employees and Students Organization (GESO) to achieve official recognition, see George Judson, "Yale Student Strike Points to Decline in Tenured Jobs," *New York Times,* January 17, 1996, late ed., p. B6; and Emily Eakin, "Walking the Line," *Lingua Franca* 6.3 (1996), pp. 52–60. For the perspective of one of the union members, see Lauren Appelbaum, "Broken Promises: Yale's Union-Busting Binge," *Dollars and Sense* (May/June 1996), pp. 26–28.

[2.] See Keith Bradsher, "Gap in Wealth in U.S. Called Widest in West," *New York Times,* April 17, 1995, p. A1.

3. The line is quoted from Yale spokesman Thomas Conroy in Alice Dembner, "Union Drive Erupts at Yale; Graduate students could be expelled," *Boston Globe,* January 10, 1996, Metro/Region, p. 17.

4. For statistical information on the 1993–94 job market for Ph.D.'s in the modern languages, see "The MLA's 1993–1994 Survey of Ph.D. Placement: Major Findings," in the *MLA Newsletter* 27.4 (1995), pp. 1–3.

5. For evidence of an increasing turn toward collective action on the part of both professors and teaching assistants, see Mary Crystal Cage, "Winter of Pickets; Unions on many campuses turn to protests as contract negotiations stall," *The Chronicle of Higher Education,* January 26, 1996, p. A15.

Independent of What?
Rethinking Academic Marginality

Laura Stempel Mumford

"For, what is it to be an academic, except to have been authorized to speak by the academy?"
—Hilary Radner, *Shopping Around*[1]

"One of the most valuable sorts of information constituting inherited cultural capital is practical or theoretical knowledge of the fluctuations of the market in academic qualifications, the sense of investment which enables one to . . . [know] the right moment to pull out of devalued disciplines and careers . . . rather than clinging to the scholastic values which secured the highest profits in an earlier state of the market."
—Pierre Bourdieu, *Distinction*[2]

A couple of years ago, I was invited by a friend to be the respondent on a conference panel she was organizing called "Questions of Margins and the Academic Marketplace." The invitation came, as you will soon understand, because of my vexed relationship to the major terms of the session's title, so I began my comments by reminding the audience that how we respond to "questions of margins" always depends on how we frame those questions: where we think the margins are, what we imagine they're marginal to, what we believe constitutes the "center." It was my fourth or fifth public appearance on a panel of this sort, and as usual, I devoted most of my remarks to an exploration of the personal significance of this tension between margin and center, explaining my commitment to making a virtue of my professional marginality. But by the end of my presentation, I realized that I'd chosen to discuss the wrong half of the title. Instead of concentrating on questions of margins, I should have been examining the ways in which, despite my apparent distance and disenfranchisement from it, the academic marketplace frames and perhaps defines my own experience as an intellectual.

I got my doctorate in 1983, and if my career had proceeded according to the conventional narratives of academic success, I would by now probably be an associate, perhaps even a full, professor somewhere. Instead, because of a variety of professional and personal exigencies—shifting academic trends, a commitment to live in the same house as my husband, and a lousy job market, about which more later—I've spent the last thirteen years working without any ongoing formal institutional affiliation, and although I've never stopped being a scholar, I abandoned the academic job search long ago. I've made a career out of writing for both academic and general audiences—spending nearly nine years, for instance, as a TV columnist for the local weekly paper, while redefining my focus as a critic and theorist from turn-of-the-century British feminist writing to contemporary cultural studies. When finances permit it, I work full-time as a writer and independent scholar; when they don't, I work full-time as a writer and independent scholar, and part-time at miscellaneous temporary jobs.

I have a history of being outspoken—even confrontational—about the issues that face those of us struggling to carve out academic identities without the financial, social, and collegial support of the institutions that comprise the traditional academy. That history includes public presentations, published essays, and the irritating habit of standing up at meetings to remind conventionally employed academics of the professional presence of people like myself. Unlike the long-term job candidates who, as what Cary Nelson calls "damaged goods," are subject to "implicit pressure . . . to hide or misrepresent their emotional condition,"[3] I want everyone to understand the damage I've suffered, to recognize the pain and also the nerve and commitment of people who continue to write without regular academic employment. When someone describes me as "a success story,"[4] I feel compelled to tell them that it all depends on your definition of success. When they express amazement at how much writing I do, I'm forced to remind them of my fear that without a teaching job, if I don't write, I barely exist on any recognizable professional horizon.

Over the years, I've been frustrated by this problematic existence and challenged by the need to describe myself and what I do, to make my presence visible in language or emotions that my real and potential colleagues can understand—to make sense, for myself and others, of the experience of working as an academic who has not been clearly "authorized to speak by the academy." By trying them all on, for instance, I've discovered that the modifiers available to me—"displaced," "unaffiliated," "independent"—presume a center of intellectual life and work to which I am by definition marginal.[5] This fact has always made me uncomfortable, yet I've also always seen a strategic advantage in embracing my marginality, if only to discomfit those of my fully employed academic colleagues who would be happier not having to remember that people like me exist. Besides, there's something appealing, even liberating about identifying myself as independent, about claiming to operate outside the regulations of the formal academy. (In the same way, despite the martial and phallic imagery, I love the idea of being a "freelance writer," of showing up with my own personal weapon, ready to do battle on my terms.) As a feminist, I also like being connected to the tradition by which excluded groups glory in not being part of the institutions that oppress them, and even better, seize the very vocabulary of exclusion and demonization—"queer," "dyke"— and turn it into an affirmation.

At the same time, though, that process of finding a name, an identity, a way to talk about my experience sometimes feels like a form of repetition compulsion. Despite countless resolutions not to go over the same ground again, despite the fact that each rehearsal of my history revives familiar feelings of exclusion and failure, I find myself unable to stop writing and speaking about my position. In their work on the downsizing of academic institutions, Wesley

Shumar and Jonathan Church help to situate my compulsion by pointing to the stigmatization of certain specific positions and identities within the scholarly community, using Erving Goffman's idea of "virtual" versus "real" selves to explicate the difficulties adjunct and temporary faculty face within the academic hierarchy. They note that "the stigmatized spend a considerable amount of time managing their identity—making the plot twist make sense,"[6] and this characterization perfectly describes and, to my amazement, makes sense of my own practice by reminding me that despite my enthusiasm for independence, my identity is after all defined by a hierarchy, a structure in whose terms I am stigmatized. I'm not merely claiming outsider status because it's fun, or for some obscure political or theoretical advantage; I really am outside of something, and I can't ignore the specific consequences that this fact has for my psyche as well as my work.

Still, the precise definition of my status continues to elude me. On that "Questions of Margins" panel, for example, I was meant to represent a self-evidently marginal position, to be the voice that speaks from the edge of the marketplace, a stance which I found comfortable, even comforting, when I agreed to take part. Yet in the interim between the session's organization and its performance, I began to rethink the question of my own marginality, moved not only by changes in my individual life, but by the growing suspicion that my experience may not have occurred quite as far out of the mainstream as it had always seemed.

Let's begin with me: A few months before that panel, my book on soap opera was published by a major university press, an accomplishment that raised my profile on the academic scene to a new level. Although it wasn't an overnight transformation, my discovery of it was sudden: People now knew who I was, what I worked on; they were reading my book, wanted to teach it, to meet me at conferences. When I tried to arrange speaking engagements around the book, I easily found people who were happy to invite me to their campuses (although it was partly my low speaking fees that attracted them!). And when a friend and I decided to organize a major conference, I quickly realized that I had a wide collegial network of support and interest on which to draw, that people were eager to answer my phone calls and e-mail messages, and even to commit themselves to participate because I'd invited them. After years of seeing myself as marginal, maybe even invisible, within my specialty, I was genuinely shocked to discover that I'd been building a public presence without understanding exactly what its components were.

I don't want to put too sunny a face on this, because at the same time, I also faced some significant setbacks—most significantly, the loss of my husband's job only weeks after my book came out, and with it, the economic security that had allowed me to spend all these years writing for little or no money. Nevertheless, I could see quite dramatically how far I'd come since the "Point of View" essay I wrote for *The Chronicle of Higher Education* in 1986, in which I'd wondered, as I left the academic marketplace, whether I could continue to be an intellectual without a teaching job.[7] The answer had obviously turned out to be yes.

And yet, while this review has given me a greater sense of myself as part of a collegial circle, my daily experience of being a scholar and writer remains fundamentally unchanged. As always, I spend most of my time sitting in my study alone, drawing no salary and paying my own expenses for photocopying and phone calls and on-line time and conference attendance. The isolation, of course, is not mine alone, for depending on your mood and temperament, it is either the cost or the benefit, but always a defining feature of being a writer. However, in happy contrast to those conventionally employed scholars who experience their solitude as alienation or estrangement from on-campus colleagues,[8] I've come to understand my professional community as composed of people I see once or twice or three times a year at conferences, with whom I exchange E-mail or occasional phone calls. In some ways, I have the best, or at least the purest, version of community, because it consists of people with whom I share specific intellectual interests or personal styles, rather than simply an office corridor.

Ironically, though, it's my increasingly secure position within that community that has created this latest flurry of identity management, for having staked out not just a public position, but practically an academic specialty based in my own apparently incontrovertible marginality, I am now faced with the unforeseen problem of integrating into my professional self-image some of the tangible and intangible signs of mainstream academic success: a book, a degree of name recognition, a sense of belonging to a collegial cohort. Even stranger, having persuaded myself that it's the work itself, rather than employment, that counts, I find myself having to excavate the entire question of my relation to the academic job market. While I'd thought that one permanently and safely buried, other people inevitably see the book as a credential for a potential and, they assume, triumphant return to the search for a teaching position. Having labored all these years to proclaim not only my independence, but my exclusion, to remind everyone that I'm out here working on the margins, all by myself, I find myself wondering whether that's still a fair characterization.

I've tried to resolve this dilemma by turning once again to the problem of naming myself, trying to invent some new term like "professional intellectual," which would move me safely away from the assumption that colleges and universities are the real sites of the work I do and focus instead on the work itself. But after all of the insights I've gained from this exercise in the past, this time it gives me little comfort. Instead, oddly, it only serves to remind me that some great, central questions remain unanswered: What does it mean to be an "academic" or an "intellectual" or a "scholar," independent, professional, or otherwise? What is the supposedly central project and identity against which we define other projects and identities as marginal? Is it teaching, research, writing, some combination of these, or something else altogether? And where do these things get defined, anyway? Who authorizes the ones we understand as central, or excludes the ones we know as marginal?

It doesn't take much imagination to realize that context is everything. Despite the public Sturm und Drang about domineering leftists and "tenured radicals," my questions are hard to answer even if we confine ourselves to ideologically loaded examples from a single, well-established discipline. Ask a graduate student with a commitment to, say, feminist cultural studies or queer theory or radical pedagogy or postcolonial literature how she feels working within a highly traditional English department and you'll get a very different answer about where the margins and the center lie, and how they got there, than you'll hear from someone committed to traditional research on the established canon, working within a department that prides itself on turning out cutting-edge theorists. And things are just as murky and contradictory when it comes to thinking about the parameters of the work itself. Ask an adjunct who's been on the job market for six years about the pleasures of pursuing research without the burden of committee work and student advising and what you hear will have little in common with the answer you get from a sixth-year assistant professor facing a difficult tenure review. The point isn't that we can one-up each other in the marginality sweepstakes, but that the geography isn't quite as clearly marked as our professional apprenticeships—or mass-media disputes about the tenure process—may have led us to believe.

This fact of academic life creates a real crisis for me, because as much as I want to locate myself at least within shouting distance of the center—wherever that is—I want to keep claiming my marginality as well, to get credit for the difficulties I've endured all these years, the efforts I've made, the hard-won achievement of simply continuing to write. But if I can't figure out where the margin is, how do I celebrate my triumph over its limitations?

It isn't an abstract problem for me, either, but one that manifests itself in the pettiest details of daily professional life. At least four times during the last academic year, for instance, I've had to correct conference organizers, session chairs, and others who have ascribed to me a specious institutional affiliation. In each case, I was more than just frustrated at a clumsy inaccuracy; I was angry about the conclusions people would draw. Some would assume that the affiliation was correct, thus endowing me with departmental office supplies, phone service, e-mail, health insurance, a salary, and perhaps even funding for the conference in question. A few of those who knew it was incorrect would figure there'd been some simple bureaucratic screwup, but others—the ones who don't know me, or who believe that an institutional connection is every academic's ultimate goal—would assume that I was trying to boost my status by appropriating the institution's name.

This matters to me not only because I want personal recognition, but because I have an ongoing commitment to reminding people that serious intellectual work occurs outside of formal academic institutions. As an assertion of my own independence, but also as a consciousness-raising exercise, I always insist that my conference name tags and program listings cite only my name and the city I live in, yet when people see that attenuated I.D., they inevitably read into it an implicit affiliation and ask me which department I'm in, apparently persuaded that I've simply forgotten to mention my employer's name. Because I've repeatedly had to insist on new name tags or program corrections or changes in the minutes, because I spend a certain amount of time at every conference I attend explaining my situation, I know that these are innocent mistakes rather than deliberate misrepresentations, and that they occur primarily because people with institutional ties simply cannot quite imagine academic life outside those formal boundaries. But this is precisely the point: at some level, people cannot quite imagine my life, even when they know its contours. No matter how much noise I make about it, the information doesn't quite sink in, and paradoxically, the more I publish, the worse it gets. The higher my public profile rises, the more casually people assume that I must be teaching somewhere. The more visible I become, the more invisible my status grows, and in this sense I remain solidly outside of the paradigm that frames people's expectations.

And yet—once again!—it's obviously far more complicated than that, for whatever tidy paradigm they're using is itself far from stable. When I first began to reconsider my own marginality, I thought about it primarily in terms of the conventional scholarly accomplishments I've already described: how marginal can I be, I asked myself, when my book's been published in a series edited by Andrew Ross, who is seen in some circles as the sine qua non of academic, not to mention sartorial, glamour? As I've thought more about it, however, I've come to recognize the dubious premises underlying my conviction that working on the institutional margins means I am marginal, and to realize that a far deeper reconsideration of both margin and center is required than I'd previously imagined undertaking. It demands first that I rethink in a fairly profound way just what importance the institutional academy has in the intellectual lives of people who practice outside its walls, how fully our theoretical and scholarly agendas, even our ideas, are defined by the work, the economics, the politics and social structures of institutions in which we don't participate.

Can I really say, for instance, that the job market has nothing to do with me when I know how frequently people choose an academic specialty precisely because they think it will get them a job? If those choices lead to presentations and publications, won't they eventually shape the work I do, despite my "outsider" status? And in that case, isn't it my responsibility to keep track of hiring and tenuring trends, to pay attention to campus politics, to acknowledge the influence of disciplinary fashions because some day these things will have some impact, however indirect, on my own thinking and writing?

These questions become increasingly urgent as the shape of intellectual and academic life changes. Recent studies have concluded that some 40 percent of faculty in the United States are not in tenured or tenure-track jobs, but despite the mass-media dissemination of this statistic,[9] I've discovered that few of my friends or colleagues were aware of it until I'd announced it in several public forums, and even those who knew the figure seemed not to have considered its implications. Yet it seems to me that such a trend threatens the very notion of what it means to be "authorized to speak by the academy"—does it mean mere paid employment? a faculty line? tenure?—and thus the long-standing definition of terms like "academic," "intellectual," "scholar." That 40 percent figure— which does not even count the people who, like me, continue to work as scholars without teaching at all—means that something quite fundamental to academic employment and therefore, necessarily, academic identity has changed. It means, I think, that adjunct and part-time and temporary teachers and "freeway fliers" and exploited graduate students and overworked lecturers and so-called "independent scholars" are now marginal more to an *idea* of what it means to be an academic than to its reality. And that demands in turn a thorough reconsideration of the familiar assumption that full-time, permanently employed faculty are at the center of the academic and intellectual universe, that their experiences define academic life, that their labors in the classroom, in the laboratory, in the library produce the work that counts.

And this is the very least it means, for accommodating the statistic also requires a seismic shift in the myth that underlies academic life, in which a Ph.D. leads ultimately to tenure and those whose experiences don't conform to that trajectory are unequivocally marked as failures. If this myth ever reflected reality, it ceased to do so years ago, but the academic community hasn't yet fully acknowledged even the fact that it is a myth. Instead, we seem constantly to rediscover, to our collective astonishment, that the academic world is not what we imagined it to be. Feminist scholars and theorists have remarked on the practice of "reinventing the wheel" when it comes to women's experience, a cycle in which new generations of feminists seem doomed to recover, almost from scratch, not only the historical contributions women have made to culture and society, but the very history of feminism itself. We explain the need for that recovery in terms of patriarchy's continual erasure of women from the public chronicle of human achievement, which feminism was until recently insufficiently powerful to remedy. But what explains the fact that, despite the almost obsessive collection and publication of hiring figures, it's taken until now for the alteration of the academic landscape to even begin to register?[10] Here, for instance, is a comment published in 1994:

> It is time for faculty members and institutions to understand what job seekers have already found out: that the current academic job crisis is very bad. It is not a temporary slump but a full-blown collapse, not a normal downswing in a healthy market cycle but a Great Depression.[11]

Yet these words, which come from a graduate student, could have been written by any of us who faced the humanities job market since the early 1970s.[12] When I was first accepted to graduate school in 1976, the letter of acceptance noted that teaching jobs were few and far between, and nearly everyone who received a doctorate in the humanities in the last two decades can tell a similar story. While this common experience might lead one to expect that a few basic lessons would have been learned about the uncertainty of our collective academic future, each generation of new Ph.D.'s seems to meet the crisis unprepared for what is in fact not just a major, but it seems a permanent, change, and one that is guaranteed not only to resonate across the employment scene, but to echo throughout the intellectual enterprise as a whole.

If this change remains undigested, its consequences do not seem even to have been ingested. Recent arguments over the existence and role of so-called ''public intellectuals'' have failed utterly to dislodge the fantasy that the only intellectual accomplishments worth taking seriously come from within colleges and universities.[13] In the winter of 1996, for example, a lengthy and quite heated discussion about the ethics of adjunct hiring took place in an academic on-line list I subscribe to, raising important issues about the job market, budget constraints, student advising, faculty responsibility, and administrative power—all considered as if intellectual life occurs only within the confines of formal academic institutions. After about two weeks, I finally intervened, with this message:

> Okay, guys, I've been sitting very quietly while you debate the current job market, the ethics of adjunct hiring, the exploitation of grad students, etc.—all *extremely* important issues, but discussed here as if all intellectual life occurs within the university, and no job = no scholarship. So I'd just like to remind you, as one of the people who does it, that intellectual work *does* take place beyond the formal institutions that comprise the academy. It's hard, it's even more grotesquely underpaid than being an adjunct or a TA, & you have to push yourself in the faces of those with jobs, who tend to forget that so-called ''independent'' or ''unaffiliated'' scholars exist. But it can be done. I don't rec-

ommend it as a way of life—& I only ended up in this
situation because the job market of the early '80s was at
least as hideous as the current one, & yet, as the recent
posts remark, I chose it, I felt I *had* to do it. And as
someone who's managed to work without institutional support for 13 years now, & publish, & establish some small
reputation in my field (TV studies), I take very seriously
my responsibility to remind everyone that I'm not the only
one. It's absolutely crucial that people with tenure & administrative power & advising responsibilities take seriously the real experiences of people not like yourselves,
that you don't erase the existence of *anyone* who isn't
in your privileged positions: grad students, adjuncts, part-
timers, untenured people, *and* those of us working outside of your institutions. We're *all* your colleagues.

Lest you imagine that this was an isolated incident, I hasten to add
that only two months later, a similar discussion occurred at the
plenary session of a conference I attended, during which a debate
about how to deal with various threats to academic freedom became
framed almost immediately by the twin assumptions that all intellectual work occurs within the university and that all university
employees of consequence are academics. Call it identity management or consciousness-raising or just plain frustration, but despite
a promise to myself not to intervene, I found myself unable to
keep silent, and ended up essentially reiterating the message I've
reproduced above.

What's interesting to me about both cases, however, isn't my
obnoxious interventions, but the fact that my remarks led absolutely
nowhere. I don't mean that I got no response at all, since, as usually
happens when I act up or out in this way, I got a few nice thanks-
for-enlightening-us posts from the on-line list, several supportive
comments from friends at the conference, and even a couple of remarks from people I ran into over the following months. Rather, I
was struck (although hardly surprised) by two specific things that
didn't happen in either forum: no member of the stigmatized pop-

ulation with which I identified myself—independent, or temporarily or marginally affiliated—publicly echoed my remarks, and neither discussion ever took up the problem of the false divide between intellectual life "inside" and "outside" academic institutions.

Experiences like these have brought home to me quite powerfully that there is some real urgency to my project of rethinking the categories of academic margin and center by reminding me that these categories have meaning and indeed hegemonic power for people other than myself. That 40 percent figure means that the colleagues who can't imagine my life render invisible not just my personal experience, but the experience of nearly half their professional peers as well, and as long as that collective experience remains invisible, we remain locked into a set of dichotomies— tenured and adjunct, affiliated and independent, inside and outside— that endangers us all. Having been acculturated alongside our non-academic friends and relatives, those of us who identify ourselves as academics and scholars are equally prone to accept the familiar metaphor of the ivory-towered intellectual whose work occurs in some sphere outside of the "real world."[14] Yet this image, which never did describe our experiences accurately, has become increasingly inapt as the brutality of the academic job market has accelerated. There are real-world consequences to this too: the prevailing, indeed escalating, popular sense that academics are self-indulgent navel gazers has been bolstered by the unwillingness of those with institutional affiliations to understand their work as linked to that of intellectuals outside of the university, for it enables those who fear or denigrate our enterprise to cordon it off in a safe little corner— The University—where it can easily be neutralized or ignored. This is—or at least should be—of particular concern to those of us on the left, not only because we're under siege, but because it is precisely our critical and theoretical practices that have illuminated the ways in which institutions work to erect artificial cultural barriers, of which this false divide is surely one.

Despite the power and appeal of those ivory tower fantasies, the academic marketplace doesn't exist in a vacuum, but in a culture that's increasingly characterized by corporate downsizing, deskilling, the erosion of benefits and job security, and the conversion of full-time permanent employees into part-timers, subcontractors, home workers, and temps. The last twenty years' changes in academic employment eerily mirror those changes in the larger society,[15] but with one crucial difference: as cultural workers, as writers and thinkers, as theorists and critics possessed of the research tools and the language needed to understand and describe our place in the world, we are uniquely placed to intervene in the debate and to make certain that these alterations in the conditions of intellectual labor are accurately understood, not only by non-academics, but by our own scholarly community. The task of rethinking what it means to be a member of that community becomes daily more urgent, as more and more of us find ourselves working outside the conventional academic boundaries. If current trends continue, institutional downsizing and the Reaganbush legacy of virulent anti-intellectualism will continue to force a significant portion of each year's Ph.D.'s to look elsewhere for either jobs or professional support, to redraw the boundaries of their scholarly or their pedagogical interests to suit the opportunities available. The odds are high that some of them will feel the same compulsion I do to maintain their scholarly work and their identities as intellectuals, regardless of their employment status, and regardless of the academy's refusal to grant them official authority to speak. And in that case, my own experience will turn out to have been far less marginal than I ever imagined.

Notes

Part of this essay was presented at the National Coalition of Independent Scholars conference, May 4, 1996, Princeton. Thanks as always to the friends who provide an intellectual community that helps to make my own work possible, among them Julie D'Acci, Ellen Berry, and Carol Siegel, for conversations both virtual and actual; JoAnn Castagna and Diane Worzala, who are endlessly willing to discuss the quandaries of independence; and Shiva Subbaraman, who made me think about this one more time, even when I said I didn't want to.

Critiques of the Academy

1. Hilary Radner, *Shopping Around: Feminine Culture and the Pursuit of Pleasure* (New York: Routledge, 1995), p. 17.

2. Pierre Bourdieu, *Distinction: A Social Critique of the Judgment of Taste*, trans. Richard Nice (Cambridge: Harvard University Press, 1984), p. 142.

3. Cary Nelson, "Lessons from the Job Wars: Late Capitalism Arrives on Campus," *Social Text* 44, Vol. 13, No. 3 (Fall/Winter 1995), p. 124. See also Jack H. Schuster's comment that "Over the past twenty years, incalculable damage has been inflicted on thousands of aspiring academics as the academic pipeline continues to disgorge people into a marketplace saturated in most fields," in "Speculating About the Labor Market for Academic Humanists: 'Once More unto the Breach,'" *Profession '95*, p. 60.

4. MLA President Sandra M. Gilbert, for instance, uses this phrase in discussing a man who, on being turned down for tenure at "an elite school," turned to novel and screenplay writing, "whose 'case history' suggests that the alternative career route can lead to interesting places." See her "President's Column," *MLA Newsletter*, Vol. 28, No. 2 (Summer 1996), p. 4.

5. I discuss naming and what constitutes academic "employment" in "Telling My Story: The Narrative Problems of Being an Independent Scholar," *Narrative* 2: No. 1 (January 1994): 53–64.

6. Wesley Shumar and Jonathan T. Church, "Marginalization and Institutional Restructuring: Struggles of a Flexible Professoriate in the New University," paper presented at the National Coalition of Independent Scholars conference, May 4, 1996, Princeton, New Jersey. Effusive thanks to them, as promised, for letting me quote from the unpublished version of the argument.

7. "The Painful Process of Letting Go," *The Chronicle of Higher Education,* November 19, 1986, p. 104.

8. David Damrosch, "The Scholar as Exile: Learning to Love Loneliness," *Lingua Franca,* January/February 1995, pp. 56–60.

9. "Yale Student Strike Points to Decline in Tenured Jobs," *The New York Times,* January 17, 1996, p. B9; Schuster, "Speculating About the Labor Market for Academic Humanists," p. 58.

10. A variety of academic associations and publications keep such records. The MLA (to cite only one of the professional organizations to which I belong) tracks and publishes these statistics annually, and recent issues of its yearly publication, *Profession,* have dealt extensively with the subject, both in the form of individual articles and through thematic groupings, such as *Profession '94*'s "Special Topic on the Job Market." For a completely different disciplinary perspective on the job-market crisis, see *Science*'s on-line Next Wave project (see Appendix for its URL address). R. Eugene Rice's "Making a Place for the New American Scholar" (AAHE New Pathways Working Paper Series, Inquiry #1), a 1996 report commissioned by the American Association for Higher Education, also acknowledges the changes I describe, but while it suggests ways in which faculty and academic institutions might accommodate them, it treats these shifts as relatively new phenomena.

11. Erik D. Curren, "No Openings at This Time: Job Market Collapse and Graduate Education," *Profession '94,* p. 60.

12. In "Lessons from the Job Wars," Cary Nelson describes the job market of the early 1970s as equally brutal (pp. 123–24).

13. A few examples from both mass media and academic sources, to indicate just how wide-ranging this discussion is: Russell Jacoby, *The Last Intellectuals: American Culture in the Age of Academe* (New York: Basic Books, 1987); Jervis Anderson, "Life and Letters: The Public Intellectual," *The New Yorker,* January 17, 1994, pp. 39–48; Janny Scott, "Journeys from Ivory Tower: Public Intellectual is Reborn," *The New York Times*, August 9, 1994, pp. A1, A13; Jay Rosen, "Making Things More Public: On the Political Responsibility of the Media Intellectual," *Critical Studies in Mass Communication,* Vol. 11, No. 4 (December 1994), pp. 363–88; Nicholas Garnham, "The Media and Narratives of the Intellectual," *Media, Culture & Society,* Vol. 17 (1995), pp. 359–84; Robert S. Boynton, "The New Intellectuals," *The Atlantic Monthly,* March 1995, pp. 53–70. One could

also cite about half the content of each *Lingua Franca* issue as a contribution, albeit not always marked as one, to this debate.

[14.] Wesley Shumar interrogates the terms of the binary oppositions that define cultural understandings of what it means to be an academic, particularly the ivory-towered "community of scholars" versus the "knowledge factory," in "Higher Education and the State: The Irony of Fordism in American Universities," in John Smyth, ed., *Academic Work: The Changing Labour Process in Higher Education* (Buckingham, United Kingdom: Open University Press, 1995), pp. 84–98.

[15.] In "Higher Education and the State," Wesley Shumar uses the notion of commoditization to explicate the relationships between recent crises in higher education and extra-academic economic changes.

Afterwords

Afterword

Louis Menand

Ph.D. program in English, The Graduate Center
of the City University of New York

applied to graduate school in 1973. My situation was typical of
graduate school applicants, both then and now, in three ways. I
had tried something else first (I was in law school at the time);
I had no special interest in becoming a professor; and I was
warned by someone who was a professor that I would not be able
to find an academic job. For by 1973 the job market in my field,
which is English, had already undergone the collapse from which,
nearly twenty-five years later, it still has not recovered.

Why did the demand curve for people with Ph.D.'s fall away
so suddenly and dramatically from the supply curve in the economy
of American higher education? Because between 1960 and 1970,
student enrollment in colleges and universities grew by 120 percent,
and to meet that need, more new faculty positions were created, in
that single ten-year period, than had existed in the entire 325-year
history of American higher education to that point. So that by the
early 1970s, the system was operating at full capacity. These new
professors were young, they were readily tenured (since slots for
them were being newly minted), and they were not going anywhere.
These were not baby boomers; these were people who had gone to

college in the 1950s and early 1960s. The baby boomers were the undergraduates who made their careers possible—and who went on, in large numbers, to graduate school themselves, only to find the road to an academic career blocked by the very people who, as their undergraduate teachers, had given them the desire to continue their educations in the first place.

As the editors of this volume note in their introduction, many people expected that the generation of professors who entered the academic economy in the 1960s would be due for professional expiration in the 1990s. But the professors who got in when universities were flush are getting out (often with attractive retirement incentives) when funding is evaporating. They are leaving, and their budget lines are leaving with them. This is due to an important feature of the current academic employment picture, which is that the growth in higher education since 1960 took place overwhelmingly in the public sector. Between 1960 and 1980, the number of public institutions of higher education in America more than doubled, from 700 to 1,600. And although there are today 1.5 million more students in private colleges and universities than there were in 1960, there are nearly 9 million more students in public institutions.

The public sector, in other words, is where all those new academic jobs were created in the 1960s, and the public sector is therefore where the crunch is being felt in the 1990s. With less reason to pour money into research and development now that the Cold War is over, and with more pressure to lower taxes and reduce spending, the federal government and many state governments are lowering subsidies to public higher education. State appropriation to public higher education in California, which has the largest system in the country, was cut 27 percent between 1991 and 1994. In the last ten years, state expenditures on higher education nationally have shrunk by 4 percent. (State expenditures on corrections have increased by 40 percent. It is not a minor irony that one of the editors of this book now teaches in a California prison.) In other words, when people looking at the future of academic employment in 1973 thought they could see, twenty years down the road, a light at the

340

end of the tunnel, it turned out that what they were looking at was actually another tunnel.

That's the demand side of the situation. On the supply side, undergraduate enrollments continue to grow. It is expected that by the turn of the century there will be 16 million college students in America (up from about 9 million back when I applied to graduate school, in 1973). Someone has to teach these people, and this has raised, once again, the hope that the market for Ph.D.s will revive (and the further hope that, cautioned by recent experience, fewer people will seek the Ph.D., thus reducing the applicant pool). But people have been predicting for twenty years that the market will take care of this problem, and it hasn't happened yet.

Why not? Because many people who apply to graduate school do so in the same spirit I did: they don't especially care, in the beginning, whether they become professors. They just love their subjects, and although, in many cases, they've tried to do something more practical with their lives, they find they can't resist a little more learning. There is not enough demand for people with doctoral degrees inside the academy and there is virtually no demand for them (apart from some traditional nonprofit and government jobs, which are vulnerable to the same economic pressures universities are) outside the academy. But there is a continued demand—measured by the number of doctoral degrees granted annually, it is in fact a growing demand—for advanced education. Thus there are not only a lot more graduate students than there were thirty years ago, there are also a lot more doctoral programs.

It is suggested, not infrequently, that one solution to the job crisis is to eliminate lower-ranked doctoral programs, on the assumption that it is their graduates who are swelling the pool of academic unemployables. This seems a bad suggestion, on two counts. It is, first, patently elitist. If qualified people want to pursue advanced degree work, then American universities ought to accommodate them. It is my own view that these people should not be penalized for life by being required to spend eight years (the current median time to a degree in the humanities) getting that education, and that doctoral programs should therefore be a lot shorter and a lot less geared to professionalization and specialization. Since this would entail changing the research requirement (in the non-sciences) from a proto-monograph to something more manageable, and since it would discourage the use of graduate students as teaching assistants (which is a big drain on time spent researching and learning), it is unlikely that the profession will do anything so drastic. The profession, after all, has nothing to lose by doing nothing. But a shorter and more focused program would not only be a more humane way to educate people; it would make the Ph.D. less of a stigma for graduates seeking jobs outside the academy, since they would have spent less time narrowing themselves to fit into academic specialties.

The second reason why eliminating lower-ranked doctoral programs is not a good solution to the job crisis is more relevant to the contemporary job market, and that is that it is not the lower-ranked programs that are having the placement problem. When the Harvard Graduate School of Arts and Sciences, which is probably the finest graduate school in the world, surveyed its 1995 recipients of the Ph.D., it discovered that only 27 percent had secured full-time teaching positions. This is very likely because all those public institutions that sprang up between 1960 and 1980 don't want Harvard Ph.D.'s. Harvard Ph.D.'s are overtrained in one sense and undertrained in another sense for the kind of work those institutions require. They are overtrained by being too specialized and cutting edge for the typical college or state university department, and they are undertrained because they have taught only Harvard undergraduates. The face of higher education has completely changed since 1960, but future professors are still being trained as though it has not—as though most academics spend four hours a week in the classroom (plus an office hour, when they can make it) and take a semester off every two and a half years to work on their books. This is not the professional reality.

Whatever they imagined when they first applied, people who have spent six or eight or ten years in a doctoral program usually find themselves pretty keenly interested in going on to a career as a professor. The first thing to say to these people is that the placement process is not, despite superstitions about it, random or fixed. It is simply not in the interests of departments hiring new assistant professors to pass over better qualified candidates in favor of a colleague's niece, or to make snap judgments about whom to offer their job to. In the end, the pegs pretty much fit into the holes that await them. The perception of "unfairness" arises from the fact that mere brilliance and scholarly accomplishment are not always the leading criteria for employment—precisely what the Harvard survey demonstrates. Schools want to hire people who are congenial in every respect, and in this market, they can wait until they find them. They know perfectly well that they no longer have to grab the first Ivy League candidate who comes along, a person who will often be gone at the first opportunity to scramble upward to the next available rung. Professors want, quite naturally and appropriately, to hire professors who are like themselves—people who want to teach where they teach and do the kind of research they do. Figuring out what this means, figuring out what the real dimensions of the advertised hole are, is the first and principal task of every would-be peg.

It is thus important for people on the academic job market to tailor their applications to the particular institutions advertising the positions they are interested in. Schools are different; job descriptions are different. An institution wants to feel that the candidate is interested in what is distinctive about it. The chances of ultimately achieving tenure may, at many places, be small enough, but there is no point in hiring someone when neither the candidate nor the school expects that person to stay. One of the most important ingredients of the application is, therefore, the candidate's own letter. This is something everyone on the search committee will read, and it needs, consequently, to be readable, and to be written with the likely members of that particular search committee in mind.

The other part of the application that invariably gets read is the letters of recommendation. (It is hard to "read" a curriculum vitae; most committees just check the dates and scan the publications. And writing samples, unless the process is very far along, are generally, well, sampled.) Candidates need to keep their letters of recommendation updated. It's a bad idea to circulate letters with last year's date on the top, since it creates the impression that the candidate has been passed over in the marketplace already. As with vegetables, so with graduate students (and contrary to the teaching of *King Lear*): freshness is all. And applicants need to be certain that their recommenders are people who understand their work and are committed to helping them get jobs. A vague and noncommittal letter from a famous professor whose seminar a candidate happens to have attended is worse than no letter at all.

The purpose of the dossier, of course, is just to get your foot in the door of the interview room, and that is where the serious selling begins. The most important thing to remember about interviews for academic jobs is that not all committees are equally experienced or competent. The interviewers are not professional personnel people. They are just professors. They like to hear themselves talk, and they can get long-winded or lapse into an inappropriate paternal/maternal mode. The candidate needs to take charge of the direction of the interview if this happens. No one is hired on the basis of what some interviewer has said, only on the basis of what a candidate has been able to say.

It is very easy, in the case of a lazy or inexperienced committee, for the interview to get sidetracked on topics like tenure possibilities, housing, local weather (the chief topic of discussion in an interview I once had with a college in New Hampshire), how many graduate courses the candidate will get to teach three years down the road, and so on. These topics may come up; the candidate may have good reasons, if there appear to be special circumstances in the case, for bringing them up. But you cannot make a good impression by the suave way you discuss, say, your housing needs. The worst thing is to let the committee get into a discussion, in your presence, about whether its job is right for you. If you have applied, you believe it's right for you. Make the point, and move on.

It's useful for candidates to know whom they can expect to be present at the interview, and candidates are entitled to ask (not too aggressively) for those names when the interview is scheduled. There may be one specialist in the candidate's field, but there will almost certainly be several people who know very little about that field. Both types need to be impressed. The hardest thing is the sixty-second synopsis of the dissertation. It requires ruthless concision and a lot of practice. The idea is to say just enough to get the ball rolling for everyone in the room—for people who know a lot about the subject as well as people who don't (or who merely think they do). It helps to know before stepping into the room which people are which.

There is always (it seems) one interviewer who wants to play-act as the devil's advocate. (Sometimes the devil himself may be present too—the professor who prides him- or herself on considering all the latest scholarship a lot of nonsense.) Candidates need to be prepared to defend the significance of their work against the usual sort of skepticism, but they should not get into a quarrel with an interviewer—even if the interviewer seems determined to get into a quarrel with them. Unless, of course, they decide they want the short-term satisfaction of blowing somebody off more than they want the position. Extremists are usually extreme because they are in a minority in their own departments. Their colleagues are used to hearing them sound off, and won't blame it on you. If they turn out to be ornery enough to dictate the decisions of the committee, you don't want to be in that department anyway.

Finally, every interview ends with ''Do you have any questions for us?'' Candidates should always be sure that they do. Schools are exactly like people. They want to feel that other people are interested in them—that they're wanted too. Candidates can help themselves enormously by making a point of expressing the enthusiasm they feel for the job being advertised. In the current market, this is not a difficult emotion to come by. No one should have to fake it.

The next thing that needs to be said is the most depressing. It has to do with what happens when no offers materialize. One reason people now take so long to get their degree is that they are likely to spend two, three, or even more years on the job market. It is almost always best, while you are on the market for a full-time position, to remain enrolled as a student—ideally a student who is, year after year, just one chapter short of finishing a brilliant disser-tation. Once the nest is left, life immediately gets a lot tougher, since schools generally prefer to pick fresh graduates rather than itinerants. This is, indeed, an unfair part of the system, but it is best not to be naive about it.

When people with doctorates don't get tenure-track positions, they often wind up either in post-doctoral programs (there are many excellent ones) or in one-year replacement positions. The mirage that sometimes arises in these latter situations is the promise of continued employment. Every once in a while, people taken on for one year end up staying a lifetime. But in general, departments cannot manufacture positions out of thin air: if they have a one-year replacement job available, that's what they have. Occasionally (and this is often the worst scenario) the one-year position will be advertised as "possibly" leading to a tenure-track appointment. Candidates should be aware, no matter how painful the fact is to contemplate, that there is a natural tropism working against inside candidates. It's not only that familiarity breeds contempt, though it does. It's that departments, in the end, don't like giving the impression, when they are conducting a national search, that the position has been promised to someone already on site.

And when you do get the offer (congratulations!): I turned out to disappoint the professor who advised me not to go to graduate school back in 1973, and to be extremely lucky—there really is no other word for it—in getting the jobs I wanted when I wanted them. But I also learned one thing that I think is worth passing along. And that is to get everything in writing. Students tend, over the many years they spend in ignorance of how departments and academic institutions actually govern themselves, to get the idea that professors know what they're doing, and that they understand how their own schools work. In reality, they usually don't. Search committee members don't know what chairpersons will do; chairpersons don't know what deans will do; deans don't know what provosts will do; and provosts and presidents don't know what trustees or state legislatures will do. And not only that. Universities tend to have all kinds of rules and policies about employment, promotion, and every imaginable perk, but they can almost always find a loophole when it suits them. No one who says an institution "can" or "can't" do some particular thing should be trusted—not because they don't mean it, but because institutions, in the last analysis (and consistent with the absolute limits of their budgets), do pretty much what they feel like doing. A verbal promise in the academy is the legal and ethical equivalent of a smile and a pat on the back. Accept the offer, but make them put everything they promised you in writing.

Afterword

Michael Bérubé
Professor of English, University of Illinois,
Urbana-Champaign

A Tale of Two Candidates

During my second year as placement director for the Department of English at the University of Illinois at Urbana-Champaign, I got a call from a woman who was one of our job candidates. Call her Candidate A. The date was December 22, 1993. The candidate asked me whether it would be worth her while to attend the MLA at all that year, since she had received no interview requests and was not sanguine about the prospects of "picking up" an interview at the convention itself. Moreover, she explained, her mother was ill, and since her mother's house lay in one direction and the MLA convention was hundreds of miles in the other direction, she thought it might be best for her to join her mother and forgo an ad hoc convention job search that would likely be futile anyway. I told Candidate A that I agreed with her reasoning completely, and that her mother's health was probably more important than anything that

348

would happen at an MLA session, so she shouldn't attend the convention simply in order to see what it was like or to get a flavor of MLA panels, overcrowded hotel rooms, and elevator delays. But I also said that she would do well to wait just one more day before making a decision, since it was not unknown for candidates to get calls for interviews right up to Christmas Eve.

The next day she received a call from a school she'd set her heart on: it was reasonably close to her family, and the job description seemed as if it had been written just for her. The teaching load was 3:2, the salary was good, and the students and the research resources seemed attractive as well. When she called me again (partly to let me know the good news, partly to thank me for advising her not to leave town for one more day), she told me that she'd been especially despondent that this school hadn't responded to her writing sample, and now was especially hopeful that her job search would pan out after all. She added quickly, however, that she knew it was only one interview; she knew it was risky to go to the MLA with only one interview; and she knew she would still wonder whether she wouldn't be better off joining her mother for the holidays. But now, at least, she had some hope.

The interview went beautifully: Candidate A was very much the person they were looking for (just as she'd hoped), and she was thrilled with the possibility of teaching at that school and living in that area. In January she was short-listed. In late February she was offered the job. Gratefully and ecstatically, she accepted.

In March, however, the university cut the funding for the position, rendering the hard work of its own search committee—and their decision, and therefore the job offer—meaningless. For Candidate A, the news had precisely the effect you'd imagine. And in the three years since that disaster, she has yet to find a full-time tenure-track job.

The story of Candidate B starts out as pretty much the same story as that of Candidate A: a candidate in despair, a late-December phone call, a good deal of ambivalence about attending the MLA with only one interview. What made Candidate B's plight look even worse to me at the time, though, was that she didn't seem interested in the school that was interviewing her, and as it turned out, they didn't seem interested in her, either. By her report, the interviewing committee had scheduled only half an hour for the interview, and spent twenty-five minutes going over basic information that was available in the college brochure, leaving the candidate a scant five minutes to describe her dissertation and her teaching experience.

Yet to her surprise, Candidate B was granted an on-campus visit in February, during which she was asked to be the "guest teacher" in a class on two 19th-century essayists well outside her envelope of expertise—an assignment that had little to do with the job for which she had applied. When she arrived to teach the class, she learned that the students had originally been slated to take an exam that day, but that the course schedule had been modified to accommodate her visit. This meant, among other things, that very few, if any, of the students had done any of the reading for the day. Displaying a resilience almost beyond belief, Candidate B somehow managed to teach a class for which she had had almost no preparation—to a group of students who were even more ill-prepared than she. To lend a touch of the surreal to the whole affair, Candidate B's hosts on campus continually marveled to her at the richness of the talent pool for new Ph.D.'s and assured their guest that if they themselves were on the market today, they wouldn't have a chance at landing a job. One wag, apparently, went so far as to say that the list of finalists for this very job was so impressive that he'd decided the best thing he could do for the profession was to gather his colleagues, find a tall building, and jump off. "But then," he noted, "we're all such lightweights, we probably wouldn't even hit the ground."

Candidate B returned to Illinois with a quiver full of questions for the placement director: What do I do with a five-minute interview? How do I guest-teach in a course I know little about for students who haven't even glanced at the assigned reading? What do I say when my prospective colleagues make jokes about jumping off buildings for the good of the profession? The placement director, a well-meaning but flummoxed fellow, had to admit he didn't have a clue.

But B's story turns out very differently from A's. Candidate B was offered the job. She accepted. She is now very happy she went to the MLA with one interview, very glad she guest-taught that course during her on-campus visit, very happy with her colleagues, and very happy to be teaching and writing, full-time, tenure-track, right where she is.

The Psychology of Candidacy

One of the morals of this tale of two candidates is that when you're on the academic job market, you never know. *You just never know.* The likeliest job gets its funding pulled; the search that looks comically futile turns out to be a surprise success. The former is the more likely outcome for job seekers these days, but as the essays in this collection show, the latter is not unknown. And that's what most people, from tenured faculty to the families of job candidates, usually don't realize about what it means to be on the market. Everyone who knows anything knows it's tough to be a Ph.D. looking for an academic job, and those who are reasonably well informed about the state of the academy know that good academic jobs are now extremely difficult to find, in part because every decent job opening draws hundreds and hundreds of applicants. But few people who haven't gone through the process themselves know how violent are the emotional vicissitudes of the market. For many new and recent Ph.D.s, the job search is a ticket to bipolar disorder, as their emotions run from despair to elation to depression in the course of a semester, a month, a day.

The essays in this collection provide, among many other things, a comprehensive introduction to the psychology of what it means to be "on the market" in the academy of the 1990s. To the job candidates, to the Ph.D. candidates of the present and the future, these essays say, *We have been there; we know what you're going through.* Whatever solace, advice, or inspiration these essays may afford, they can tell prospective job candidates how to prepare—

materially and psychologically—for a prolonged job search in an uncertain market. Have a trusted faculty friend vet your letters of recommendation; personalize your letter of application; stress different aspects of your record—teaching, research, extramural activities—to different prospective employers; arrive on campus prepared for anything; and remember above all else: *you never know*. The school that looks perfect may be a chimera, and the school that looks like a dead end might be just what satisfies your soul—and repays your student loans.

But the value of these essays—their *market value*, I should say—is not solely a function of their value for job seekers. On the contrary, some of the people who might benefit most from reading this collection, some of the people for whom this collection should be *valuable,* aren't on the academic job market at all. The families of unemployed and underemployed Ph.D.'s who wonder, like Mrs. Hopewell in Flannery O'Connor's ''Good Country People,'' what all those years of advanced education were for; the journalists who lampoon aspiring Ph.D.'s as sycophants and toadies trying to butter up (or just reproduce the scholarship of) their mentors in the hopes of impressing a cloistered, narcissistic professoriate; the tenured faculty who have no contact with graduate education, or who think themselves exempt from the general collapse, or who believe that times have *always* been tough for new Ph.D.'s and don't know that part-time teachers have grown from 22 to 45 percent of the professoriate in the past twenty-five years (or, more astonishingly, from 36 to 45 percent since 1989 alone)—these are the people for whom this book should have great market value—and great intellectual value.[1]

I presume that few readers who've picked up this book, or who've gotten this far in it, are utterly clueless about the job crisis in the American academy: you, dear reader, know what's happening, and chances are you're worried about what it means. But even among those who have turned their attention to the job crisis, there are still some strains of denial that bear addressing here. One strain involves the long-term lament that the oversupply of Ph.D.'s has been a problem since 1970: true though this may be, it does not warrant the conclusion that the current crisis is nothing new under the sun. As I noted above, the very character of academic jobs has changed radically since 1970. The result, as we are beginning to see, is that the profession of college teaching has been so eroded by the use of part-time and adjunct labor that "professional" disciplinary organizations are no longer able to promote or sustain professional working conditions for their members. (Larry Hanley of CCNY calls ours "the last generation of college professors" for this reason.) In other words, there has indeed been a "job crisis" in academe since 1970; but only since 1989 or so have academic jobs *themselves* been a substantial part of the crisis.

The second strain of denial involves what I call the "gun to head" defense. It goes something like this: What are these Ph.D.s complaining about? They knew the market was tough—and they went to graduate school anyway. Nobody put a gun to their head; they paid their money, they took their chances.

I want to discuss this second strain of denial for a moment, partly because it is so prevalent in the general population (inside and outside academe) and partly because the essays in this collection do such an effective job of exposing its mendacity. For if there's one note that resonates throughout this book, it's the note of betrayal: "We heard there was going to be a faculty shortage in the 1990s," say the Ph.D.'s of last year and next, "and we were told we could combine our love of learning with a hope of steady, secure, gainful employment." This is not the place, I think, to debate the accuracy or the methodology of the studies that, however cautiously, predicted a faculty shortage; those studies now look remarkable in that they never considered whether universities would continue to replace retiring faculty with tenure-track assistant professors or whether they would "downsize" and "outsource" faculty labor by relying increasingly on adjuncts and graduate teaching assistants, but there's not much point in pawing over the details of, say, William G. Bowen and Julie Ann Sosa's 1989 *Prospects for Faculty in the Arts and Sciences*. The point is that in the mid- to late 1980s, the news, however garbled and tinged with wishful thinking, went out in media and by word of mouth: There will be a faculty shortage to rival that of the mid- to late 1960s. Graduate school is a sound investment. Sign up now and there will be a good job awaiting you at the end of your six, seven, or ten years of solitary labor. So go ahead and pursue your love of archaeology, psychobiology, analytic number theory, or world literature: your services will be needed when your formal studies are through.

And then think of what this meant to graduate students! Think of what it takes to finish a doctorate, to finish a book-length thesis that actually contributes to the store of human knowledge! Think of the self-doubt, the self-deprivation, the determination, and the naive faith that defines the life of the average Ph.D. candidate! Or look at the contributors to this collection, and think of how proud Ingrid Steffensen-Bruce was to join the ranks of those who hold the highest degree in the land, and to have earned the degree with distinction; think of the sacrifices made by spouses, the interminable marital stress, and then the triumph of finally completing the damn degree. And then think of what it means to cast about for a few more years looking for a decent job *after* you've attained the goal you sought so long, your self-esteem varying inversely with your sense of betrayal: after all, you were told that society would value your talents, your teaching, your years of training and research. But the best you can do is to cobble together a few introductory courses at a local college at $1,200 a pop, together with a continuing education gig at a community college three nights a week for $1,000 per course. (Brian Caterino's essay is especially relevant here.) And you think, Is this the life I dreamed of when I was writing my term papers and lining my carrel with resource material for the dissertation?

The sorry truth is this: very few graduate students have any idea what kind of academic job market they'll be getting into as they make their way through graduate school, and very few graduate programs make a comprehensive effort to tell them what kind of ordeal awaits them at the end of their years of study. It is true that not even the most farsighted and well-intentioned faculty could have predicted, in 1990, how desolate and forbidding the job market would look by 1995. But it is nonsense to maintain, as some of my colleagues have done, that the Ph.D.'s who are now on the market are people who walked into a desperate situation with open eyes. By and large, the graduate students of the late 1980s and 1990s were lured by two things: the promise of pursuing an exciting, important intellectual endeavor that would be challenging, expansive, and fulfilling—*and* the promise of living in a world in which people who pursued such endeavors, and who had the talent and determination to succeed in them, would be rewarded with an academic job as challenging and as fulfilling as was the discipline, field, or inquiry itself.

The first lure is a good one: as far as I'm concerned, the more people who are convinced of the intellectual value of advanced graduate study, the better the society they live in. This may sound foolish, but it's among my cardinal beliefs that on the whole, humans have done a good thing in creating institutions that can foster the free exercise of human intellectual faculties regardless of the object or product of those institutions. The problem, though, is that people—even budding intellectuals—have to eat, find shelter, and (in extreme cases) raise children, and so the first lure winds up looking pretty bad if the second one turns out to be a sham. Because if there really isn't any gainful employment awaiting the reasonably accomplished Ph.D. candidate at the end of his or her studies, then graduate school doesn't look like a noble institution that fosters the free exercise of human intellectual faculties; it looks like a place where graduate students can be deployed as cheap labor for introductory college classes while the tenured faculty go about cultivating *their* intellectual faculties. There should be, then, no mystery about the bitterness felt by many recent Ph.D.'s: they were sold a vision of liberal education and self-advancement, and they found themselves on a market in which "liberal education" is a phrase tossed around in brochures produced by colleges half of whose labor force is made up of part-time faculty and graduate teaching assistants working at the poverty line with little or no benefits or job security.

What we need now in academe, then, whether we work in subatomic physics or cultural studies, is a three-point plan: a rigorous defense of tenure and a vocal, organized protest against what I will call the *adjunctification* of the professoriate; a truth-in-advertising program for graduate degree programs; and, not least, a reduction in the number of Ph.D.'s granted each year *combined with* a reevaluation of the function of the M.A. degree—rather than the Ph.D.— for employment outside academe.

The Function of Graduate Study at the Present Time

Points one and two of this three-point plan are symbiotic: we need to roll back the adjunctification of the professoriate even as we warn prospective graduate students about it. This means it will no longer suffice to tell graduate students, either personally or in admissions materials, that their job prospects are "uncertain." Truth in advertising now requires, I believe, that we give our students some sense not only of our employment statistics by discipline, but also a sense of what *kind* of employment universities and colleges are now offering holders of the Ph.D.—the low pay, the 5:5 teaching loads, the limited benefit packages, the *very* limited opportunities for advancement or promotion. We have not been honest enough about the nature of those jobs, either to our students or to anyone else who might be listening. Recently, in fact, I learned that at one school, our stiff-upper-lip policies on this score had had a rather grotesque consequence: a Ph.D. program was targeted for closing by a state Board of Regents on the grounds that it had not placed a sufficient number of its recent Ph.D.'s in tenure-track jobs. In coming to this conclusion, the Board of Regents refused to recognize the program's Ph.D.'s who had secured part-time employment. Let me rephrase that: the Regents would not regard the holders of non-tenure-track academic jobs as legitimate "placements" even though such jobs now account for almost half of what college teaching *is* in this country—including, of course, in the very state in which this Board of Regents was doing its work.

In the modern languages, the MLA is exemplary for compiling such statistics for part-time, full-time, and tenure-track jobs; however, the MLA produces its numbers by counting the number of jobs advertised and the number of new Ph.D.'s granted annually, rather than by counting funded jobs and *actual* job seekers—that is, job seekers who earned their Ph.D.'s in previous years and are still on the market. The result is that the MLA's numbers suggest that roughly 50 percent of new Ph.D.'s are finding tenure-track jobs each year, but do not say how many of the unemployed 50 percent of the previous five years, say, are still looking for jobs as well. My purpose here is not to debate methodology; my purpose is to persuade faculty with large graduate programs to inform their graduate students that the nature of academic employment has changed radically over the past twenty years, so much so that in many cases, prep school teaching has become a more secure and rewarding (intellectually and financially) means of employment than college teaching. A number of essays in this collection testify eloquently to this strange development, and I hope those essays are read carefully and disseminated widely.

But it's point three that I'd like to address here, for a number of reasons. My colleague Cary Nelson and I are now widely (and rightly) associated with the position that Ph.D. programs in the humanities and social sciences should be reduced in size, and that some truly marginal programs should be eliminated altogether (though not solely on the basis of their placement rate). There are any number of people who think that Nelson and I are utterly out to lunch on this one, and some of them may even be contributors to this book. So let me ask two obvious questions: who am I to make such a suggestion, and how can I defend it in the context of a collection of essays like this? I have a secure and comfortable job, and there are legions of new and recent Ph.D.'s out there who've accomplished far more, in professional terms, than I had in 1989 when I was on the market (with one published essay, no conference presentations, and scanty teaching experience to my credit). For that matter, at the entry end of graduate programs, there are any number of prospective students who have better records now than I did in 1983 when I began my studies at Virginia: in 1992, for instance, when Illinois received over five hundred applications to a graduate program that then admitted fewer than thirty students (we are the smallest program in the Big Ten), I realized that my 1983 numbers—that is, my GREs and GPA—would probably not qualify me for the first cut, the round in which the admissions committee begins reading applicants' writing samples. What had happened in the interim? Well, between 1985 and 1990 alone, the average graduate program in English experienced an astonishing 50 percent rise in the number of applicants, from 120 to 181.[2] And one curious thing the late-1980s boom in graduate studies in English had done, I realized, was that it had raised the entry-level qualifications so high that I would very likely not be admitted to the graduate program at the very institution that had hired and tenured me. So, again, who am I to close the sluice gates, to call for reductions, to restrict access to the Ph.D.? Wouldn't I do better to demand *expanded* access to doctoral programs for all students, and then to suggest that Ph.D.'s should fan out from academe into jobs in media, publishing, service organizations, government, think tanks? If I'm so concerned with "public access" to the academy and academics' access to the public, can't I imagine a flood of smart Ph.D.'s reinvigorating the public sector and the public sphere?

The essays in this collection, I think, give us some idea of how difficult it is to change the social meaning of the Ph.D. for prospective employers outside academe: all too often, the degree signifies a kind of specialization and rarefied training that is looked upon with a mixture of admiration, indifference, and suspicion. "It's very impressive that you received a Ph.D. from Johns Hopkins and that your dissertation makes an original contribution to musicology. But how precisely does that qualify you for the position of assistant manager in the city symphony's budget office? Aren't you somewhat overqualified for the job?" In some cases, it is possible for doctoral candidates, having spent the better part of a decade devoted to their studies, to find meaningful and fulfilling employment outside the academic disciplines for which they were trained. In other cases, however, the Ph.D. weighs like an albatross around the neck of talented job seekers trying to move into non-academic jobs. One of my colleagues on the academic left once told me that there is no dishonor in getting a Ph.D. in an academic discipline and then taking the degree elsewhere, into law, public service, the media, or any other ideological state apparatus. Indeed, said my colleague, whether we're progressive activists or just educators interested in fostering the enterprise of critical thinking, we should *want* new Ph.D.'s to take jobs outside the academy wherever they can get them. A nice and noble sentiment, I replied, but somewhat blinkered: yes, there is no "dishonor" in completing a Ph.D. and getting a job outside academe; the problem, however, often lies in getting the job outside academe. One of my friends from graduate school at Virginia, having bailed out of the academy after a decade of doctoral work and a few years of working temporary teaching jobs, applied to law school four years ago and is now an attorney; but when he began to look for positions at law firms he found that his Ph.D. in English literature was sometimes so serious a liability—"You spent ten years doing *what*?"—that he had to take it off his résumé altogether.

Of course, shrinking the size of graduate programs will not help my friend now, nor will it solve the overproduction of Ph.D.'s in the past ten years. And shrinking the size of graduate programs will not help the Ph.D.'s of the future, either, unless the professoriate also pursues humane, well-negotiated early retirement agreements for those tenured faculty who are no longer meeting the minimum professional requirements of their departments and disciplines. If the academic job market is going to improve in any substantial way, both the supply *and* the demand sides of the academic market equation need to be readjusted, and certainly there can be no early retirement program for *any* faculty unless university administrations agree to replace all retiring faculty with tenure-track faculty. I am not, in other words, calling for austerity measures in graduate programs and on university faculties; I *am* calling for more of a planned economy in higher education.

There is a real danger in reducing the size of graduate programs, however, and quite a few graduate students have spoken to me about it. Shrinking a program necessarily puts more weight on the decisions of admissions committees, and no committee has such foresight as to know which of its applicants will actually go on to stellar careers in academe. The danger in narrowing the sluice gates at the point of graduate school admissions, then, is that it will miss the "late bloomers," the talented researchers, analysts, and teachers of the near future who don't look as good on paper as some of their peers at age twenty-two or twenty-five but who will, given the chance, shine in any doctoral program and develop into brilliant teachers who make real contributions to knowledge. Some early retirement programs for faculty are fine with us, say my graduate student colleagues, as long as they're pegged to performance and they're not simply cost-cutting measures that brain drain the faculty of everyone over fifty-five (like the controversial early retirement program pursued by the University of California system); but reductions in graduate programs will only make the system more elitist, more dependent on GREs, letters of recommendation, and the prestige of the institution from which applicants receive their undergraduate degree. This is a meritorious complaint, and if I were advocating across-the-board cuts in enrollments, I would agree with it; but I'm not advocating that kind of reduction. I want to keep access to the M.A. as open as possible, partly so that graduate faculty can judge which students are promising enough to go on to the Ph.D. on the basis of their actual graduate work. It's the size of the *doctoral* program I'm worried about.

I should put my cards on the table here: in 1983 I applied to five graduate programs, and the only two that admitted me—Virginia and Columbia—had a policy of admitting large numbers of students and then winnowing them out before admitting them to Ph.D. candidacy. The year I started at Virginia, 1983–84, I was one of seventy entering students (Columbia admitted a similar number); the next year, 1984–85, Virginia admitted an incredible *one hundred and twenty-six*. I did not enter graduate school with the expectation that I would definitely go on toward the Ph.D.; I entered graduate school with the sense that I would try it out for a year or two and see whether I was any good at this literary criticism stuff. And I know perfectly well that if graduate programs were barred from admitting more than, say, twenty students in 1983, I would never have been admitted to graduate study at all. I have, therefore, a great deal of sympathy with the position that graduate students should be evaluated on the basis of whether they can thrive *in graduate school,* rather than on the basis of whether they look good to admissions committees before they arrive. At the same time, though, I still want to insist that in a profession where leading graduate programs admitted fifty to one hundred students a year even in the early 1980s, when the job market was as bleak as it is today, it is sane and salutary to suggest that such programs could be significantly reduced in size.

Here, then, is what I would hope for. We can still be generous, to a point, when it comes to admitting students to programs; we should give as many people as possible the chance to develop their passion for and their knowledge of whatever field of human inquiry they desire. But if we're going to be generous on this register, then we must be far less generous in admitting students to advanced study beyond the M.A. degree. Beyond the M.A., graduate student apprenticeship too often becomes simple exploitation, as Ph.D. candidates are assigned to teach introductory undergraduate courses at low pay while their eventual prospects for full-time, tenure-track employment after the Ph.D. get dimmer with each passing year. It seems clear to me, then, that the Ph.D. is not the degree we should be trying to redefine in the global marketplace; the degree we need to think about is the M.A. And one crucial reason to reconceive the M.A. is that as good jobs in college teaching become fewer and less available, graduate programs will need, at the very minimum, to establish (or reestablish) good working relationships with private and public secondary schools.

I hope this collection does at least two things for my faculty colleagues. One, I hope it calls attention to systemic and abusive labor practices in academe, practices to which I have given the ungainly name ''adjunctification.'' And two, I hope it impels all of us, but especially those of us involved in graduate education, to rethink secondary school teaching as a career path for some of our students. I don't want to glorify high school teaching; I simply think the characteristic disdain with which the academy treats high school teaching, as a career for Ph.D.'s and ABDs, is disastrous and unsustainable. If it makes sense to think of "alternative career paths" for Ph.D.'s (and this book, I hope, will help to show faculty how to begin thinking this way), it obviously makes sense to give high priority, among those alternative paths, to getting our students teaching jobs outside universities.

Secondary schools are not the magic answer to the many problems enumerated in this book; neither are early retirement programs for faculty or smaller doctoral programs for prospective students. But these are partial answers, and they do not preclude other solutions to the job crisis. I would be quite happy, in fact, to see the nation's unemployed and underemployed Ph.D.'s fan out into law, media, public service, and any other ideological state apparatus. I would be happier still if there were more jobs like mine available for new Ph.D.'s. But until there are, I propose that today's college faculty have a few tasks before them: to resist the adjunctification of the profession; to conduct job searches fairly and ethically; to reduce the size of doctoral programs; to ameliorate the exploitation of graduate teaching assistants, and support the creation of graduate student unions; and to encourage the adoption of "alternative career paths" for advanced graduate students—with special emphasis, for now, on the employment prospects in secondary schools. As Gene McQuillan's essay makes clear, this will mean that college faculty will have to concern themselves more closely with the state politics of teacher certification (McQuillan, you will recall, had taught for six years at the college level but could not count that experience toward a teacher's license because he had taught part-time). That won't be easy. Especially for those sectors of the profession that currently disdain even *undergraduate* instruction, preferring to focus entirely on graduate studies and the cutting edge of the discipline, it will seem impossible—or perhaps distasteful—to consider "alternative career counseling" an enterprise sufficiently noble to merit serious attention. But this is only one of the many things my generation of college professors will need to do if we want to keep graduate study alive—and meaningful, and fulfilling, and widely accessible—in the next century.

362

Notes

[1.] See Ernst Benjamin, "A Faculty Response to the Fiscal Crisis: From Defense to Offense," in Michael Bérubé and Cary Nelson, eds., *Higher Education Under Fire: Politics, Economics, and the Crisis of the Humanities* (New York: Routledge, 1995): 57.

[2.] See Bettina Huber, "Recent and Anticipated Growth in English Doctoral Programs: Findings from the MLA's 1990 Survey," *ADE Bulletin* 106 (1993): 44–63. According to the survey, to which 88 percent of all departments replied, 77 percent of graduate programs reported that their applicants were better qualified for graduate study in 1990 than in 1985, and only 2 percent reported a drop in the qualifications of their applicants.

Appendix of Useful Resources for the Academic Job Search

Books and Articles

(Note that most disciplinary organizations publish guides to careers in their fields. These can be obtained by mail order from the organization itself, or through their websites, some of which are listed below. See also the endnotes of individual essays for additional sources relating to the job market.)

Bérubé, Michael, and Cary Nelson, eds. *Higher Education Under Fire: Politics, Economics, and the Crisis of the Humanities.* New York: Routledge, 1995.

Caplan, Paula J. *Lifting a Ton of Feathers: A Woman's Guide to Surviving in the Academic World.* Toronto: University of Toronto Press, 1993.

Careers in Sciences and Engineering: A Student Planning Guide to Grad School and Beyond. National Academy of Sciences, 1996.

Darley, John M., and Mark P. Zanna, eds. *The Compleat Academic: A Practical Guide for the Beginning Social Scientist.* New York: Random House, 1987.

Deneef, A. Leigh, and Craufurd D. Goodwin, eds. *The Academic's Handbook.* 2nd ed. Durham: Duke University Press, 1995.

Fiske, Peter S. *To Boldly Go: A Practical Career Guide for Scientists.* American Global Publications, 1996.

Garber, Linda, ed. *Tilting the Tower: Lesbians/Teaching/Queer Subjects.* New York: Routledge, 1994.

Heiberger, Mary Morris, and Julia Miller Vick. *The Academic Job Search Handbook.* 2nd ed. Philadelphia: University of Pennsylvania Press, 1996.

Horwitz, Tony. "Class Struggle: Young Professors Find Life in Academia Isn't What It Used to Be." *The Wall Street Journal,* LXXV, No. 87, February 15, 1994, pp. A1, A6+.

Hotaling, Debra. "New Ph.D.'s Can Find a Life Outside Academe." *The Chronicle of Higher Education,* Vol. 41, No. 7 (October 12, 1994), pp. B1–B2.

Kindrow, G. [pseud.]. "The Candidate: Inside One Affirmative Action Search." *Lingua Franca* (April 1991), and *Debating Affirmative Action: Race, Gender, Ethnicity, and the Politics of Inclusion.* Ed. and intro. Nicolaus Mills. New York: Dell Publishing, 1994.

The MLA Guide to the Job Search: A Handbook for Departments and for Ph.D.s and Ph.D. Candidates in English and Foreign Languages. Revised ed. New York: Modern Language Association, 1996.

Nelson, Cary. "Lessons from the Job Wars: Late Capitalism Arrives on Campus." *Social Text* 44, Vol. 13, No. 3. (Fall/Winter 1995), pp. 119–34. The second part of this essay is published in the special issue of *Academe* listed below.

Newhouse, Margaret. *Outside the Ivory Tower: A Guide for Academics Considering Alternative Careers.* Cambridge: Office of Career Services, Harvard University, 1993. Available by mail order from the Office of Career Services, 54 Dunster Street, Harvard University, Cambridge, MA 02138; (617) 495-2595.

Rose, Suzanna, ed. *The Career Guide for Women Scholars*. New York: Springer, 1986.

Thomas, Trudelle. "Demystifying the Job Search: A Guide for Candidates." *College Composition and Communication* 40:3 (October 1989), pp. 312–26.

Timmerman, John H. "Advice to Candidates." *College English* 50:7 (November 1988), pp. 748–51.

Special Issues of Periodicals

Academe, the Bulletin of the American Association of University Professors, often has articles on the job market, including the special issue in November/December 1995 that continues Cary Nelson's essay from *Social Text,* which is listed above.

ADE Bulletin, from the Associated Departments of English, published a special issue on the job market, Volume 111 (Fall 1995).

Concerns, the journal of the Women's Caucus of the Modern Language Association, has published several special issues devoted to essays on the job market, including Volume 24:1.

Lingua Franca: The Review of Academic Life. This essential periodical often covers the job market and lists current hirings by field in every issue. It also regularly covers graduate student/ adjunct faculty union movements. See, for example, Emily Eakin's "Walking the Line" 6:3 (March-April 1996), pp. 52–60, on the graduate student strike at Yale in 1996.

Profession. The Modern Language Association's annual magazine often has special issues on the job market. See *Profession '94* and *Profession '96*, for example.

Science magazine devotes a special section to the job market every fall. See, for example, "Careers '95: The Future of the Ph.D.," Vol. 270 (October 6, 1995), pp. 121–46. See also its associated web page, listed below.

Online Resources for Job Listings, Information, and Support

The Internet has become an abundant source of job listings, information, and discussion for everyone involved in academia. The sources listed below just scratch the surface of available resources, but they all include links to other sites and discussion groups about academia and alternative careers. We have not included websites that do not provide significant job hunting help, but it is worth checking your professional organization to see if it recently added a new feature. Web addresses change frequently, so if an address no longer works, try searching for it by title or subject with one of the major web search engines, like Yahoo! (http://www.yahoo.com) or AltaVista (http://www.altavista.com).

General

Academic Employment Network
　　http://www.academploy.com
Academic Position Network
　　http://www.umn.edu/apn
The Chronicle of Higher Education, available on-line with searchable job listings and excerpted articles
　　http://chronicle.merit.edu
The National Adjunct Faculty Guild hosts two e-mail discussion groups (ADJUNCT, with weekly topics, and ADJUNCT FACULTY, with no specified topics) and has links to other resources for adjunct faculty.
　　http://www.sai.com/adjunct/NAFGE.html
WMST-L, a women's studies listserv, is a supportive community that often hosts discussions of the job market. To subscribe, send the message SUB WMST-L ''your name,'' with no subject header, to listserv@umdd.umd.edu

Humanities

American Anthropological Association, with on-line job listings
  http://www.ameranthassn.org/carplc.htm
American Philological Association, with on-line job listings
  http://scholar.cc.emory.edu/scripts/APA/frontpage/position-
  info.html
e-Grad, the listserv of the Modern Languages Association's graduate
  student caucus, includes discussion of many job-related issues.
  To subscribe, send the message SUBSCRIBE E-GRAD "your
  name," with no subject header, to Listproc@listproc.bgsu.edu,
  or visit their home page.
  http://www.bgsu.edu/departments/english/GSC_MLA/
  egrad.html

Mathematics

American Mathematical Society Employment Information, with job
  listings, guidance, and a registry for job seekers
  http://www.ams.org/committee/profession/employ.html
The Young Mathematician's Network hosts meetings as well as a
  weekly e-mailed newsletter, *Concerns of Young Mathematicians.*
  http://www.ms.uky.edu/~cyeomans

Sciences

American Astronomical Society, with job listings and other career
  services
  http://www.aas.org
American Chemical Society, with a link to a job bank for members
  http://www.acs.org
American Physical Society, with discussion forums and job listings
  http://www.aps.org/jobs/index.html
Geological Society of America, with on-line job listings
  http://www.geosociety.org/index.html

The Network of Emerging Scientists sponsors an e-mailed newsletter for scientists, as well as a website of on-line resources.
http://pegasus.uthct.edu/nes/nes.html

Science's Next Wave, the website of *Science* magazine, includes weekly forums, an archive of past articles and discussions, and features on alternative career options.
http://www.nextwave.org

The Young Scientists' Network provides job listings, archives of past issues and discussions, information on alternative careers and grants, and an e-mailed newsletter.
http://www.physics.uiuc.edu/ysn/httpd/htdocs/ysnarchive/index.html

Social Sciences

American Political Science Association, with links to order APSA's career guides
http://www.apsanet.org

American Sociological Association, with on-line job listings
http://www.asanet.org

Progressive Sociologists' Network sponsors a graduate student forum and a listserv for discussion of professional issues.
http://csf.colorado.edu/psn

About the Contributors

Joseph O. Aimone recently completed his Ph.D. in English with a Designated Emphasis in Critical Theory at the University of California, Davis, where he is currently a lecturer. He was the president of the Graduate Student Caucus, an allied organization of the Modern Language Association, in 1996.

Eleanor B. Amico has had a checkered career which has placed her so far, even at the age of forty-nine, in the realm of the economically marginal, even while she has lived continuously in the overeducated professional middle class. Early adulthood was taken up with the traditional (at that time) female demands of homemaking and child raising. In the 1980s this was supplemented (though not replaced) with a rigorous eight years in graduate school, which included working as a teaching assistant and later, during the dissertation stage, as an underpaid, under-resourced coordinator of Women's Studies at the University of Wisconsin-Oshkosh. This job continued for a few years after she obtained her Ph.D. in Hebrew and Semitic studies with a minor in Women's Studies from the University of Wisconsin in 1989. She later spent a year unemployed before securing a contract with Fitzroy Dearborn Publishers to prepare a *Reader's Guide to Women's Studies*. After a one-year teaching position in the Women's Studies Department at the University of Wisconsin-Whitewater, she is again unemployed.

Lesliee Antonette is currently an assistant professor of English at East Stroudsburg University in Eastern Pennsylvania. She graduated with a Ph.D. in American literature, early and modern, and Rhetoric, with an emphasis on Composition theory, from the University of California at Riverside. Her dissertation, entitled *Multiculturalism in the American University: The Rhetoric of Diversity and the Traditions of Literary Study*, examines the academy as an institution that serves to promote a monocultural, patriarchal tradition of knowledge and knowledge-making systems.

Eliene Augenbraun got her doctorate in medicine in 1986 (from the New York College of Osteopathic Medicine) and a Ph.D. in Biology in 1992 (from Columbia University). She worked as a medical researcher at Johns Hopkins School of Medicine for two years, then as an exhibit developer at the Maryland Science Center for a year. She is now working in Washington, D.C., as an American Association for the Advancement of Science Diplomacy fellow. After her fellowship she will turn exceptional science into extraordinary news as chief executive officer of ScienCentral, a media production company.

Kurt T. Bachmann is an assistant professor of physics at Birmingham-Southern College, where he teaches and advises undergraduate students and supervises their projects in the physical sciences. His primary research concerns solar activity and the acoustic oscillations inside the sun, and he is first author of four publications in *The Astrophysical Journal* and *Solar Physics*. He is also a coauthor on many papers in the *Physical Review* and other journals as a result of his graduate work in high-energy neutrino physics. His teaching interests include the general physics curriculum, especially the introductory calculus-based course for pre-professional students, and

372

physical science courses for non-science majors such as astronomy and the physics of music. He is an avid piano player and he enjoys many sporting activities.

Joseph J. Basile was born on Christmas Day, 1965, in Brooklyn, New York. Wanting to be an archaeologist since he could walk, he enrolled at seventeen in the Department of Archaeology at Boston University and graduated with a B.A. magna cum laude in Archaeological Studies in 1987. Joe then received an A.M. (1990) and a Ph.D. (1992) in Old World Archaeology and Art at Brown University. Since that time he has lectured and published articles in his field of specialty (Italic and Roman sculpture) and taught in the Department of History at the Boston University Academy before taking his current position as full-time faculty member in the Department of Art History of the Maryland Institute, College of Art. Some readers may be happy to know that since writing "Remembering the Battlefront" Joe's three-year contract with the Institute has been renewed and that he received another (larger) grant this summer to excavate with Brown University at the Southern Temple, Petra, Jordan.

Barbara Bennett earned a Ph.D. from Arizona State University and is now an assistant professor of English at Marian College in Fond du Lac, Wisconsin. Her areas of research and publication include Southern literature, gender studies, and humor theory. Her book *Comic Visions, Female Voices: Contemporary Women Novelists and the Humor of the New South* will be published next year by LSU Press.

Michael Bérubé is professor of English at the University of Illinois at Urbana-Champaign. His most recent book is *Life As We Know It* (Pantheon, 1996) and he is currently completing a new collection of essays, *The Employment of English: Theory, Jobs, and the Future of Literary Studies* (forthcoming from New York University Press).

Marilyn Bonnell is the daughter of a very blue-collar family, and her first job was arranging oil filters into artistic displays in the window of her father's gas station. Because she did not knock her classmates unconscious, as did her brother and sister, she was dubbed "the smart one" and, indeed, school was her salvation. Although her parents were pleased with the docility that her good grades implied, they refused to contribute any money toward her college education. It would be wasted when she got married. When she was finally accepted to graduate school at Penn State, her sister wanted her to stay in their hometown and drive a school bus with her—tag team sisters like in wrestling! As hard as that offer was to decline, she did get a doctorate—to the continual puzzlement of her family, who would rather tell people that she is a beautician in a funeral parlor—at least the work is steady! She has a Ph.D. in English with a minor in Women's Studies, a fat c.v., a thin wallet, no husband, no children, no parents, no credit cards, a good attitude, and a great life.

Daniel Born, associate professor of English at Marietta College in Ohio, is author of *The Birth of Liberal Guilt in the English Novel: Charles Dickens to H. G. Wells* (University of North Carolina Press, 1995) and his articles have appeared in journals including *Conradiana, Novel,* and *Nineteenth-Century Prose.* He holds a Ph.D. in English from the Graduate Center of the City University of New York (1990).

Christina Boufis received her Ph.D. in English literature from the Graduate Center of the City University of New York, where she specialized in Victorian literature and Women's Studies. She has published several essays on nineteenth-century girlhood and feminism, as well as general audience articles on women's issues. Currently, she is an Affiliated Scholar at Stanford University's Institute for Research on Women and Gender, and an instructor at City College of San Francisco. She lives in San Francisco.

Carrie Tirado Bramen is assistant professor of English at the University of Buffalo, SUNY. She took her Ph.D. in modern thought and literature from Stanford University in 1994; she also has an

M.A. in critical theory from the University of Sussex and a B.A. in English from the University of Connecticut. She has published on Puerto Rican–American literature in *New Immigrant Literatures of the United States*; on Dominican fiction in *Callaloo;* and she is currently at work on a book entitled *Uniquely Different: Pluralism and the Rhetoric of Distinctiveness, 1880–1920.*

Adam Bresnick received his Ph.D. in comparative literature from the University of California, Berkeley, in 1992. He has published articles on Diderot, Hoffmann, Balzac, and James. He currently resides in New York City, where he teaches English at the Collegiate School and at Fordham University, where he is an adjunct assistant professor.

Daniel Brownstein was recently awarded a doctorate in history from the University of California, Berkeley, and he still believes in the future of the humanities. He lectured in the departments of History and Italian Studies at U.C., Berkeley, over the past academic year.

Brian Caterino has studied philosophy and political theory and holds a Ph.D. in political science from the University of Toronto. He has taught at the University of Rochester and SUNY-Brockport and offers courses in the DIAL Program at the New School for Social Research. He has published articles and reviews in the areas of contemporary social and political theory. His work has appeared in *Constellations, Theory and Society,* and *Canadian Journal of Social and Political Theory*. His recent publications include "Cognition and Ethics: Lyotard on Addressors and Addressees" in *Transitions in Continental Philosophy*. He currently holds the Walter Benjamin Folding Chair.

John Dixon was born in New York City and received an A.B. from Harvard College, and a Ph.D. in English literature from Boston University in 1995. He specializes in eighteenth-century British literature and wrote his dissertation on Samuel Johnson's moral essays. He currently lives in the Boston area with his wife, who is finishing her dissertation in American literature. They have both been working at part-time teaching positions, and will continue looking for full-time academic jobs.

Diana Dull received her Ph.D. in Sociology in 1995 from the University of California at Santa Cruz, where she has served as Lecturer, teaching courses in the areas of ethnography, social inequality, and the family. She has published articles concerning her research on the relations between women and cosmetic surgeons, as well as her study of community disaster response to the Loma Prieta earthquake. Her current research deals with the dynamic relations between ethnicity, identity, and place in the Italian neighborhood of North Beach, San Francisco. She has a joint appointment as Lecturer in Sociology and Women's Studies at Sonoma State University. She reports: "I'm happy to have landed even a temporary job in California during these troubled times, though I'll admit finding something permanent would have made me downright giddy."

Elizabeth Freeman received her Ph.D. in English at the University of Chicago in 1996. She has published articles in *boundary 2, Arizona Quarterly, Radical Teacher,* and *Women in Performance.* She is now a part-time, tenure-track member of the faculty at Sarah Lawrence College, teaching Gay and Lesbian Literature.

Elisabeth Rose Gruner is assistant professor of English and Women's Studies at the University of Richmond, where she also coordinated the Women's Studies Program from 1993 to 1996. She received her Ph.D. from U.C.L.A. in 1992. She has published articles on Frances Burney and Wilkie Collins, and is currently working on a project about the sibling relationship in Victorian novels, especially novels by women.

Martha Hollander has taught at Yale University, Parsons School of Design, Pratt Institute, the School of Visual Arts, and the State

University of New York, Albany. She is currently assistant professor of Art History at New College, Hofstra University. She is the author of articles on seventeenth-century Dutch art, and a book of poems, *The Game of Statues* (Atlantic Monthly Press, 1990), which won the Walt Whitman Award from the Academy of American Poets.

Allen G. Hunt was born in 1954 and attended Riverside City College and the University of California at Riverside, where he received his B.S. in 1977, his M.S. in 1980, and his Ph.D. in physics in 1983. He taught physics part-time at various local colleges and universities from 1983 to 1985 and then spent 1985–87 in the Federal Republic of Germany at Philipps-University in Marburg with a Fulbright Research Fellowship for research in condensed matter physics. He got married in Germany and returned to the United States to teach physics part-time at the University of California, Irvine; California State University, Fullerton; and California State University, San Bernardino. He began post-doctoral research in soil sciences in 1992 and in 1995 entered the graduate program in geology at Duke University, where he received an M.S. in geology in December 1996. He is currently teaching physics part-time at UC Irvine and doing additional post-doctoral work in soil sciences at UC Riverside.

Anahid Kassabian is assistant professor of Communication and Media Studies at Fordham University. She is editor of *and the walls come a-tumblin' down: Music in the Age of Postdisciplinarity* (a special issue of the *Stanford Humanities Review*) and coeditor of the forthcoming *Keeping Score: Music, Disciplinarity, Culture* (University Press of Virginia, May 1997). Her book on film music and identification processes, *Tracking Identities: Hollywood Film Music of the 1980s and 90s,* is forthcoming from Duke University Press. With David Kazanjian, she also writes on Armenian diasporic identities and mass media.

Gene McQuillan received his Ph.D. in American Studies from the Graduate Center of the City University of New York in 1991. Since then he has taught American Studies, ESL, and Basic Writing at

Queens College and Kingsborough Community College (CUNY). He has published articles on Thoreau, Diane Ackerman, Shelley, and *Dances with Wolves*. He is currently completing a book entitled *Demanding a Different World: Essays on Adventure, Tourism, and Landscape*, as well as an article on relations between part-time and full-time college teachers.

Louis Menand is Professor of English at the Graduate Center of the City University of New York.

Anne M. Menke, assistant professor of French at Swarthmore College, is currently a visiting scholar at the Institute for Research on Women and Gender at Stanford University. She is revising a manuscript entitled "The Taming of the Prude: The Emergence of French Erotic Fiction." She is coeditor (with Alice Jardine) of *Shifting Scenes: Interviews on Women, Writing, and Politics in Post-'68 France,* and translator of Julia Kristeva's *Language, the Unknown.*

Laura Stempel Mumford is an independent scholar and writer living in Madison, Wisconsin. She has written about television, style, feminist theory, and the experience of working outside the formal institutions of the academy, and is the author of *Love and Ideology in the Afternoon: Soap Opera, Women, and Television Genre* (Indiana University Press, 1995) and co-organizer of The Style Conference (July 1997). She is currently at work on a book of critical personal essays called *Sitting Like a Girl: Style, Femininity, and Why I Don't Play the Guitar.*

Lisa Nakamura received her Ph.D. in English from the CUNY Graduate Center in 1996 and is currently an assistant professor of English at Sonoma State University. She has published articles on Victorian fiction, race, and ethnicity in cyberspace, and feminist theory. She lives in San Francisco with her husband.

Michael O'Donovan-Anderson holds a Ph.D. in philosophy from Yale University. He is the editor of *The Incorporated Self: Inter-*

disciplinary Perspectives on Embodiment and author of the forth-coming monograph *Content and Comportment: On Embodiment and the Epistemic Availability of the World,* but (believe it or not) he found writing the piece contained herein much more fun. He has taught philosophy at Yale, Harvard, and Stonehill College, and was a member of the scientific staff at Language Engineering Corporation, a language and computing think tank and software development company in Belmont, Massachusetts. But then came a last-minute, late-August tenure-track offer from St. John's College in Annapolis, Maryland. So there he is. (Which is to say: it ain't over till it's over.)

Victoria C. Olsen received her Ph.D. in English in 1994 from Stanford University, where she specialized in Victorian women's studies. She has published in *Victorian Poetry* and *The San Francisco Chronicle,* and is currently working on a biography of the Victorian photographer Julia Margaret Cameron. She lives in San Francisco with her husband and daughter.

Ingrid Steffensen-Bruce earned a Ph.D. in art history from the University of Delaware, an M.A. in English literature from Yale University, and an undergraduate degree from the University of Virginia. She has taught courses in art history at Bucknell University and at Manhattanville College; her dissertation will reappear sometime in 1997 as *Marble Palaces, Temples of Art: Art Museums, Architecture, and American Culture, 1890–1930* from Bucknell University Press. She learned, with great amusement, of her new job and the publication of the present essay within the same week, and is happy to report that, starting in the fall of 1996, she will be teaching art and architectural history in a tenure-track position at a community college in New Jersey.

Sivagami Subbaraman did her graduate work at the University of Illinois, Urbana. After teaching at different universities, she is currently an Affiliate Scholar in Women's Studies, University of Maryland, College Park, while working at a local retail mall to support herself. She has made several presentations at the conferences of the Modern Language Association, the American Studies Association, the Midwest Modern Language Association, and the National Women's Studies Association, and published in the *Centennial Review* and *The Feminist Companion to Literature in English*. Apart from talking about the crises in the profession, she "persists" in writing on "American" literature, including African-American, and feminist theory, and has articles forthcoming in *Signs* and the MMLA *Journal*.

Brian Ulicny received bachelor's degrees in Electrical Engineering and Philosophy from the University of Notre Dame in 1986. In 1993, he was awarded a doctorate from the Department of Linguistics and Philosophy at MIT. He is currently employed as a computational linguist with Inso Corporation in Boston, Massachusetts.

Barbara Louise Ungar received her Ph.D. in English with a Women's Studies certificate from the Graduate Center, CUNY, in 1995. She is an assistant professor of English (American Literature and Creative Writing) at the College of Saint Rose in Albany, New York. She has published poetry in many journals, such as *The Minnesota Review, Calliope, Asylum Annual, Global City Review, Cream City Review*, and *The Literary Review*.

Julie Vandivere is an assistant professor of English and Women's Studies at Bloomsburg University in Pennsylvania. She has published articles on English- and Spanish-speaking twentieth-century women novelists, and is currently completing a book on lesbian modernists in English- and Spanish-speaking cultures. Active in community queer politics, she lives with her partner and their children in Lewisburg, Pennsylvania.

Veronica Vazquez Garcia is a native of Mexico City and received her Ph.D. in Sociology from Carleton University in 1995. Her dissertation examines the dynamics of class, gender, and ethnicity in a native community of southern Veracruz, Mexico. She presently teaches part-time at the University of Ottawa and has a four-month contract with the International Development Research Centre to co-ordinate applied research on drinking water and sanitation systems in Latin America. In January of 1997 she will take a job at the Colegio de Posgraduados in Texcoco, Mexico, and will start working on a participatory action research project on gender, poverty, and the environment in the southern Veracruz region. Her work has appeared in the *International Journal of Canadian Studies,* the *Canadian Journal of Development Studies,* the *Revista Mexicana de Ciencias Politicas y Sociales,* and *Cuadernos Agricolas.*

Howard Wachtel earned his Bachelor of Arts degree in mathematics at Washington University in St. Louis, his Master of Arts degree in mathematics at the University of Wisconsin at Madison, and his Doctor of Arts in mathematics at the University of Illinois at Chicago. His research interest is in the evaluation of teaching effectiveness in college mathematics. At the time of this writing he is assistant professor of mathematics at Bowie State University in Maryland.

Dave Williams grew up in upstate New York and attended Cornell University as an undergraduate. He later worked as a histology technician in a Rochester hospital, and moved to Boston to find work in theater. In 1982, he received an M.F.A. from the Dallas Theatre Center, at that time affiliated with Trinity University. He held various jobs in and out of theater until 1987, when he was offered the chance to teach English at Liaoning University in Shenyang in the People's Republic of China. Here, he met and married Xu Xiaoxia. He also took advantage of his vacations to travel the length and breadth of the country by rail. Returning to the United States in 1988, he earned his Ph.D. in Theatre Arts from Cornell University in 1994. He now teaches English and Theatre at Providence University in Taichung on Taiwan. In his spare time, he enjoys running, computer games, and actively guiding his children, Linus Clark Minhao Williams and Vivian Celeste Jiayun Williams, into productive and enjoyable adulthood.